DISPUTES ON HUMAN RIGHTS VIOLATION BEFORE THE ECOWAS COURT OF JUSTICE

Alioune SALL

DISPUTES ON HUMAN RIGHTS VIOLATION BEFORE THE ECOWAS COURT OF JUSTICE

Translated from French by
Emmanuel Kofi NKANSAH

L'Harmattan Sénégal

10 VDN, Sicap Amitié 3, Lotissement Cité Police, DAKAR

http://www.harmattansenegal.com
senharmattan@gmail.com
senlibrairie@gmail.com

ISBN: 978-2-343-17955-1

EAN: 9782343179551

To budding jurists,
Ousseynou and Assane El Bachir.

SUMMARY

PART I

THE CASE LAW OF THE COURT

PART II

REFLECTIONS ON THE COURT FROM THE POINT OF VIEW OF DOCTRINE

PART I

THE CASE LAW OF THE COURT

The case law of the Court is examined here from three angles: the key figures of the trial (Chapter 1), the jurisdiction of the Court and admissibility of applications (Chapter 2), and how the Court handles the cases (Chapter 3).

CHAPTER 1

THE KEY PLAYERS IN THE TRIAL

We are concerned here with the entire stream of persons who may feature as the key participants or stakeholders in the trial: the parties themselves (Section 1), as well as their representatives, and the interveners and *amici curiae* (Section 2).

SECTION 1

THE PARTIES

We will naturally have to deal with the person formally bringing a request before the Court – the applicant (Paragraph 1), and the defendant (Paragraph 2).

Paragraph 1

The applicant

In the terms of Article 10 of the 19 January 2005 Supplementary Protocol A/SP.1/01/05, access to the Court is open to: "... individuals on application for relief for violation of their human rights …"

There is no doubt that this may be applicable to natural persons. The capacity for legal persons to appear before the Court however gave rise to jurisprudential hesitations for some time. Rather fortunately, no doubt subsists today, as to corporate bodies being qualified applicants before the Court (A)[1].

A second condition is however required from the applicant: that he possesses, as locus standi, a definite interest at stake, of having suffered a harm himself (B).

---

1 With regard to this point, see article: **Remarks on the status of the applicant before the ECOWAS Court of Justice**, ibid, Part II of this work.

A. - Who may feature among the category of applicants?

Private individuals, as human beings, may apply to bring a case before the Court.

An issue was raised concerning access of legal entities before the Court, and the Court initially refused to grant them access as possible applicants.

In its Judgment of 8 July 2011, in *Ocean King Nigeria Ltd.* v. *Republic of Senegal,* ECW/CCJ/JUD/07/11, the Court followed the argumentation of the Republic of Senegal according to which a company – Ocean King Ltd. – which is a legal person, cannot bring claims regarding 'human rights', in line with a very narrow interpretation of the concept of human rights, according to which the rights in question related exclusively to "human beings", physical human beings made of flesh and bones:

> §50: "Thus, by expressly giving access to only individuals, the Supplementary Protocol sought to give that right exclusively to individual human beings who are victims of human rights abuse to the exclusion of all others ..."
>
> §72: "The Court further decides that Article 10(d) of the 1991 Protocol, as amended, is not open to corporate bodies as victims of human rights abuse; that is open to only human beings."

It must however be made known that the Court later departed from this case law, and the turnaround must indeed be commended. The restricted meaning previously assigned to the concept of human rights culminates certainly in a considerable reduction of the legal guarantees inherent in the concept itself. In the case concerning *Ocean King,* which was just cited, the Court, in following the reasoning of the Defendant State, clung to a very abstract, not to mention, very academic conceptualisation of the notion of human rights. Apart from the fact that similar courts had already recognised the right of legal persons – companies, associations, political parties, etc. – to lay claim to provisions drawn from instruments of human rights protection, one may take note of the unrealistic nature of the restricted stance adopted by the Court. For, who dares to support the argument that an association with interest in protection of the abuse of childhood cannot file a case in court on that same matter of interest when children have in actual fact been abused? Can one reasonably maintain the stand that a political party which has been banned from participating in elections – as was the case of the party of the former President of Burkina Faso, which was banned from participating in national elections, upon the relinquishing of power by the President in October 2014 – is disqualified from claiming the rights of its party members to vote and to be voted for during the elections? Or that a measure restricting the right to the freedom of expression of the members of the same political party, does not breach the right to free expression as stipulated in several international conventions? And where a profit-making company is unfairly dispossessed of its assets or properties, can one deny that such company shall not be entitled to a claim of violation of its right to property? Whereby the Court, in certain rulings, such as in *Case Concerning Tidjani* **v.** *Republic of Niger*, had decided the case at hand by taking a stand for the claim of "human rights"?

In fact, subsequently, the jurisprudence of the Court had to undergo a variation in regard to this stance, and the Community judge eventually allowed certain corporate bodies to come before the Court with claims on human rights violation, as evidenced in Judgment of 17 December 2009, *National Co-ordinating Group of Departmental Representatives of the Cocoa-Coffee Sector* (CNDD) **v.** *Republic of Côte d'Ivoire* (ECW/CCJ/JUD/05/09):

> §23 : "The Court holds that the said text talks of "toute personne victime" without stating whether it is a question of natural person or legal person, or still, whether it is the two at the same time ; but the Court would like to emphasise, moreover, that the word "victime", and more precisely the concept of "victime" enables one to understand that it is a question of adjudicating on complaints from any person who may claim that he/it has been harmed and that he/it has suffered from violation of his/its recognised rights to freedom."
>
> §24: "Whereas if it is trite that rights and freedoms guaranteed by international instruments relating to human rights are so made for individuals, it is nonetheless the case that legal persons equally have rights they can claim."

§28: The Court further cites, specifically, the provisions of Article 1(h) of the Protocol on Democracy and Good Governance thus:

> "The rights set up in the African Charter on Human and Peoples' Rights and other international instruments shall be guaranteed in each of the ECOWAS Member States; each individual or organisation shall be free to have recourse to the common or civil law courts, a court of special jurisdiction, or any other national institution established within the

framework of an international instrument on human rights, to ensure the protection of his his/her rights."

§62: "Whereas in a matter of application for human rights violation, the Court cannot grant such right to natural persons only, to the exclusion of legal persons."

Such access granted to legal entities was later confirmed in Judgment of 6 November 2013, *Chude Mba* **v.** *Republic of Ghana*, ECW/CCJ/JUD/10/13:

§66: "Unlike other provisions of the Charter, the text just quoted above does not specify whether or not the right to property is only guaranteed to individuals or people. It has therefore not excluded legal persons, which include corporations…"

Political parties, notably, were then able to have access to the Court.

One can cite Judgment of 23 April 2015, *Convention Démocratique Sociale, alias CDS Rahama* **v.** *Republic of Niger* (ECW/CCJ/JUD/03/15), or yet still Judgment of 13 July 2015, *Congrès pour la Démocratie et le Progrès (CDP) and Others* **v.** *Burkina Faso* (ECW/CCJ/JUD/16/15), wherein the Court declared that:

§20, 21: "As to the claim of inadmissibility of the matter before the Court, regarding the right at stake – the right to participate in elections and in the management of public affairs – that it is a personal right and not a right of a political party, the Court must first of all recall that it is not seised in the instant matter by political parties only, but equally by citizens of Burkina Faso. But even if it were seised by associations of a political nature, the Court is of the view that nothing would prevent it from sitting on the case, for the reason that such restriction on the enjoyment of such right may breach the rights of a political party, which is a body whose mission consists precisely of insisting on citizens' right to vote in political elections and to participate in the management of public affairs. Not only that the texts governing the Court do not exclude legal entities from bringing cases before the Court – on condition that they come before the Court as victims (Article 10 (d) of the 2005 Protocol on the Court), but it would be purely artificial and unreasonable for the Court to deny political parties the right to bring their cases before it, once the rights relating to their assigned mission of participating in the electoral race are violated.

Hence, the claim in respect of inadmissibility of the Application, as maintained by Burkina Faso, is hereby dismissed."

It is not necessary, in bringing an application before the Court for human rights violation, to possess the nationality of a Member State.

It shall be worthy to commend the stand taken to set aside every consideration relating to nationality. Initially, however, in the course of the early years which followed the 2005 reform granting the Court powers on human rights violation, some doubts still subsisted on the requirement of the nationality of a Member State, for, via the style of writing, the judgments delivered systematically mentioned, in their introductory portions, the nationality of the persons bringing the case before the Court. That form of detail could give the impression that for bringing an action before the Court, possessing the nationality of a Member State was a prior condition to be fulfilled. Now, the deeply rooted notion of *human right* is a universal one. The naturalistic background of the concept of human rights demands that every attempt at ascribing particular considerations to it be banished, notably nationalistic factors. Thus:

- In Judgment of 4 March 2010, *Mahamat Seid Abazene* **v.** *Republic of Mali, African Union, Afro-Arab Cultural Institute* (ECW/CCJ/JUD/02/10), the Applicant is of Chadian nationality;
- In Judgment of 18 November 2010, *Hissène Habré* **v.** *Republic of Senegal* (ECW/CCJ/JUD/06/10), the Applicant is equally of Chadian nationality;
- In Judgment of 6 November 2013, *Chude Mba* **v.** *Republic of Ghana* (ECW/CCJ/JUD/10/13), it is stated that the Applicant had a dual nationality: Nigerian and British (§1). But, if one should refer to the provisions of the 1982 Protocol on citizenship of ECOWAS, the Applicant is not a "Community citizen" since he had not yet renounced his British nationality. Despite that, his action was admitted before the Court.
- In Judgment of 6 March 2014, *Bassam El Najjar* **v.** *Republic of Togo* (ECW/CCJ/JUD/08/14), the Applicant was of Lebanese nationality, but he was established in Togo (§10).

Once the identity or physiognomy of the applicant is determined, we must now turn our attention to another required condition: *locus standi*, which refers to the necessity for the applicant to have personally suffered a harm arising from the violation of a right.

B.- Locus standi: necessity of an impending personal harm and (or) a mandate to act on behalf of other victims

One must have suffered a prejudice oneself. That is the reason why, in bringing actions before the Court, entities like NGOs cannot assume the position of the victims.[2]. Article 10 (d) of the 2005 Supplementary Protocol explicitly provides that only victims may file a case before the Court. The person bringing a case before the Court shall not be any other than the person or entity affected, in his (its) being or his (its) legacy, by the violation alleged.

However, the right of access to the Court may be delegated, by way of authorisation whose authenticity shall systematically be verified by the Court. The point must be made absolutely clear here: the person vested with the power of attorney shall not be "unaffected" by the violation alleged, he must himself be a victim, for Article 10 of the 2005 Protocol talks of 'victims' (*personne victime* in French), and such is the interpretation upheld by the Court. What the Court seeks to avoid here is the total "disappearance" of the victim(s) behind a protective screen mounted by the mandated person, a suit filed upon the unilateral decision of a person or an entity not connected in any way to the violation at stake. There shall be no trace of *actio popularis* granting anyone whatsoever the right to file a case before the Court.

In practice therefore, the scenario is that of a situation where the universal set of victims is required to be represented by only one of the victims or by a group of the victims. This requirement is quite formal: the name or names of one or more of the victims must appear on the initiating application. Naturally, it is not a requirement for the applicant or applicants to be physically present in court, except where the Court requests so; at any rate, the mere indication of the identity of the victim or victims, suffices, in principle. It thus goes without saying that this requirement is without influence on the issue of representation before the Court, which may be assumed by lawyers or agents, and the latter may be entities for the promotion of human rights.

---

2 However, as we shall explain further, much later in our work, such NGOs may possibly act as agents of the victims, pursuant to the provisions of Article 12 of Protocol A/P1/7/91, which remain in force, and as such, does not distinguish between "States" and "private individuals" or "natural persons". But the function of an NGO would thus consist, as a counsel, of pleading a cause, and not to substitute itself for the victim.

The necessity of a personal harm, as justification for the cause of action, has been emphasised several times by the Court[3] :

- **In Judgment of 9 May 2011, *Center for Democracy and Development, Center for Defence of Human Rights and Democracy* v. *Mamadou Tandja and Republic of Niger* (ECW/CCJ/JUD/05/11):**

§ 28: After citing the terms of Article 10 of the 2005 Protocol, the Court holds that: "... it can be deduced from the points of the case, that the Applicants are legal persons incorporated under the laws of the Federal Republic of Nigeria and of the Republic of Benin, as regards, respectively, the Centre for Democracy and Development and the Centre for the Defence of Human Rights and Democracy in Africa. Now, in the circumstances of the case, even if one should suppose that the said association possess the legal status in their respective countries, they have not evinced their status as victims nor justified that they are qualified to act on behalf of the victims whose mandate they must have received."

§29: "... The Court finds that the decisions taken by Mr. Mamadou Tandja have effect on only the nationals of Niger and possibly on the residents of the said country. But, the Applicants are not Associations formed from the laws of Niger and do not have any justification either as constituting a part of the Republic of Niger. The said decisions cannot therefore be against them and does not concern them either intimately or remotely; they cannot therefore constitute victims of the consequences of such decisions. Ultimately, they cannot be identified as victims."

---

3 The Court asked for the fulfilment of this condition in various procedures where cases were filed for human rights violation, and relating, for example, to challenging the legality of an act by the Community or a default in contractual liability. See Judgment of 16 May 2008, *Odafe Oserada Case, represented by Kolawole O. O. James, in court, against ECOWAS Council of Ministers, ECOWAS Parliament and ECOWAS Commission* (ECW/CCJ/JUD/01/08), § 31 : "*... it cannot reasonably be held that the promoter of a project will be the most qualified to occupy the post of Secretary General of ECOWAS Parliament, much less when he has not demonstrated, on his own, any interest in the said post; whereas legally speaking, an interest in a case must be personal, direct and certain.*"; or, again, Judgment of 16 May 2012, *Oluwatosin Rinu Adewale v. ECOWAS Council of Ministers, President of ECOWAS Commission, President of the Community Court of Justice, Director of Administration of the Community Court of Justice* (ECW/CCJ/JUD/07/12), §45, where the case was dismissed because it was decided that if the person in cause was not directly and immediately affected by the act whose annulment was being requested, it cannot be admitted that that same person files the complaint, within the terms of Article 10 of the Protocol on the Court.

- **Judgment of 12 February 2014, *Oumar Mariko* v. *Republic of Mali* (ECW/CCJ/JUD/03/14):**

The Court adjudged that Oumar Mariko could not assume the status of a victim of the violation of his human rights (…) since he could not have been a candidate for the presidential elections, within the meaning of the electoral laws of Mali. The Court therefore dismissed the case (§29).

Similarly, in the instance where the victim or victims decide to delegate the right to come before the Court, producing the power of attorney to that effect is required by the Court. This is apparent in the following decisions:

- **Judgment of 17 March 2011, *Bakary Sarré and 28 Others* v. *Republic of Mali* (ECW/CCJ/JUD/03/11) :**

> §37 and 38: "It follows from this provision (Article 10 of the 2005 Supplementary Protocol on the Court, as cited in the above-stated judgment), that the admissibility of an application is linked, among other criteria, to the status of the victim. This condition necessarily entails that the applicant, acting on personal grounds as a result of a legally protected injured interest, reserves the right to come before a judge to have his claims examined; alternatively, an applicant, authorised to act by virtue of a power of attorney on behalf of another person or for a group of people whose legally protected interests have been harmed, shall exercise the power of representation in the action (…). Bringing an action before a court of law is a vested power, and it is up to the holder of that prerogative either to execute it himself or entrust that power to a third party (…). Thus, the said power of attorney which accords joint powers of representation does not confer on Mr. Bakary Sarré any legal title to act before the Court of Justice of ECOWAS on behalf of the said year-group. As a result, there are grounds for concluding that Mr. Bakary Sarré does not have the locus standi for lodging the instant case in the name of the judges of his year-group."

- **Judgment of 31 January 2012, *Aziablévi Yovo and 31 Others* v. *Société Togo Telecom and Republic of Togo*, (ECW/CCJ/JUD/04/12):**

§10 and 11: The Court found that the heirs to the deceased Applicants had indeed given the required power of attorney to another party to act on their behalf. If the Court set their aside case, it was solely because the authorisation to act on their behalf "*was given after the filing of the case*" before the Court.

- **Judgment of 12 February 2014, *Bouréima Sidi Cissé* v. *Republic of Mali* (ECW/CCJ/JUD/04/14) :**

Page 10 (French version): The Court adjudged that since the Applicants had no mandate to represent the other Applicants (i.e. the Co-Applicants) in the case before the Court, the Application brought by them in their capacity as Applicants, was inconsistent with the relevant provisions of the texts relating to the Court. The Court thus declared their Application inadmissible, in as much as filed on behalf of the Co-Applicants by the Applicants.

- **Judgment of 30 June 2015, *167 Former Workers of SONIDEP Represented by Eli Haggar and B. Kanfideni* v. *Republic of Niger and SONIDEP* (ECW/CCJ/JUD/15/15):**

§ IV.13, 15: The Court observed that the Application had indicated that the 167 former officers of *Société Nigérienne des Produits Pétroliers (SONIDEP)* were represented by Messrs. Haggar and Kanfideni, and yet for the proceedings, the mandated persons (i.e. Messrs. Haggar and Kanfideni) did not prove that they possessed any authorisation for doing so. The Court held that it had no record of any power of attorney having been granted to the said representatives by the 167 former officers of SONIDEP, and that Messrs. Haggar and Kanfideni provided no justification for representation before the Court, of the former workers. Therefore, as decided by the Court, the Applicants had no locus standi for pleading the case on behalf of the Applicants.

The harm suffered must therefore be "personal", or "direct", if one prefers. Shall the harm suffered, in any case, be current or simply possible?

In the very beginnings, the standpoint adopted by the Court was not crystal clear, and Judgment on *Hissène Habré* **v.** *Republic of Senegal* particularly portrays the hesitation being referred to here. Then came illumination in the jurisprudence of the Court, which may, today, be captured in summary terms as follows, in quite classical terms, at any rate: in principle, the harm must be current – the Court at times states that it must be "concrete" – but in exceptional cases, the Court will be satisfied with a "possible" or "potential" harm. As one may guess, it is upon such degree of "likelihood" or "probability" that the judicial argumentation will be hinged. In Judgment of 13 July 2015, *Congrès pour la Démocratie et le Progrès (CDP) and Others* **v.** *Burkina Faso* (ECW/CCJ/JUD/16/15), the latest on the point in issue, the Court attempts to fix in clear terms, its doctrine on the status or degree of harm the applicant is required to have suffered.

The following decisions symbolise the same attempt at clarification:

- **Judgment of 27 October 2008, *Hadijatou Mani Koraou* v. *Republic of Niger* (ECW/CCJ/JUD/06/08):**

The applicant, having devoted the greater part of her argumentation to the necessity for the Republic of Niger to adopt laws that will provide greater protection for women against discriminatory customs, the judges of the Community Court responded thus:

> § 60: "As regards the Applicant's first plea-in-law, the Court finds that it does not have the mandate to examine the laws of Member States of the Community in abstracto, but rather, to ensure the protection of the rights of individuals whenever such individuals are victims of the violation of those rights which are recognised as theirs, and the Court does so by examining concrete cases brought before it."

- **Judgment of 18 November 2010, *Hissène Habré* v. *Republic of Senegal* (ECW/CCJ/JUD/06/10):**

§29, §30, §36, §38, §47, §48: The Court ruled that as at the material stage where Hissène Habré's case was being adjudicated upon by the ECOWAS Court of Justice, no process or proceedings had been instituted against him, as affirmed by the Republic of Senegal, and not refuted by Hissène Habré himself; the Court, noting at the same time that the principal concern of Hissène Habré therein being essentially, that fresh proceedings may *possibly* be instituted against him.

The Court decided thereby that the violations alleged by the Applicant (i.e. Hissène Habré) were borne out of a hypothesis, enabling the Court to adjudge therefore that the allegations made were no more than a potential case. Again, the Court found that Hissène Habré had not pleaded any concrete proof for backing the claims of violation of his right to effective remedy, and the Court equally adjudged that the mere act of a State envisaging amendments to its Constitution may not be invoked by any individual as constituting a violation of his rights, in absolute terms. The Court thus deduced that considered in that light, the violation alleged by Hissène Habré was not only anchored on a hypothesis, but remained abstract in nature. The Court went further, not only to cite its case law in its judgment in *Hadijatou Mani Koraou* **v.** *Republic of Niger*, where it held that its jurisdiction did not consist of examining cases of human rights violation in abstracto, but concrete occurrences of human rights violation, and equally confirmed its reasoning along the same lines as those found under the case law of the European Court of Human Rights.

- **Judgment of 13 July 2015, *Congrès pour la Démocratie et le Progrès (CDP) and Others* v. *Burkina Faso* (ECW/CCJ/JUD/16/15):**

The applicants brought their case before the Court after the new authorities in power in the country had adopted laws excluding them from participating in national elections, upon the pretext that they supported a constitutional amendment (termed "anti-constitutional change") granting the former President, Compaoré, the opportunity to seek a further term in office.

The Court takes the stand that the harm alleged must be real, and cannot but be imminent only:

> § 15, 16, 17, 18: "As regards the allegation by Burkina Faso that the Court lacks jurisdiction to adjudicate on the case before it, as a result of the non-concrete nature of the claims of violation brought by Burkina Faso, the Court has always held that it only makes rulings, in principle, on cases of human rights violation which are concrete, real and proven, and not on violations claimed to be possible, contingent or potential. One may thus be tempted, in the instant case, to question whether or not the matter before the Court is indeed well grounded, because as at the time the Court was seised with the case, no violation had as yet been committed, nor had any case of actual rejection of candidature been brought before the Court, and no individual candidature had been set aside in accordance with the new provisions; that, in a word, there is no real prejudice caused.
>
> It would amount to consigning its own time-held case law to oblivion if the Court should rule that it may legitimately entertain violations which have not yet occurred, but are very imminent. In the instant case, the alleged violation has not yet been committed, but could very soon be. Going by the indications provided to the Court, the electoral process is to open seventy (70) days before the scheduled date for voting (i.e. 11 October 2015), on the fateful day of 1 August 2015. The Court was therefore seised with the case on grounds of urgency. In the present circumstances of the case, if the Court were to wait for the applications of candidature to be possibly rejected before acting, if it had to wait for the exhaustion of the effects of any transgression before stating the law, its jurisdiction in a context of urgency would have no sense, because the

electoral rights of the presumed victims for participating in the electoral race would inexorably be breached.

At any rate, this position of the Court, regarding the nature of harms it entertains, was clearly stated in its judgment on **Hissène Habré v. Republic of Senegal,** delivered on 18 November 2010. The Court recalls therein its case law in **Case Concerning Hadijatou Mani Koraou v. Republic of Niger**, where it ruled that it has no jurisdiction to examine cases of violation in abstracto, but concrete cases of human rights violation. Therefore, in principle, a human rights violation is found à posteriori, by way of the evidence that the violation in question has already occurred (§48). The Court has further ruled however that it may occur that in specific circumstances, the risk of a future violation confers on an applicant the status of a victim (§49). Thus, there may be reasonable and convincing indications of the probability of the occurrence of certain actions (§53). Given such specific circumstances, which the Court considers akin to the conditions surrounding the instant case, the Court can perfectly adjudicate on the case.

It is therefore wrong for Burkina Faso to claim that the Court cannot make any pronouncement on the case because none of the rights at stake has as yet been violated."

After all these considerations on the applicant – his identity and the harm he must have suffered – we need to look at another party in the proceedings for human rights violation.

Paragraph 2
The defendant

The variety of persons that may feature as applicants in proceedings for human rights violation sharply contrasts with the invariable nature of the status of the defendant, who must systematically be a State (A). That is so because the applicable law in such an instance remains public international law, the law that States, principally, enact, and which are binding on them (B).

A.- Only one form of defendant: the State

Again, the early days of the jurisprudence of the Court were marked by uncertainties in regard to this point. Numerous applications, insufficiently informed about the realities of the ECOWAS Court of

Justice, unduly cited persons or institutions as defendants, suing them before the Court. They are considered unduly sued for the simple reason that they are not under any obligation whatsoever, in international law, to observe human rights. It is commendable that in the recent past, the Court has systematically declared such persons or entities as having no case to answer before the Court, and improperly sued, even if the names assigned to some of those suits do not always reflect the accuracy of the preliminary work done towards expunging the disqualified defendants from the proceedings[4]. This very significant point is the fruit of the following judgments, among others:

- **Judgment of 17 December 2009, *National Co-ordinating Group of Departmental Representatives of the Cocoa-Coffee Sector* (CNDD) v. *Republic of Côte d'Ivoire* (ECW/CCJ/JUD/05/09):**

§34:"The Court recalls, on this issue, that the ECOWAS Member States, as contracting parties of the ECOWAS Community law, or as guarantors for the implementation of the human rights recognised in the Revised Treaty of ECOWAS, are obliged to subscribe to these rights, and may in that regard be sued before the principal legal organ of ECOWAS, i.e. the Community Court of Justice. Consequently, the Court declares that an individual may bring proceedings against a Member State of the Community, before the Community Court of Justice."

- **Judgment on the *Peter David Case,* 11 June 2010 (ECW/CCJ/RUL/04/10) :**

§42: "... the Court recalls that the international regime of human rights protection before international bodies relies essentially on treaties to which States are parties as the principal subjects of international law...."

- **Judgment of 8 November 2010, *Mamadou Tandja* v. *General Salou Djibo and Republic of Niger* (ECW/CCJ/JUD/05/10):**

Page 121 (Law Report (2010) CCJELR, last 2 paragraphs):

"Article 9(4) of the Supplementary Protocol of 2005 on the Court provides that: the Court has jurisdiction to determine cases of human rights violation that occur in any Member State;

---

4 Hence, it would be desirable to adopt as a custom at the Registry of the Court, the practice of taking account of any parties that may be declared by the Court as "false defendants", and to note therefore that the Court is not bound to use the same appellations for the suit as may have been used by the applicant at the time of bringing the case before the Court for the first time, since the name assigned to the case by the applicant may turn out to be incorrect.

Whereas, it is commonly admitted that proceedings relating to human rights violations are initiated against Member States, and not against individuals. Indeed, the obligation to respect and protect human rights is placed upon Member States. The obligations of respect for and protection of human rights are derived from international conventions which were accepted and ratified by Member States."

- **Judgment of 9 May 2011,** ***Center for Democracy and Development, and Center for Defence of Human Rights and Democracy*** **v.** ***Mamadou Tandja and Republic of Niger*** **(ECW/CCJ/JUD/05/11):**

§31: "Furthermore, the Court recalls that when an application on human rights violation is brought before it, it is so done necessarily by a person who is a victim of the said violation against one or several Member States of the Community, and not against individuals, natural or legal persons."

- **Judgment of 17 May 2016,** ***Marie Molmou and 114 Others*** **v.** ***Republic of Guinea*** **(ECW/CCJ/JUD/16/16) :**

Page 7 (English version): "A point must be made clear here concerning the citing of SOGUIPAH (a limited liability company registered under the laws of Guinea) as a party in the instant case. It is apparent that SOGUIPAH was sued as a defendant before this Court, for human rights violation. Now, even if it is manifest that SOGUIPAH as a company maintains an overriding interest in the action brought before the Court, since it is SOGUIPAH which has been benefiting from the disputed land expropriation, SOGUIPAH cannot, as such, constitute a party in the proceedings, for the reason that only States may be cited as defendants in proceedings for human rights violation. This principle is easily explicable: the international instruments, international by definition, as invoked by those bringing the action, do remain instruments binding only on States; the States concerned are the only entities which signed those instruments, and thereafter, either ratified them or declared allegiance to them. Such instruments cannot therefore, by definition, be invoked against any other entities than the States concerned, for they shall not be binding on those other entities."[5]

If the State holds, as such, the monopoly of the position of defendant, it is by virtue of the fact that the law on human rights violation may only be applied against States.

---

5 It may be mentioned in passing (see page 10 of the judgment, English version), that the Court disagreed with the Applicants on the status of "a people" under international law.

B.- A corollary: application of public international law before the Court

The principle in force at this stage is as follows, and can be broken down into two assertions, corroborated by the following decisions of the Court: the Court applies the norms of *international law* which are *binding on the States*.

If, unfortunately, it had occurred before, that the Court did not strictly consider to set aside references made, either to the domestic law of the States or to an international law not binding on the Member States of ECOWAS – attributable to the flutter in the early years of an evolving jurisprudence, without doubt[6] – one can however observe, for some time now, that the Court pays particular attention in pointing out the sole norms of reference it applies, which are the international legal instruments binding on the States concerned. Decisions of the Court which may be cited in support of this assertion are simply numerous:

- **Judgment of 17 March 2011, *Bakary Sarré and 28 Others* v. *Republic of Mali* (ECW/CCJ/JUD/03/11) :**

> §34: "The Court equally reaffirms that in accordance with its consistently held case law, once human rights violations constituting international or Community obligations of a Member State are brought against any Member State, the Court declares its jurisdiction to examine such violations."

- **Judgments of 11 June 2012, *Sikiru Alade* v. *Federal Republic of Nigeria* (ECW/CCJ/JUD/10/12):**

> §25: "The rights in the said African Charter are not the only rights that the violation of same will fall under Article 9 (4) of the Protocol on the Court as amended. Those UN Conventions and Charter on Human Rights acceded to by Member States of ECOWAS are recognisable rights

---

6 One may cite for example Judgment of 28 January 2009, *Djot Bayi Talbia and 14 Others* **v.** *Federal Republic of Nigeria, Attorney General of the Federation, Chief of Naval Staff, Inspector General of Police, Comptroller General of Prisons* (ECW/CCJ/JUD/01/09) where the applicant relied heavily on the naval code of Nigeria and several provisions of the Constitution of Nigeria ; or Judgment of 26 January 2012, *El Hadji Mame Abdou Gaye* **v.** *Republic of Senegal* (ECW/CCJ/JUD/03/12), where it is unfortunately, an issue concerning the European Convention on Human Rights (§14,22,39), etc. etc. Such errors should have been avoided, with the full assumption of the powers of the Court in matters relating to human rights.

that the violation of which will fall within the ambit of Article 9(4) of the Protocol of the Court, just to mention a few."

- **Judgment of 23 April 2015, *Eli Haggarmi* v. *Republic of Niger* (ECWCCJ/JUD/04/15):**

Page 8 (French version): The Court declared that the facts invoked by the Applicant must be examined in the light of the African Charter on Human and Peoples' Rights, and not in relation to the provisions of the national law, as the Defendant seemed to maintain.

- **Judgment of 24 April 2015, *Pascal A. Bodjona* v. *Republic of Togo* (ECW/CCJ/JUD/06/15):**

§ 37: "Similarly, the Court shall note as irrelevant, all the references made to the domestic law of Togo by the Parties in their written pleadings. The Constitution of Togo in particular was frequently cited by the two Parties. Now, the Court has no powers to assess the constitutionality or legality of instruments adopted by the national authorities. That mandate is assigned to the domestic courts of the Member States, and the ECOWAS Court of Justice cannot assume their role. In examining the cases brought before it, the ECOWAS Court of Justice shall refer exclusively to the norms of international law as binding on the Member States which have subscribed thereto. …"

- **Judgment of 30 June 2015, *Bourama Sininta and 119 Others* v. *Republic of Mali* (ECW/CCJ/JUD/13/15) :**

§ IV.17, p.12 (French version): The Court noted that the 1789 Declaration of the Rights of Man and of the Citizen is a national norm, originally applicable to Franc, finally adopted by other national legal orders, and thereby not applicable before the ECOWAS Court.

The Court declared that only applicable before the Court, are international legal instruments to which the Defendant State is signatory, in accordance with the Court's settled case law.

§IV.29, p.15 (French version): The Court held that the European Convention on Human Rights may not be invoked before it, for the simple reason that neither the Defendant State, nor the Economic Community of West African States (ECOWAS) in general, are signatory to that international treaty.

- **Judgment of 7 October 2015, *Wiayao Gnandakpa and Others* v. *Republic of Togo* (ECW/CCJ/JUD/18/15):**

§16: The Court pointed out that the Applicants invoked, in support of their requests, a number of texts from the national legal order, and ruled that the stated case law of the Court demanded that forthrightly, such references to the national law be set aside, since its jurisprudence holds that the judges of the ECOWAS Court of Justice shall not make any rulings on the constitutionality or legality of acts or actions undertaken by the States; that the ECOWAS Court shall rely solely on the international norms binding on the States, which justifies the fact that only the States shall constitute themselves as defendants in cases of human rights violation brought before the Court;

- **Judgment of 16 February 2016,** ***Abouzi Pilawike and 183 Others*** **v.** ***Office Togolais des Recettes (OTR) and Republic of Togo*** **(ECW/CCJ/JUD/01/16) :**

§20: The Court recalled that the rules it applies in disputes on human rights violation – of which the case cited above was an example – remain the rules of public international law, deriving from international conventions signed by the States bound by the conventions in question. Therefore, it was out of question that reference may be made to violations committed by entities other than States. The Court did not contest the possibility of the alleged violations being committed by persons clearly distinguishable from a State, but it was the view of the Court that on principled and formal grounds, only States may be sued before the Court to answer for any blames that may be laid against them as arising from international instruments binding on them. The Court so declared, as constituting its time-held case law.

- **Judgment of 16 February 2016,** ***Konso Kokou Parounam*** **v.** ***Republic of Togo*** **(ECW/CCJ/JUD/02/16):**

§23, 24, 26, and 27: The Court ruled as follows:

That, first of all, the Applicant relied on the national norms of Togo, particularly the Constitution of Togo, whose Articles 16 and 21 were referred to, in relation to respect for human beings and the prohibition of cruel, inhuman and degrading treatment.

In that connection, the Court recalled that disputes on human rights violation which it could adjudicate upon, relate only to rules invoked notably from international conventions binding on the States. That the Court had no mandate, in principle, to watch over the application of the national law, that mandate being specifically assigned to the domestic courts of the Member states. Therefore, as the Court had decided in other judgments, so it was that it had to set aside any argument which drew its strength from the domestic law of Togo.

That the Applicant equally invoked, in support of his claims, a number of international instruments whose legally applicable status remained doubtful. The Court held that more precisely, the texts would rather be classified among "soft laws", texts which are merely of persuasive or advisory significance, and would intrinsically be devoid of every form of obligation, and thereby, not likely to be binding on States. Such instruments are of course not completely valueless to the Court; they may contain precious indications for appreciating a "consensus" on certain given rules, notably towards the emergence of an international custom, an undoubted source of law. But in themselves, declaratory instruments are not binding on States, and the Court has always insisted on the fact that human rights allegations must be based on texts which indeed place obligations upon the States concerned. The Court again gave a reminder of its declaration in its judgment on the *Peter David Case* of 11 June 2010, in the terms of which:

> "... the Court recalls that the international regime of human rights protection before international bodies relies essentially on treaties to which States are parties as the principal subjects of international law."(§42). Similarly, in the above-cited judgment of 13 July 2015, Congrès pour la Démocratie et le Progrès (CDP) and Others **v.** Burkina Faso (ECW/CCJ/JUD/16/15), the Court held that "(...) its mandate is restricted to sanctioning States' disregard for the obligations arising from the international texts binding on them." (§25).

Hence, the Court set aside three instruments relied upon in the Application, instruments whose scope of application did not entail, as such, binding obligations upon the States:

> Body of Principles for the Protection of All Persons under Any Form of Detention or Imprisonment (19 December 1988); Basic Principles for the Treatment of Prisoners (adopted on 14 December 1990); and, the Declaration of Basic Principles of Justice for Victims of Crime and Abuse of Power.

- **Judgment of 20 April 2016, *Samba Barry* v. *Republic of Côte d'Ivoire* (ECW/CCJ/JUD/06/16):**

IV.20, p.13 (French version): The Court declared that the three-year statute bar invoked by the Defendant in the case cited above, is a concept originating from the domestic law; that such national norms are not applicable before the ECOWAS Court of Justice, and that indeed, the Court refers solely to international legal instruments which the Member States of ECOWAS are signatory to.

- **Judgment of 17 May 2016, *Marie Molmou and 114 Others* v. *Republic of Guinea* (ECW/CCJ/JUD/16/16):**

Page 7 (English version): "A point must be made clear here concerning the issue of citing of SOGUIPAH (a limited liability company, registered under the laws of Guinea) as a party in the instant case. It is apparent that SOGUIPAH was sued as a defendant before this Court, for human rights violation. Now, even if it is manifest that SOGUIPAH, as a company, maintains an overriding interest in the action brought before the Court, since it is SOGUIPAH which has been benefiting from the disputed land expropriation, SOGUIPAH cannot, as such, constitute a party in the proceedings, for the reason that only States may be cited as defendants in proceedings for human rights violation. This principle is easily explicable: the international instruments, international by definition, as invoked by those bringing the action, do remain instruments binding only on States; the States concerned are the only entities which signed those instruments, and thereafter, either ratified them or declared allegiance to them. Such instruments cannot therefore, by definition, be invoked against any other entities than the States concerned, for they shall not be binding on those other entities."

It may be mentioned in passing, (page 10 of the judgment, English version), that the Court disagreed with the Applicants on the status of "a people" under international law.

- **Judgment of 17 May 2016, *N'Guessan Yao* v. *Republic of Côte d'Ivoire* (ECW/CCJ/JUD/15/16):**

§24 and 25: "Now, the Court recalls that its mandate is not to adjudicate in terms of the most correct interpretation to be assigned to the domestic laws of Member States of ECOWAS, but to examine whether the manner in which the law was applied infringed upon the rights of the Applicant, as guaranteed by the international legal instruments invoked.

Similarly, the Court, in line with its case law, always held that it is not within its human rights protection mandate to re-examine and substitute its decisions for those whose facts may already have been submitted before the domestic courts and decided upon."

- **Judgment of 1 July 2016, *Djibril Yipéné Bassolé* v. *Burkina Faso* (ECW/CCJ/JUD/22/16) :**

Page 7 (English version): "Indeed, the written pleadings of the two Parties reveal numerous references to the domestic law of Burkina Faso, be it the Constitution or many other codes. The Applicant in particular meant to contest certain measures taken against him by virtue of provisions of the Constitution. On its part, the Defendant State invoked a number of texts – such as Law 061-2008/AN of 27 November 2008, Regulations on Networks and Electronic Communication Services in Burkina Faso, or the Burkinabe Civil Code – to justify, notably, the tapping of the telephone conversation.

Now, the norms referred to by the Court are, in principle, the norms of international law binding on the Member States. At any rate, that is the reason why only States are defendants in proceedings before the Court for human rights violation. Therefore, and in accordance with a well-established jurisprudence, all the points of argumentation based on the domestic law must be set aside."

The idea that the Court only applies the rules of public international law binding on States, has a corollary, which is the exclusion from the disputes coming before the Court, private disputes capable of being tried on the rules of civil law, commercial law or others. It has occurred at times that a case is brought before the Court claiming certain rights incontrovertibly arising from the jurisdiction of the domestic courts, in proceedings in private law, or perhaps private international law. Every abuse is therefore not amenable to trial proceedings under the international law of human rights, and some of such disputes under private law incidentally, very scarcely, brings into play issues concerning human rights. Thus, the Court, in such instances, carefully declines jurisdiction:

- **Judgment of 6 March 2014, *Bello Aminu Balla Kalto* v. *Republic of Niger* (ECW/CCJ/JUD/06/14):**

The Applicant is indeed a party in a civil suit, on a land issue, which has experienced numerous ups and downs, and she drags the Republic of Niger before the Court because she blames the State judicial services of the Republic of Niger for admitting the initiation of other procedures into the case, as a form of "delay tactics". The Court declares the Application inadmissible[7] :

§22: "It can be deduced from the Application for human rights violation filed by Madam Amina Balla Kalto against the Republic of Niger, that all the allegations on human rights violation made therein are either

[7] It is permissible to ask whether, further to the inadmissibility of the Application, it was not the Court's lack of jurisdiction, rather, which was at stake here.

concerned with, or related to civil procedures between her and Mr. Lamoudi Amadou in the dispute over ownership of Land Title No. 1417.

§23: "The Court thus finds that the matter brought before it concerns civil trials in respect of private interests between the Applicant and her contestant in that matter, and that the Republic of Niger is completely and absolutely outside the matter at stake. (...) That in such civil procedures where the law guarantees equal chances to each of the contesting parties, it is not plausible to invoke human rights violations against the State."

§25: The Court finally declared "(...) the Application for human rights violation lodged by Madam Amina Balla Kalto (...) inadmissible."

- **Judgment of 20 April 2015, *Les Etablissements Vamo and Kuekia Pascal* v. *Republic of Benin* (ECW/CCJ/JUD/12/15) :**

The case in reality deals with a dispute on lease. The Applicant is the leaseholder vis-à-vis *Office de Gestion du Stade de l'Amitié* (OGESA). The Court declares that it has no jurisdiction to adjudicate on the case.

IV.21- "... Indeed, the facts are presented as difficulties resulting from the execution of a lease agreement concluded between a Department of the State of Benin (Office de Gestion du Stade de L'Amitié (OGESA)) and Les Établissements VAMO and Mr. Pascal Kuekia, who managed their business activities at the rented premises;

IV.22- It is therefore a lease for professional purposes which came to an unhappy end resulting from implementation of the terms involved;

Moreover, the Plaintiff were so much conscious of that as to title their application as "a request for compensation";

IV.25- Nowhere in the provisions of Article 9 of Supplementary Protocol A/SP/01/05 of 19 January 2005 is it mentioned that one of the areas of the jurisdiction of the Court shall be in the instance where a dispute arises from the execution of a private contract concluded between an individual and a Member State;

Clearly, an application for compensation is not within the jurisdiction of the Court ..."

IV.26- In the light of the foregoing, it is clear that the facts stated by the Plaintiff cannot be construed as violation of human rights and the Court therefore has no jurisdiction to adjudicate on such matter..."

- **Judgment of 17 May 2016, *La Société du Pont de Kayes* v. *Republic of Mali* (ECW/CCJ/JUD/14/16):**

The Applicant blames the Malian authorities for aborting the execution of a concessionary contract on the toll bridge of *Kayes*, whereas the Applicant, the concessionaire, had contracted a loan to fulfil his obligations (construction of the bridge notably). The Republic of Mali cites the incompetence of the Court over the matter. The following ensues from the argumentation of the Republic of Mali:

Pages 5-6 (French version): The Court declared its competence as based on Article 10 of the 2005 Protocol. The question to ask is whether the default in fulfilling a contractual obligation is, per se, capable of being described as a "human rights violation".

The Court was of the view that the two areas cannot be mistaken, one for the other. A careful look at the arguments and pleas in law of *Société du Pont de Kayes* reveals that despite its attempts to place the harms it had allegedly suffered on the terrain of human rights violation, it cannot but constitute a matter of non-execution of commitments previously agreed upon.

Supposing the Applicant was actually entitled to any claim which may have been unlawfully denied him, such denial cannot necessarily be characterised as "human rights violation", since the concept of "human rights" is precise and makes reference to a catalogue of given prerogatives. The Court eventually upheld the position of the Defendant in declaring that the dispute submitted before the Court had nothing to do with "human rights", but that it remained a contractual issue, and thus, did not lend itself to an action being filed before the Court under Article 10 of the 2005 Protocol.

The Court held that any injury of economic nature, any undue loss of profit or earnings, does not necessarily amount to "human rights violation", and concluded that the dispute must be filed before judicial bodies other than the ECOWAS Court of Justice, and that it was not incumbent upon the ECOWAS Court to indicate such bodies.

- **Judgment of 17 May 2016, *Abdoulaye Koba* v. *Republic of Niger* (ECW/CCJ/JUD/09/16):**

The Applicant brought his case before the Court following bank operations which erroneously turned his account into debit balance. The decisions made by the domestic courts went against him, and he sued the Republic of Niger before the Court.

Naturally, the Court declined jurisdiction, since it was a purely private dispute:

Page 4 (French version): The Court pointed out that the dispute related to the payment of a sum of money which was due, in connection with bank operations. As things stood, the Application, purporting to bring the case under Article 9 of the 2005 Protocol, does not only expressly invoke a human rights violation, but as well, does not cite any provision of an international instrument which may serve as the basis for the claim.

In those circumstances, the Court ruled that it will be in order if one may ask whether the trial in question was truly within its remit, and in that sense, recalled its jurisprudence.

In Judgment of 2 November 2007, *Chief Frank C. Ukor* **v**. *Rachad Laleye* and *Republic of Benin*, the Court, after recalling that the two parties were engaged in business relations, ruled that there was no issue whatsoever of human rights violation, but simply contractual relations, and thus concluded that it had no powers for resolving the matter.

In *Case Concerning Mrs. Alice R. Chukwudolue and Others* **v**. Republic of Senegal (Judgment of 22 November 2007), the Court equally declined jurisdiction "... on the grounds that the present dispute does not concern human rights" (§54).

The *Abdoulaye Koba Case* cited above, without doubt, is a case in point. The Court, thus, did not hesitate in declaring that it had no powers to adjudicate over the case.

Such categorical dismissal of disputes on private relations has a fundamental consequence on the system of human rights protection guaranteed by the ECOWAS Court of Justice: it fends off the spectre of *drittwirkung*, and discountenances the theory of horizontal effects of human rights, that is to say, the application of human rights to relations among private individuals. The improbability of drittwirkung in the ECOWAS judicial system of human rights protection arises from several factors.

The first relates to the huge variety – the overbearing range of varieties – of the norms of reference relied upon by the ECOWAS judge. The absence of a single pointer of orientation, for the norms relied upon, the plurality of the texts that may well be invoked, prevents the judge from engaging in a continuing and deep-seated exegesis, the kind of exegesis that may enable one to discover all the potentialities of a text, and to extend the rights in cause beyond the initial entity the rights were meant for, the signatory State. It is easier for courts which work principally on the basis of only one text – as the European Court does with the European Convention on Human Rights, or the American Court, the American Convention on Human Rights – to explore to the hilt, the resourcefulness of the given text, its maximal potentialities, where drittwirkung is indeed one of such potentialities. In other words, what the mandate of the ECOWAS judge gains in width – a very wide spectrum of texts of reference – it loses in depth; in having recourse to many an instrument for a reference text, the ECOWAS judge loses full grasp of any of them – "grasp all, lose all" – as the saying goes.

A second factor has to do with the fact that the texts ordinarily brandished before the Court – essentially the various Conventions of the United Nations, and the African Charter on Human and Peoples' Rights – are not particularly designed with an intention for integration, since they are not specially made for the judge in the domestic court, who adjudicates on cases between private persons, nor do those instruments seek to affect the national judicial orders. Not necessarily incorporating the nationally guaranteed rights, they have a little less chance of being applicable to disputes arising among private persons. One of the rare instances – probably the only one – where these norms may be taken into account in the handling of disputes among private persons, is where they are integrated into the "constitutional bloc", that is to say, when they get "converted" into constitutional rights. Yet still, the national system will need to empower such private persons to institute constitutional proceedings, notably by way of referrals for preliminary determination on constitutionality.

The third factor which tends to buttress the improbability of drittwirkung in the ECOWAS judicial system is the absence of any mechanism of referrals for preliminary determination in respect of disputes on human rights violation. The duty assigned the Court, as well as the effects the Court ascribes to the rights in cause could have affected the situation of private persons if the Community judge were empowered to have a say, even incidentally, in domestic judicial procedures submitted before the national courts, concerning opposing interests of private persons. Such collaboration between the national level and the Community level does indeed exist for other categories of disputes, but not for disputes on human rights.

Finally, the manner in which the Court itself conceives of its mandate constitutes an obstacle to the emergence of horizontal effects. In handling the cases submitted before it, the Court manifests a certain timidity in the use of its powers. It limits itself to finding violations, and almost invariably, orders reparation in monetary terms. No indication of measures – notably of a legislative order – to the States, nor directives to the national judges, borne out of an interpretation of the texts. The handling of the disputes does not go beyond the international sphere, and does not have a prophylactic ambition for a sort of structural purge, the eradication of an original canker, sometimes embedded in the legislations, or found in a consolidated but questionable judicial interpretation.

For all these reasons, it becomes plausible to consider that the granting of horizontal effects will not be for tomorrow. That, again, offers an opportunity for evolving the jurisprudence of the Court.

SECTION 2

REPRESENTATION OF PARTIES AND THIRD-PARTY REPRESENTATION

After the parties themselves, we need to turn our attention to the other actors in the proceedings for human rights violation: the representatives of the parties themselves (Paragraph 1), and the third-party interveners known as *amici curiae* (Paragraph 2).

Paragraph 1

Representation of parties

The issue is settled by Article 12 of Protocol A/P1/7/91 of 6 July 1991, which provides:

> "Each party to a dispute shall be represented before the Court by one or more agents nominated by the party concerned for this purpose. The agents may, where necessary, request the assistance of one or more Advocates or Counsels who are recognised by the laws and regulations of the Member States as being empowered to appear in Court in their area of jurisdiction."

In truth, as couched, this provision could give the impression that the representation in question is done in principle by "agents", with "advocates" or "counsels" given the possibility of assisting them. In practice, there is nothing of that nature. Agents and advocates or counsels are placed strictly on equal footing, and rather fortunately, the Court's interpretation of the said Article remains flexible and liberal: not only is representation possible for either category, but every form of discrimination by the litigants among these categories is forbidden, the idea having emerged that only States may appoint "agents", to the exclusion of other litigants.

That being the case, the very phenomenon of representation before the Court – what one may call the "office of the agent, lawyer or counsel", remains a mandatory requirement before the Court, as illustrated in the following decision:

- **Judgment of 17 March 2011, *Bakary Sarré and 28 Others* v. *Republic of Mali* (ECW/CCJ/JUD/03/11) :**

> §40: "... in the instant case, the Court notes that Mr. Bakary Sarré did not nominate a duly constituted agent or lawyer. Consequently, his Application does not follow the due process, in terms of formal presentation; the Application is therefore inadmissible."
>
> §41: "The Court, (...) adjudges that the criteria for representation before the Court were not respected by Mr. Bakary Sarré, since he was neither represented by an agent nor a lawyer."

A.- Lawyers

The only condition laid down by Article 12 of the 1991 Protocol is that the lawyers must be recognised by the laws and regulations of the Member States as being empowered to appear in court in their area of jurisdiction. It must indeed be noted that unlike other international African courts, it is not an issue of "having one's name registered on a list of persons called to the Bar in a Member State", which is a more onerous requirement than the one stated here. Having the right to plead in a given country is, without doubt, easier than being registered on the Bar of that country, since this latter condition may even imply that the person concerned must have passed a competitive qualifying examination to become a lawyer, subject to the existence of conventions of co-operation among the States, thus granting the right to plead to the lawyers of the signatory States[8].

---

8 See for example, for comparison purposes, Article 22 of Regulation N°01/96/CM/UEMOA of 5 July 1996 on Rules of Procedure of the Court of Justice of UEMOA, which, on its part,

Consequently, the right to plead before the Court is acquired by every citizen of a State which, for example, has signed an agreement of co-operation with a Member State of ECOWAS, once such agreement provides, of course, for the possibility for lawyers to plead cases in court. One can safely bet that with such a rule, there is a great number of lawyers potentially qualified to plead before the ECOWAS Court of Justice, in view, both, of the number of conventions of such nature concluded by the States (notably with the western States), and of the sufficiently current nature of the right to plead in court, which such conventions make provision for.

B.- Agents

The existence of such a notion may be a cause for surprise. Without doubt, the framers of the Protocol were influenced by the practice, in force before the International Court of Justice at The Hague[9], of the appointment of "Agents" by the States. To the extent that an issue was raised as to whether, once the 2005 reform had opened the doors of the Court to private persons, such right of appointing "Agents" should not be maintained for the States only.

The text being thus silent in that regard, sides were taken towards a literal interpretation – a textual interpretation, in fact – resulting in maintaining or affirming the right of private persons to appoint an "agent", irrespective of their right, unchallenged, to appoint a "lawyer" or "counsel".

In truth, the very nature of the Court and the typical mandate assigned it, towards the safeguard of human rights, called for such generosity. Procedures for the defence of human rights often lay emphasis on the intervention of third parties, for and on behalf of the applicants – "direct" or "personally injured" victims – willingly uninformed or even penniless, and who will therefore need to be "assisted". By maintaining the right of private persons to appoint "agents", the Court clearly took the option to carve a place, in the proceedings, for human rights bodies, who thus saw conferred on them the prerogative, following the path laid out for the "lawyers", to plead a case before the Court. The "agent" thus becomes the "lawyer" who, for one reason or the other, one could not gain access to. In adopting that stance – which certainly deserves to be maintained –

---

states the obligation for every lawyer pleading a case before the said Court to be "... a registered member of the Bar of one of the Member States."

9 Article 42 §1 of the Statute of the International Court of Justice

the ECOWAS Court of Justice did not only keep faith with current procedural practices in matters concerning the judicial safeguard of human rights, but equally sought to strike a balance regarding the restriction made mention of above, consisting of opening its doors to only "direct" or "personally harmed" victims to bring their cases before the Court – another rule which shall not be unreasonable to maintain, in view of its mandate as a court – and not a "militant" body – with the ever present risk of *actio popularis*, which may culminate in an overload of cases before the Court.

Such position, which, in all its nuances, appears balanced and wise, should, in our estimation, be maintained.

We will add two more points, in finalising. First of all, nothing defines the status of an "agent". The Court, in following the example of its senior institution, the UNO, defers to the will of the applicant in conferring the status on such individual or entity, and the Court does not really exercise any control on the assignment of that status. Secondly, the actual case law of the Court tends to be particularly demanding on the issue of the rights to defence and the necessity of being assisted by a lawyer, in the Member States. As we shall see, one of the most rigorous aspects of the jurisprudence of the Court is hinged on such right to defence and the corollaries thereto. Under such conditions too, the Court is bound to grant access to applicants. It thus occurred that a party had to be represented only by an "agent" and not by a "lawyer":

- **Judgment of 27 October 2008, *Hadijatou Mani Koraou* v. *Republic of Niger* (ECW/CCJ/JUD/06/08):**

§2: Counsel for the Applicant was SCPA Chaibou-Nanzir (A Professional Partnership of Lawyers), a legal firm registered with the Court of Appeal of Niamey, in the Republic of Niger. The Applicant was *"... assisted by Mrs. Helena Duffy and Mr. Ibrahima Kane of Inter Rights, London."*

- **Judgment of 17 March 2011, *Bakary Sarré and 28 Others* v. *Republic of Mali* (ECW/CCJ/JUD/03/11) :**

§20: It was the Ambassador of Mali to Nigeria, described as *"Agent"* of the Republic of Mali, who defended the Republic of Mali in court.

- **Judgment of 8 July 2011, *Ocean King Nigeria Ltd.* v. *Republic of Senegal* (ECW/CCJ/JUD/07/11), Judgment of 26 January 2012, *El Hadji Mame Abdou Gaye* v. *Republic of Senegal* (ECW/CCJ/JUD/03/12):**

§1: The Republic of Senegal was represented and defended, in the two cases, by a person who was not of the status of a "lawyer", and was a deputy "State Judicial Officer" of his country.

Paragraph 2

Third parties

The third parties concern (A) Interveners in the trial proceedings, and (B) *amici curiae*.

A.- Interveners

As currently provided by the texts, intervention, strictly speaking, is reserved for States, as is apparent from Article 21 of Protocol A/P1/7/91:

> "Should a Member State consider that it has an interest that may be affected by the subject-matter of a dispute before the Court, it may submit by way of a written application a request to be permitted to intervene."

Article 89 of the Rules of the Court states the various conditions under which an intervention shall be submitted: it must be made within six weeks of the publication in the *Official Journal of the Community* of the notice of registration of application initiating proceedings (Article 13(6) of the Rules of the Court makes it an obligation to publish such notice of registration of the initiating application in the said journal); an indication of a minimum set of pieces of information relating to the intervener; a statement of the circumstances establishing the right to intervene (which means that there is no acquired right of intervention, contrary to the impression one may have upon an initial reading of Article 21 of the 1991 Protocol); the decision of the Court either to admit or not to admit the application for intervention, once the matter comes before the President of the Court; and in case the Court allows the application, a prescription of the time period within which the intervener may submit a statement in intervention. The content of the statement in intervention is equally determined by the same Article 89.

In one of the rare cases where the Court had to deal with an application for intervention, the Court declared it inadmissible (Judgment of 18 November 2010, *Hissène Habré* **v.** *Republic of Senegal* (ECW/CCJ/JUD/06/10)).

B.- Amici curiae

According to *le Dictionnaire du droit international public,* (Dictionary of Public International Law) *amicus curiae,* an expression which stands for "friend of the Court", is originally "a legal concept of Anglo-American domestic law which refers to the prerogative accorded a personality or body not constituted as a party to the judicial procedure, to furnish information of such nature as to enlighten the court on questions of fact and law."[10].

Nowhere in the texts organising the ECOWAS Court of Justice do we find a single provision devoted to the practice of *amicus curiae*. Irrespective of the silence of the texts on the subject-matter, the Court has, at least on two occasions, admitted certain "friends of the Court" to its proceedings: in *Case Concerning Tokumbo Lijadu-Oyemade* **v.** *Executive Secretary of |ECOWAS and Others* (Judgment of 10 October 2005, ECW/CCJ/JUD/02/08) and in *Case Concerning Linda Gomez and 7 Others* **v.** *Republic of The Gambia* (Judgment of 14 February 2014, ECW/CCJ/JUD/05/14). One can equally cite another case, pending as at the time these lines are being written: *Federation of African Journalists and 3 Others* **v.** *Republic of The Gambia* (General List, ECW/CCJ/APP/36/15).

Conversely, the Court refused such admittance to its procedure, in *Case Concerning CDP and Others* **v.** *Burkina Faso* (Judgment of 13 July 2015, ECW/CCJ/JUD/16/15)[11].

Such jurisprudential disparities are regrettable. This is why it is urgent, in our view, that the issue be resolved once and for all, by taking into account the practice of amicus curiae procedure, and ensure that the amicus curiae norm becomes a firmly regular feature of the Court, so as to avert the deviations the concept has engendered before other courts, be they national or international. It indeed appears necessary to us that the ECOWAS Court adopt a stand in consonance with the practice of comparable international courts, by being open to modern judicial trends which, in actual terms, entail the practice of *amicus curiae* procedure.[12].

---

[10] SALMON J. (dir.) ; Bruxelles, Bruylant, 2001, p.62.

[11] It seems, in that respect, that the Anglo-Saxon tradition may be more inclined to admit an amicus curiae to its trial proceedings than the Romano-Germanic tradition, as may appear to have been demonstrated by the very attitude of judges of the Court classified as belonging to either of the two legal traditions.

[12] Certainly, indeed Article 16 of the 1991 Protocol in particular, exists, and provides that the Court may have recourse to expert opinion during its trial proceedings; but, apart from such

It would be unfortunate if the Community Court, whose essential mandate consists, in contemporary terms, of handling disputes on human rights violation, should operate only on the fringes of an evolving trend which does take into account the difficulty and increasing complexity of the task of trying cases, notably in an international context where States have lost the monopoly of access to the law courts, with the reforms of 2005 marvellously illustrating the removal of the dominance of the State in the judicial procedure within ECOWAS.

The multiplicity of voices generated by international trial proceedings; the emergence of various voices differing from those of the litigants in the trial; the progressive banishment of a strict bilateral logic in the confrontation of interests; the consideration given, when trying cases, to issues which cannot be confined to the strict interests of the parties in the case; the multiateralisation of such judicial procedure; – all, do surely beckon the West African Court towards adopting a friendly approach which must practically translate into making provision for welcoming willing third parties, so as to lend a hearing ear to a differing judicial tone which cannot but enrich the decisions of the Court. Being in line with modern trends, more especially, beyond merely seeking to be in vogue; acknowledging the increasingly complex nature of the job of trying cases, and thereby demonstrating humility, in listening to other voices, and thus incorporating legitimate concerns other than the purely judicial and technical; – all would enable the ECOWAS Court evolve its methods and procedures towards resolving the complex cases which will come before it. Further on, we will find in the present work, shades of reflection on the subject-matter of amicus curiae, which may constitute outlines of a legal framework in the direction being advocated here.[13].

---

power being conceived here from a rather "technical" standpoint, of "measures of inquiry", the abundance of clear details as to what *amicus curiae* is all about, does favour a clearly independent introduction of the amicus curiae procedure, distinct from mere "measures of inquiry".

13 See article entitled: "**Prospects of *amicus curiae* before the ECOWAS Court of Justice**" infra, Part II of this work.

CHAPTER 2

THE JURISDICTION OF THE COURT AND ADMISSIBILITY OF APPLICATIONS

The Court is indeed required to make a pronouncement, beforehand, on these two points.

SECTION 1

JURISDICTION

There may exist, first of all, hurdles on the path of the Court to be cleared, in the exercise of its jurisdiction. It is natural that, given the "public order" nature of the exercise of the jurisdiction of the Court, the latter may, on its own motion (Paragraph 1) state such hurdles, as a means of declaring that it has no jurisdiction over a matter brought before it. But, the Court is always bound by duty, even where it can be assumed that there is no manifest obstacle in the exercise of its jurisdiction on a matter before it, (Paragraph 2) to uphold, in express terms, its jurisdiction to adjudicate on the case at hand, in the sense of establishing the basis of such competence to sit on the case, and provide justification for that, before exercising the judicial function of trying the case, in the practical sense of the word.

Paragraph 1

Hurdles in the exercise of jurisdiction

Such hurdles may notably arise from the fact that, it may be: (A) a national, or (B) an international authority, that is competent to adjudicate on the matter, and not the Court.

A.- Vis-à-vis domestic political or judicial authorities

The obstacles to every form of jurisdiction exercisable by the Court, as understood here, are of a twin nature: either the Court asserts its lack of jurisdiction for making pronouncements on the legality or otherwise (in the broad sense of the word) of acts and instruments made by the national authorities of ECOWAS Member States, or the Court expresses its incompetence to sit on the matter as an appellate court or a *cour de cassation* (court of cassation) to adjudicate over decisions already made by the domestic courts of the ECOWAS Member States. These two points will be discussed one after the other.

1.- The Court lacks jurisdiction over the domestic law of Member States

The statement according to which the Community Court is not competent to make judgments on the legality or illegality of certain issues, within a given scope, is very often cited in its case law. The temptation is indeed real for a litigant – who, we can easily imagine, is asking for justice from outside his country because the national authorities of his country have denied him his rights – to ask for redress for a breach of legality. It must however be admitted that it was especially in the early stages of its functioning mechanism that the Court encountered that sort of problem. Once that stage is gone, the Court has not ceased to affirm its lack of jurisdiction in matters of that nature:

- **Judgment of 27 October 2008, *Hadijatou Mani Koraou* v. *Republic of Niger* (ECW/CCJ/JUD/06/08):**

The Applicant devoted an entire portion of her argumentation to how necessary it was for the Republic of Niger to adopt laws more capable of protecting women against discriminatory customary practices.

> § 60: "As regards the Applicant's first plea-in-law, the Court finds that it does not have the mandate to examine the laws of Member States of the Community in abstracto, but rather, to ensure the protection of the rights of individuals whenever such individuals are victims of the violation of those rights which are recognised as theirs, and the Court does so by examining concrete cases brought before it."

- **Judgment of 9 May 2011, *Center for Democracy and Development, and Center for Defence of Human Rights and Democracy* v. *Mamadou Tandja and Republic of Niger* (ECW/CCJ/JUD/05/11):**

§38: "The Court, (...) declares its lack of jurisdiction to make a declaration on the legality or constitutionality of the acts made by the authorities of Member States, pursuant to the provisions of their domestic law."

- **Judgment of 22 February 2013, *Abdoulaye Baldé and Others* v. *Republic of Senegal* (ECW/CCJ/JUD/04/13):**

§70: "(...) the Court holds that the dispute between the Parties in regard to violation of the right to fair trial cannot compel the Court to examine the domestic laws of the Republic of Senegal as to illegal wealth."

§72: "(...) the Court recalls its consistently held case law that it has no mandate to examine the national laws of Member States or to review decisions made by the domestic courts of Member States."

- **Judgment of 19 July 2013, *Karim Meissa Wade* v. *Republic of Senegal* (ECW/CCJ/JUD/09/13) :**

§75: "The alleged violation must have resulted from an actual implementation of the law, to the detriment of the applicant in question. To that effect, mere presumptions or conjectures do not suffice. As such, the Court, in its Judgment of 22 February 2013, has already held that it has no jurisdiction to examine in abstracto Law No. 81-53 and Law No. 81-54 of 10 July 1981 relating to the Combat of Illegal Wealth and the creation of the Anti Illegal-Wealth Court (...)"

§76: "(...), the Court adjudges that it lacks the jurisdiction to examine virtual or potential human rights violations as alleged by Mr. Karim Meissa Wade."

- **Judgment of 1 July 2016, Judgment of 1 April 2016, *Djibril Yipéné Bassolé* v. *Burkina Faso* (ECW/CCJ/JUD/22/16):**

Page 15: "The Court notes that even if the two Parties did profusely argue on the very principle concerning restricting the right to privacy through the instrumentality of tapping conversations on the telephone, the two Parties did not in any way indicate with certainty, the impact such recorded telephone conversations may have had during the procedure.

Given the circumstances of the case, it will not suffice to demonstrate the mere existence of such conversations, as to having been tapped, so as to win one's case; it must still be proved that the recorded conversations did indeed seriously affect the rights of the Applicant.

The act of tapping telephone conversations is not in itself illegal. Several judicial systems admit the principle underlying it, for the purposes of the necessities of an inquiry. In such circumstances, one cannot criticise its mere application, but adduce evidence to the effect that at a given time of the procedure, the conditions under which it was applied violated the rights of the person targeted. Without that convincing requirement, without any proof of concrete violation, the Court would purely and simply be making pronouncements on the domestic legislations of the Member States, but to engage in such an exercise is contrary to the time-held case law of the Court."

2.- The Court is neither an appellate court nor a Cour de cassation (Court of cassation) over the domestic courts of Member States

- **Judgment of 22 March 2007, *Moussa Léo Keita* v. *Mali* (ECW/CC/JUD/03/07):**

§26: "In reality it (i.e. the Application filed by the Applicant) makes no demand on any Community text. Moussa Léo Keïta complains of being a victim of injustice committed by his State, and of the malfunction or poor running of the justice system of his country. In this perspective, the Community Court of Justice is powerless: it cannot adjudicate upon the decisions of the national courts."

- **Judgment of 4 March 2010, *Dr. Mahamat Seid Abazene* v. *Republic of Mali, African* (ECW/CCJ/JUD/02/10):**

To challenge his dismissal, and upon exhausting all the avenues available to him for seeking redress, the Applicant decided to bring his case before a Malian judge (at the Administrative Section of the Supreme Court of Mali), who, on 17 January 2008, declined jurisdiction on the matter brought. The Applicant is of the view that the Malian judge made his judgment "under duress from the African Union (AU)" (alleging that the President of the AU Commission must have persuaded the Institute, his employer, from engaging in a judicial procedure which would "turn out to be long and costly"), and from the Republic of Mali (alleging that the Republic of Mali must have ordered the Supreme Court of Mali "in diplomatic terms", to declare that it had no jurisdiction to adjudicate on the matter). The Applicant equally avers that the Republic of Mali must have organised the attack on him as well as his "kidnapping" by the Bamako police on 5 August 2008. He further alleges that he was denied justice. One notes the following statement in the resulting judgment:

§ 28: "(…) the Community Court of Justice, ECOWAS is not an Appeal Court before which cases decided by the Courts in Member States could still be brought, in order to determine the jurisdiction of the latter."

- **Judgment of 17 March 2011, *Bakary Sarré and 28 Others* v. *Republic of Mali* (ECW/CCJ/JUD/03/11):**

The Court notes that the Applicants sought to ask it to: "(…) *sit afresh, by examining Judgments No. 188 and 116 of the Supreme Court of Mali* (§26)."

The Court recalls the terms of its Judgment of 7 October 2005, *Jerry Ugokwe* **v.** *Nigeria and Christian Okeke* (ECW/CCJ/JUD/03/05):

> §32: "Appealing against the decisions of the national courts of Member States does not form part of the powers of the Court (…). The ECOWAS Court of Justice is not a court of appeal or a court of cassation."

The Court equally recalls the terms of its Judgment of 22 March 2007, *Moussa Léo Keita* **v.** *Republic of Mali* (ECW/CCJ/JUD/03/07):

> §26: "(…) the Community Court of Justice … cannot adjudicate upon the decisions of the national courts."

- **Judgment of 7 October 2011, *Cheikh Abdoulaye Mbengue* v. *Republic of Mali* (ECW/CCJ/JUD/08/11):**

> §38 : "The Court observes that the requests to re-open the judicial inquiry and annul the arrest warrant derive from the sphere of the domestic judicial competence of the Republic of Mali, and that in that respect, the Court recalls its consistently held case law and declines jurisdiction on any application brought seeking to overturn decisions of the domestic courts of ECOWAS Member States; this Honourable Court is neither an appeal court nor a court of cassation of the domestic courts of the ECOWAS Member States."

- **Judgment of 26 January 2012, *Elhadj Mame Abdou Gaye* v. *Republic of Senegal* (ECW/CCJ/JUD/03/12):**

§46: The Court recalled its time-held case law according to which the ECOWAS Court is not an appellate court over decisions made by the national courts of the Member States, and went further to rule that even if it is competent to examine human rights violations relating to the conduct of the procedures carried out before the national courts while ensuring the observance of human rights for persons under investigation, the mandate of the Court is strictly limited to examining the violations alleged.

- **Judgment of 3 July 2013, *Aziagbede Kokou and 33 Others, Atsou Komlavi and 4 Others, Tomekpe A. Lanou and 29 Others* v. *Republic of Togo* (ECW/CCJ/JUD/07/13):**

> §38, 39, 40: "As things stand, the Court may not make any finding (...) or ascribe any blame whatsoever against the Republic of Togo, without unduly interfering in the conduct of the proceedings pending at the national level, and without violating the freedom of the judge at the domestic court.
>
> (...) the Court is (...) of the view that for it to set that mandate in motion, consideration must be given to the pragmatic approach whereby appropriate importance is accorded to the proximity between the charges made and the judge at the domestic court, just as the same importance must be given to the prerogatives of the judge at the domestic court.
>
> The Court finds that it is not within its human rights protection mandate to substitute its own viewpoint on the facts of a case for that of the domestic courts seised with the same case (...)."

- **Judgment of 3 July 2013, *Kpatcha Gnassingbe and Others* v. *Republic of Togo* (ECW/CCJ/JUD/06/13):**

> §36: "Furthermore, the Court declares that since the Republic of Togo relied on its own Constitutional Law to justify the procedure used against Kpatcha Gnassingbe (procedure for flagrant offence), it is outside the mandate of the Court to examine a decision adopted by a domestic court of a Member State in accordance with the constitutional provisions of that Member State."
>
> §68: "(...) Furthermore, the Court considers that it is not within its remit to adjudge whether the charges for which the Applicants were arrested and detained were established or not, so as not to run the risk of usurping the powers of the domestic courts of the Member State in question, which would be contrary to the established and consistently held case law of the Honourable Court. The jurisdiction of the Court simply lies in examining whether the detention and related arrest of the Applicants had a legal basis."

It is the same doctrine which has been upheld, despite the reservations one may entertain regarding the equation: *arbitrary detention = absence of legal basis*, which seems established by the Court[14].

---

14 One cannot but agree with the Court when it reaffirms its creed here, which consists in refraining from constituting itself as an appeal court or a cour de cassation over the

- **Judgment of 28 January 2014,** ***Alimu Akeem*** **v.** ***Federal Republic of Nigeria*** **(ECW/CCJ/JUD/01/14) :**

> §40, 41, and 42: "The Court notes that it is within the jurisdiction of the criminal martial court before which Alimu Akeem appeared, to determine whether he is guilty or not for the incidents which occurred in the performance of his functions.
>
> The instant Court is not seised with the same facts. The Court is rather seised in regard to the detention imposed on him in the course of the procedure for the determination of that case, which he considers long, illegal, a violation of human dignity, and notably a violation of Article 6 of the African Charter on Human and Peoples' Rights. On the other hand, he brings his Application in regard to alleged physical torture amounting to violation of Article 5 of the said Charter.
>
> Similarly, it is the view of the instant Court that under such circumstances, the findings or conclusions established or yet to be established by the martial courts of Nigeria seised to determine whether Alimu Akeem is guilty or not, and to sentence him, do not have any determining effect on the Court's adjudication upon the grievances and requests brought by the Applicant. At any rate, the Application before the instant Court has no criminal connotation. As such, the criminal nature of the action instituted against Alimu Akeem in Nigeria cannot be

---

decisions of the national courts. One must however regret the drift eventually engaged in by the Court – and which had already been the case at the beginning of paragraph 68, where it is written that: "*The Court considers (...) that since the detention of the Applicant had a legal basis, it cannot be described as arbitrary*" – thus bringing to light the confusion or the equation: "arrest made on a legal basis = non-arbitrary arrest". Unfortunately, it was not the first time that the Court had yielded to the temptation to sound "empirically factual" in recognising the mere existence of a norm while setting aside its "relevance" or "value". In the same judgment, it reiterates in paragraph 65, that "*... arbitrary detention implies that a person has been detained without legal basis (...)*". Further, in Judgment of 22 February 2013, in *Abdoulaye Baldé and Others* **v.** *Republic of Senegal* (ECW/CCJ/JUD/04/13), the Court had already posited that the ban imposed on the applicants to prevent them from going outside the national territory was "*... unlawful because it had no legal basis.*" (§77). Now, it is not accurate to say that every arrest effected on the basis of a text constitutes a non-arbitrary denial of freedom. It suffices to imagine a scenario, somewhat disconcerting, but perfectly capable of occurring, of a law which in actual fact "would legitimise" arbitrariness, in enacting for example, a legal instrument empowering the police to arrest persons on the basis of their ethnic group or home town. Such absurdity would theoretically "have a legal basis", but who may argue that it is "not arbitrary"? Rendering "having a legal basis" synonymous with "non-arbitrary" is, without doubt, somewhat misplaced, and for the Court to simply insist on its avowed position not to retry cases that have already been settled by the domestic courts of the ECOWAS Member States, it will not be necessary for it resort to such equation or synonymy.

admitted as a ground for declaring the Application which the instant Court is seised with as inadmissible. (…)

(…) The instant Court is therefore not asked to re-examine the decisions of the martial courts of Nigeria. Consequently, this plea in law must equally be set aside."

- **Judgment of 31 January 2014, *Avocats sans frontières - France and ThankGod Ebohs* v. *Federal Republic of Nigeria and Edo State Government* (ECW/CCJ/JUD/18/14) :**

§50: The Court ruled that the issue as to whether or not the Court may adjudicate as an appellate body upon decisions made by the domestic courts, was irrelevant in the case at hand, since the Court had on numerous occasions clearly indicated in its case law that the scope of its judicial powers does not extend to appeal sittings on decisions made by the national courts.

- **Judgment of 24 April 2015, *Agriland* v. *Republic of Côte d'Ivoire* (ECW/CCJ/JUD/07/15):**

§44: "… it is important to recall that the Honourable Court, a Community Court of Justice, has no mandate to examine decisions made by the domestic courts of Member States, much less to interpret the provisions of their domestic law; (…) indeed, the Court has, in several judgments it has delivered, held that adjudication on applications seeking to reverse decisions of the domestic courts of Member States falls outside its jurisdiction."

- **Judgment of 13 July 2015, *Congrès pour la Démocratie et le Progrès (CDP) and Others* v. *Burkina Faso* (ECW/CCJ/JUD/16/15):**

§24, 25 and 26: "The first of these principles, which assumes a particular significance in the case submitted before the Court, is the Court's refusal to assume the role of a judge over the domestic law of the Member States. The Court has indeed always recalled that it is not a body set up with a mandate for settling cases whose subject-matter is the interpretation of the law or the Constitution of the Member States of ECOWAS. Two effects arise therefrom.

The first is that the present judicial argumentation must be devoid of every form of reliance on the domestic law, be it on the Constitution of Burkina Faso, or on any norms whatsoever related to the Constitution of Burkina Faso. In their written pleadings, the Applicants indeed made reference to both the Constitution of Burkina Faso (Article 1) and the Charter of Transition (Article 1). Such references shall be deemed as inappropriate before the judges of the ECOWAS Court of Justice. As an International Court, its mandate is restricted to sanctioning States' disregard for the obligations arising from the international texts binding on them.

The second effect is that there can be no question, in the instant case, of seeking to examine the meaning which must be ascribed to the new Article 135 of the Burkina Faso Electoral Code. It is tempting, given the relative ambiguity of the text complained of, to engage in a legal exegesis of the Burkina Faso Electoral Code, to ascribe to it a certain meaning, or to orient the construction of that domestic law along a given path."

- **Judgment of 1 December 2015, *Mamadou Moustapha Kakali* v. *Republic of Niger* (ECW/CCJ/JUD/26/15):**

Pages 6 and 7 (French version): It appeared to the Court in its judgment on the case that the grievance brought, regarding violation of the right to fair trial, was simply used as a means to criticise the very basis of the decisions which had been made previously. The Court found that the Application submitted before it further dealt with the framing and basis of the rulings and judgments delivered by the judge in the domestic court of Niger, and also that the justification can be found not only in referring to the very letter of the argument put forward by the Applicant, but to the requests he makes at the end of his Application.

Therefore, the Court concluded that the Applicant was asking the Court to interfere in the domestic judicial procedures of the Member State, and to constitute itself, in one way of the other, into an appeal court or a court with powers to quash or revise the decisions made by the national courts of a Member State. Thus, the Court eventually ruled that it cannot grant the requests made by the Applicant, in line with its consistently held case law.

The Court does not merely dismiss the applicants' submissions when the requests made therein consist, in explicit terms, of asking the Court to re-examine the decisions made by the national courts. The Court goes much further. It indeed does occur that while avoiding a clear and direct request for such re-assessment of the rulings of the national courts, an application tends to train the judge on this field of reforming national judiciary decisions.

The Court carefully uncovers the applicant's hidden agenda, by shedding light, somewhat, on the truth hidden behind the requests made, in declaring the actual consequences of the applicants' own demands, before dismissing the claims brought, and affirming once again, its incompetence to adjudicate over the matter. There is a string of decisions in which the ECOWAS judge proceeded to remove the camouflage on the requests made by the applicants, by deciphering and unmasking the claims submitted before the Court. The following judgments may be cited in that regard:

- Judgment of 17 March 2011, *Bakary Sarré and 28 Others* **v.** *Republic of Mali* (ECW/CCJ/JUD/03/11):

> §31: "The Court concludes that it can be deduced from the Application filed by Mr. Bakary Sarré and 28 Others against the Republic of Mali, that the said Application substantially seeks to obtain from the Court of Justice of ECOWAS, a reversal of Judgments No. 188 and No. 116 as delivered by the Supreme Court of Mali and it seeks to project the Court of Justice of ECOWAS as a court of cassation over the Supreme Court of Mali. Viewed from that angle, the Honourable Court declares that it has no jurisdiction to adjudicate on the matter."

What is interesting here is the use of the word "substantially". Indeed, the Court could have said "implicitly". What the Court is driving at is that granting the request made in the application will objectively result in a reform of the decisions in question, as made by the national courts.

- **Judgment of 7 October 2011, *Ameganvi Manavi Isabelle and Others* v. *Republic of Togo* (ECW/CCJ/JUD/09/11):**

The Applicants are parliamentarians challenging their dismissal from the National Assembly following adverse circumstances encountered by their political party. They had resigned from the UFC (Union of the Forces of Change) of Gilchrist Olympio, and joined a new party, the National Alliance for Change (ANC), formed by J. P. Fabre. Letters of resignation from the National Assembly, alleged to have originated from the said parliamentarians, were addressed to the President of the National Assembly by a new Chairman of the UFC parliamentary group. The Chairman of ANC thus transmitted the letters to the Constitutional Court. The Applicants contest the authenticity of those letters, claiming that they are altered documents which must have been supplemented with their surnames and first names.

They blame the Constitutional Court for merely endorsing the so-called "resignations" and gone ahead to replace them as Parliamentarians, instead of assessing the validity of the resignation letters in question. They aver that the Court thus disregarded provisions of the Rules of Procedure of the said Constitutional Court, and trampled on their right to be heard before being judged. On its part, the Defendant State argues that the provisions of the Electoral Code were respected, and that the ECOWAS Court of Justice is not an appellate body with a mandate to make rulings over decisions made by the national courts.

In the operative statement of the judgment delivered by the Court, the Court, in substance:

- Dismissed the objection regarding incompetence of the ECOWAS Court of Justice, as raised by Togo;
- Declared that it had jurisdiction to examine the allegations of human rights violation.

And, on the merits of the case:

- Adjudged that the Republic of Togo violated the fundamental human rights of the Applicants regarding their right to fair hearing, as provided for under Article 10 of the Universal Declaration of Human Rights and Article 7 of the African Charter on Human and Peoples' Rights.

However, the Court cautiously "avoids" the judgment delivered by the Constitutional Court of Togo, and makes no comment on it, so as not to challenge, thereby, the decisions made therein, even if, in examining the same procedure of the said Constitutional Court, the ECOWAS Court uncovered a violation which the judges at the domestic court did not find: disregard for the Applicants' right to be heard during a judicial or quasi-judicial procedure.[15].

---

[15] This judgment is interesting in the sense that it illustrates the subtle dialectics between the national law and the law applied by the ECOWAS judge. It is known that in principle the ECOWAS Court is neither an appellate court nor a *cour de cassation*, a court for quashing decisions made by the national courts. It is equally known that the ECOWAS Court refrains from every form of assessment as to the legality or otherwise of the domestic law of the authorities of the Defendant State.

The dilemma arising from the case was however for the Court to resolve the issue brought before it without encroaching upon the jurisdiction reserved for the domestic courts, given that the Constitutional Court of Togo had already delivered a judgment on that same dispute. The ECOWAS Court is going to remain faithful to its doctrine, in "refraining from every comment on" the decision made by the national court, by carefully abstaining from bringing the said decision under the critical searchlight of the ECOWAS Court of Justice. But the Court is going to find something which the national judge does not bring out, which leads to the ECOWAS Court sanctioning the Togolese authorities: violation of the Applicants' right to be heard in a judicial proceeding.

In other words, respecting the decisions of the national courts by no means places an obligation on the Court to think along the very lines of the national judge; the national court has no binding obligation on the Community judge's power to examine the case. Respect

- **Judgment of 13 March 2012, *Isabelle Manavi Ameganvi and Others* v. *Republic of Togo* (ECW/CCJ/JUD/06/12):**

This Application is a follow-up from the judgment already delivered by the ECOWAS Court on 7 October 2011. It was submitted under the guise of an "application for revision", purporting that the Court may have omitted to adjudicate on one of the reliefs sought by the Applicants: their re-admission into the National Assembly.

The Court stood firm in describing the facts and orders sought before it:

> §10: The Court describes the application thus made as "*asking the Court to adjudicate on an omission in adjudication*" and not "an application for revision".
>
> §19: "Consequently, the Court declares that the presumed omission to adjudicate on the issue of reinstatement, as brought by the Applicants, has no grounds, and must therefore be dismissed."

---

for the decision of the national court is therefore not the same as deference or reverence for the decision. In no way whatsoever does it connote a presumption of an established legal truth being assigned to the national court decisions, but simply consists of "abstaining" from "touching" the national judicial instrument; it consists of "taking account" of the existence of such instrument and not challenging it. One can see that we are not exactly in the domain of legality but that of "judicial courtesy", which is no more than another name for respect for the sovereignty of the States, an essential component of which is the judicial power of the State. The position of the Court must therefore be situated within its exact confines, it must be understood within its true sense: the Community judge shall abstain from questioning the judgment delivered at the national level – 'questioning' here meaning indeed employing mechanisms for reforming or overturning the decisions made – but that does not debar the Court from, within the limits of the matters brought before it, and of its powers and norms of reference, going farther than the national judge, or expressing a point somewhat different from what the national judge may have stated. The "red line", which it never crosses, and which it must never cross, so as to remain consistent with its creed, is that of questioning the existence of the decision made by the national judge. Like "Adam's Apple", such a step remains for the Community Court, a "forbidden" fruit.

A word must indeed be said concerning the respective "norms of reference" at stake. What must be emphasised therefore, and which ensures that the doctrine of legal non-interference remains safe, is that, whereas the judge at the domestic court adjudicates on the basis of the national norms – Codes, the Constitution –, the ECOWAS judge always refers, as he regularly affirms, to the international law binding on the States – especially the international treaties. In that sense, the distinction between the sources of legal reference suffices, on its own, for creating the seeds of divergence in the examination of the cases to be adjudicated upon, even if, it must be made clear, the judge in the national court is also expected to apply the international law. In *Case Concerning Ameganvi and Others* **v.** *Republic of Togo*, the judge at the national level referred to the Electoral Code and the Constitution of Togo – national norms –, whereas the ECOWAS Court cited violation of the provisions of the 1948 Universal Declaration of Human Rights and the African Charter on Human and Peoples' Rights – international norms.

In truth, the situations where the ECOWAS Court will be able to "come against" a judgment made by the judge in the domestic courts of the Member States are extremely rare. One of such situations however occurred recently: it had to do with a case where the decision of the domestic judge constituted a manifest and gross violation of a right. Under such circumstances, one finds oneself on the verge of what may be called "a judicial assault and battery", the judgment delivered constituting more or less a negation of the very idea of a right. What therefore occurs in that instance is a kind of turbulence in the reference points and principles, just like the repercussions of the concept of "assault and battery" on the ordinary rules of administrative law[16], and the judge at the Community level comes out of his reserved domain to "thwart" such decision which, to put it that way, "goes beyond the bounds of accepted limits".

It would be inaccurate however to believe that even in such a scenario, the Court becomes an appellate body or a court of cassation. In other words, the doctrine of non-interference in the national judicial decisions remains, at least in part, safe. Indeed, it is never going to be a matter of "reforming" or "quashing" the decision of the domestic court per se, it will never be a question of overruling the judgment, "quashing" it, putting it out of existence, nor, in subsequent terms, order for a retrial of the case, but simply, a removal of the transgression it carries and a sanction of that particular transgression.

Such sanction will thus be applied against the State – for the blame shall indeed lie with the State, as a result of the decision emanating from its court or tribunal – and not, as we have said, with the judicial act itself, through a measure of censure, nor with the actual author of the decision, the national judge.

It is this subtle logic which was implemented in Judgment of 17 May 2016, *Farimata Mahamadou and Others* **v.** *Republic of Mali* (ECW/CCJ/JUD/17/16).

The Applicants brought their case before the Court because they had suffered transgressions in an inheritance procedure in Mali, under the pretext that they were females and so could not claim inheritance to the same extent as the males. The Malian courts (the Court of Appeal and the Supreme Court), had been seised with the case but did not remedy the harm suffered, but rather "confirmed" it. The Court recalled that it is not

[16] Here, we are of course dealing with a particular subject-matter, French administrative law, which the non-Francophone jurists may not be familiar with.

a body set up to hear appeals on cases decided by the domestic courts or to quash judgments delivered by them, but considering the peculiarity of the case at hand, it felt the need to make certain points clear:

> §43 to 50: That the Court, in its case law, has always refused to examine the decisions made by the national courts, on the ground that it is not a court with a mandate for examining those decisions, and that such prerogative stays within the ambit of the superior courts of judicature of the Member States;

That the fact that the Court excludes revision of the decisions of the national courts from its scope of competence cannot be construed in absolute terms;

That indeed, when a court decision violates human rights, it is only natural that the judge at the Community Court, who has been entrusted with a mandate to protect the human rights of the Community citizens, cannot have any other option than to intervene and condemn it. That the Court cannot remain inactive before a flagrant violation of human rights, regardless of the instrument from which such violation may have emanated;

That here, it is not a matter of seeking to determine whether a judgment given by the national court is legal or illegal, but finding the manifest violation of human rights contained in the judicial act;

That indeed, a distinction must be made between censorship carried out on the legality of a decision made by a national court, and finding a violation of human rights emanating from a court decision;

That if the judge at the Community court has no powers to determine the correct application of the texts of the domestic law by the judge at the national level, he remains competent to find human rights violations even where such violations trace their origins to a decision made by a judge in the domestic court of a Member State;

That the human rights judge that he is would not be fulfilling the role of a guardian of human rights if he should gloss over flagrant violations contained in decisions of the national courts;

That moreover, court decisions shall not constitute an open door for human rights violation, and that court decisions may be regarded as acts adopted by the judicial authorities, and as such, may be of such nature as to constitute a violation of human rights; in such circumstances, the judge at the Community Court of Justice shall find the manifest violation.

The doctrine of non-interference in the national judicial procedures assumes its full expression in a particular domain, that of trial processes, considered within the context of criminal procedures. The ECOWAS Court of Justice systematically avoids meddling with such criminal inquiries, except, of course, where serious and manifest violations of human rights occur. In a world of such proximity, convenience and individualisation of measures, as that of the trial judge, interference by the supranational court will be unwelcome, as demonstrated in the following case law:

- **Judgment of 7 October 2011, *Cheikh Abdoulaye Mbengue* v. *Republic of Mali* (ECW/CCJ/JUD/08/11):**

§38 : "The Court observes that the requests to re-open the judicial inquiry and annul the arrest warrant derive from the sphere of the domestic judicial competence of the Republic of Mali, and that in that respect, the Court recalls its consistently held case law and declines jurisdiction on any application brought seeking to overturn decisions of the domestic courts of ECOWAS Member States ; this Honourable Court is neither an appeal court nor a court of cassation of the domestic courts of the ECOWAS Member States."

- **In Judgment of 26 January 2012, *El Hadji Mame Abdou Gaye* v. *Republic of Senegal* (ECW/CCJ/JUD/03/12), the Court ruled as follows:**

§43 and 44: That the Applicant affirmed having provided guarantees of representation to serve the purposes of a provisional release, which was consistently rejected.

That the Court held, as to this very point, that it is not within its powers to examine, in time and place, for the national judge, the nature and scope of guarantees to be provided by an individual under detention. The Court again emphasised that it is the mandate of the judge entrusted with the trial of the case to assess the materials at stake and accept or not the guarantee of representation and, *in fine*, grant or refuse the provisional release.

§46: That according to its established case law, the Court is not an appellate body with power to review decisions made by the national courts of Member States, and that even if the Court has jurisdiction to examine human rights violation in the trial proceedings of cases conducted before the national courts, while seeing to the observance of the human rights of the persons being tried, the Court's intervention is strictly limited to examining the alleged violations.

- **Judgment of 23 March 2012, *Barthélémy Dias* v. *Republic of Senegal* (ECW/CCJ/JUD/05/12):**

§18: The Applicant pleads violation of presumption of innocence by the investigating judge, who allegedly brought him under a committal order and disregarded his guarantees of representation.

§25: The Court held that all the notions advanced in the argumentation made reference to appraising the facts of the case in relation to the natural persons indicted in the case, and therefore the case was exclusively under the jurisdiction of the national courts, and not within the jurisdiction of a Community court, seised with a matter on human rights violation vi-à-vis a Member State of the Community.

- **Judgment of 3 July 2013, *Aziagbede Kokou and 33 Others, Atsou Komlavi and 4 Others, Tomekpe A. Lanou and 29 Others* v. *Republic of Togo* (ECW/CCJ/JUD/07/13):**

§38, 39, 40: "As things stand, the Court may not make any finding (…) or ascribe any blame whatsoever against the Republic of Togo, without unduly interfering in the conduct of the proceedings pending at the national level, and without violating the freedom of the judge at the domestic court.

(…) the Court is (…) of the view that for it to set that mandate in motion, consideration must be given to the pragmatic approach whereby appropriate importance is accorded to the proximity between the charges made and the judge at the domestic court, just as the same importance must be given to the prerogatives of the judge at the domestic court.

The Court finds that it is not within its human rights protection mandate to substitute its own viewpoint on the facts of a case for that of the domestic courts seised with the same case (…)."

- **In Judgment of 31 October 2012, *Baldini Salfo* v. *Burkina Faso* (ECW/CCJ/JUD/13/12), the Court stated that:**

§59: The legitimacy of the measures and their chances of success are principles which guide the Court. When examining a case related to a judicial procedure pending in a Member State, the decisions made by the Court are not intended to interfere with the decisions the national courts would be required to make. The Court cannot order measures whose implementation would result in weakening or wiping away the authority and independence of the national judge in the conduct of the cases brought before him.

- **In Judgment of 22 February 2013, *Simone Ehivet and Michel Gbagbo* v. *Republic of Côte d'Ivoire* (ECW/CCJ/JUD/03/13), the Court found:**

§96: That Mr. Michel Gbagbo, following his term of house arrest, was charged by an investigating judge and detained for other causes in the course of a judicial procedure before the national courts; that in line with its established case law, the Court could not grant the said measure, and consequently dismissed the request for provisional release of Mr. Michel Gbagbo

- **Judgment of 19 July 2013, *Karim Meissa Wade* v. *Republic of Senegal* (ECW/CCJ/JUD/09/13) :**

§95(9): "(...) Adjudges, consequently, that the Court may not grant the Applicant's request to be released, since the procedure is still pending before the domestic courts."

- **Judgment of 23 April 2015, *Convention Démocratique et Sociale Rahama (CDS-Rahama)* v. *Republic of Niger* (ECW/CCJ/JUD/03/15):**

§27 and 28: "The Court is of the view that it is a normal occurrence, in the course of a proceedings instituted before a court, for the court to adjourn once or several times, either on its own motion (suo motu) or upon a request by a party to the proceedings. As such, adjournments may indeed appear to be buttressed in rights held by the parties pleading their case before the court, but they are not so exclusively limited. Adjournments actually constitute, as well, judicial-administration measures which form an integral part of the mechanism for directing the procedure, or for preparing the causes in subsequent hearings. In that light, whether or not an adjournment or a suspension of deliberation shall be granted remains a matter to be determined within the sovereign powers of the judge in charge of the case. Thereby, it is not within the ambit of an international court like the ECOWAS Court to determine the relevance of the adjournment of a case, or else to assume the role of the domestic judge in adjudging the appropriateness or otherwise of a measure of judicial administration at the domestic level (...) Furthermore, if the ECOWAS Court of Justice were to commit itself to examining such measures as complained of by the Applicant, the Court would very soon find itself in an awkward position vis-à-vis the stand it has taken above not to act as a court of appeal or as a cour de cassation over the domestic courts of Member States; for the simple reason that, the measures sought for by the Applicant, if granted by the Court, may take the form of a court decision, notably the form of "an order of court"."

- **Judgment of 24 April 2015, *Pascal A. Bodjona* v. *Republic of Togo* (ECW/CCJ/JUD/06/15):**

> §37: "For the same reason, the Court shall discountenance the point of defence put forth by the Applicant in relation to producing an exhaustive list of the measures involved in Togo's judicial probation. It is a known fact that Mr. Bodjona contests the ban imposed on him in regard to going out of the national territory, on the ground that it is not among the measures that may be adopted in connection with serving judicial probation. It naturally implies that the Court cannot but abstain from making a pronouncement on that issue; in reality, to do so would amount to assessing the legality or otherwise of the judicial instruments and legal measures adopted by the Judiciary of the Republic of Togo."

- **Judgment of 16 February 2016, *Ibrahim Sory Touré and Issiaga Bangoura* v. *Republic of Guinea* (ECW/CCJ/JUD/03/16):**

> §78: "Whereas it is not within the powers of the Community judge to examine the grounds for the extended detention ordered by the investigating judge, given that the Community judge is not appellate court."

- **Judgment of 1 July 2016, Judgment of 1 April 2016, *Djibril Yipéné Bassolé* v. *Burkina Faso* (ECW/CCJ/JUD/22/16):**

> Page 15: "Furthermore, the Court has always held that it lacks the jurisdiction to interfere with the acts of trial judges in the domestic courts of Member States, except where such acts substantially affect the rights of a person. The Court has therefore had to decline the jurisdiction for examining certain measures of trial proceedings."

But as we indicated earlier, the doctrine of non-interference in the national judicial affairs must be understood in relative terms, for certain circumstances and situations may arise where the judge at the national level may have to take into consideration the decision of the ECOWAS Court of Justice, particularly due to the fact that through the workings of the rule of non-exhaustion of local remedies, national judge may well be in the act of carrying out his judicial duties whereas a decision from the ECOWAS Court more or less related to the dispute he is handling may well come up. As regards the details of this point, we refer to our subsequent discussions (Chapter 3, section 2, § 2, A) related to the question of independence of the trial proceedings at the international level, as compared with that at the national level.

The Court does not decline its jurisdiction before the national judge only, as we have sufficiently seen. The Court may also declare lack of jurisdiction on account of a possible or actual intervention by another International Court.

B.- As regards other International Courts

The ECOWAS Court is not only going to affirm its lack of jurisdiction to adjudicate on a matter when, for a given case, there are other judicial fora specifically competent to sit on the case. Declining jurisdiction in such circumstances is a form of beckoning – or, more than a beckoning, a call to make a move – addressed to another International Court. Again, there are numerous illustrations in this regard:

- **Judgment of 4 March 2010, *Mahamat Seid Abazene* v. *Republic of Mali, African Union and Afro-Arab Cultural Institute* (ECW/CCJ/JUD/02/10):**

§30: "The Court (…) rules that (…): The termination of Dr. Mahamat Seid Abazene's appointment falls within the purview of the Public Service of the African Union (…) It lacks jurisdiction to examine the case."

- **Judgment of 9 February 2011, *El Hadj Tidjani Aboubacar* v. *Banque Centrale des Etats de l'Afrique de l'Ouest (BCEAO) and Republic of Niger* (ECW/CCJ/JUD/01/11) :**

§31: "The Court finds further that this provision ('i.e. Article 15 (5) of the Rules of Procedure of the Court of Justice of UEMOA') attributes exclusive competence to the Court of Justice of UEMOA, when its institutions or officers are in issue as regards the exercise of their functions; that since the facts in the case are essentially constituted by Decisions and Acts made by the monetary authorities of UEMOA, in the exercise of their functions, Article 15 paragraph 4 of the Rules of Procedure of the Court of Justice of UEMOA are binding; that if the Honourable Court does not decline its avowed rationae materiae jurisdiction, it will inevitably be led to assume a right it is depositary of and whose implementation is conferred expressly and unequivocally on another Regional Court."

§32: "The Court is also of the opinion that although its rationae materiae jurisdiction is relevant, it is incumbent upon it to decline that jurisdiction in view of the exclusive jurisdiction of the Court of Justice of UEMOA over the facts of the instant case."

- **Judgment of 23 March 2012, *Laurent, Simone and Michel Gbagbo* v. *Republic of Côte d'Ivoire and Alassane Ouattara* (ECW/ CCJ/ RUL/ 07/12):**

Lodgment of the Application was on 20 July 2011, but on 30 November 2011, Côte d'Ivoire, in compliance with the international arrest warrant issued against Mr. Laurent Gbagbo by a Chamber of the International Criminal Court (ICC), decided to transfer the former Head of State to The Hague.

On the basis of what the Court calls "a new fact", the Judges decide to disjoin the two proceedings and order the suspension of the procedure in *Case Concerning Laurent Gbagbo* **v.** *Côte d'Ivoire*, pending the determination of the proceedings before ICC.

In paragraphs §27, 28 and 29, the Court held:

That Mr. Laurent Gbagbo was at that material time sued before the International Criminal Court whilst Mrs. Simone Ehivet Gbagbo and Monsieur Michel Gbagbo were still detained in Côte d'Ivoire;

That the result of that situation was the change in circumstances arising from the absence of the condition where all the other Applicants were linked to Mr. Laurent Gbagbo;

That for an efficient administration of justice, it was appropriate to disjoin the two proceedings: *Laurent Gbagbo* **v.** *Côte d'Ivoire* on one hand, and *Simone Ehivet et Michel Gbagbo* **v.** *Côte d'Ivoire* on the other hand.

Again, in paragraphs §31, 32, 33, the Court ruled:

That if the Court were to adjudicate further on the case and arrive at the conclusion that Mr. Laurent Gbagbo's right to freedom was violated, it would be in vain for it to order his release, since at that material moment, he had been detained at The Hague by the International Criminal Court;

That it could not undertake an exercise in futility;

That it was in the interest of justice to suspend the procedure *Laurent Gbagbo* **v.** *Côte d'Ivoire* pending the outcome of the case before ICC.

- **Judgment of 1 July 2016, Judgment of 1 April 2016,** ***Djibril Yipéné Bassolé*** v. ***Burkina Faso*** **(ECW/CCJ/JUD/22/16):**

> Page 10: "The Court must first of all recall that it has no mandate whatsoever to act as a watchdog over the legality of a sister organisation such as UEMOA. In every instance it has been requested to interfere in the relations among organs of UEMOA, or to assume the role of any such organ of UEMOA, notably the Court of Justice of UEMOA, the ECOWAS Court of Justice has declined jurisdiction in the matter, in due regard for those alternate legal or judicial orders.

The Court must reaffirm that position of principle in the case at hand. The ECOWAS Court of Justice has no mandate to keep watch over a legal system obtaining in the same sub-region but for which specific mechanisms of sanction are provided. The ECOWAS Court of Justice cannot therefore arrogate to itself the duty regarding the observance of the Rules of Procedure of UEMOA."

In the four decisions we have just referred to, the ECOWAS Court declines its jurisdiction and allows other courts or quasi-courts – organ of the African Union, Court of Justice of UEMOA and the International Criminal Court – to exercise theirs. The reasons behind the declarations of incompetence are however far from being the same in the various cases. If there is no doubt, in *Case Concerning Dr. Mahamat Seid Abazene* **v.** *Republic of Mali, African Union, Franco-Arab Cultural Institute*, that one can hardly fathom the ECOWAS Court assuming the role of a judge over the legality of issues under the purview of another international organisation – the AU, it must be admitted that, regarding ICC, and to a much less extent, regarding the Court of UEMOA, the Community judge, rather than strictly considering the issue of jurisdiction, resorted instead to a form of judicial courtesy, cross-bred with practical concerns relating to the very impact the Court's decision could possibly have. Incidentally, in *Laurent, Simone and Michel Gbagbo* **v.** *Republic of Côte d'Ivoire*, the Court admits that through its judgment, it temporarily ceded jurisdiction for purely practical purposes.

- **In paragraphs §31, 32, 33, the Court indicates:**

That at that material time, Mr. Laurent Gbagbo had been sued before the International Criminal Court whilst Mrs. Simone Ehivet Gbagbo and Mr. Michel Gbagbo were still detained in Côte d'Ivoire;

That the result of that situation was the change in circumstances arising from the absence of the condition where all the other Applicants were linked to Mr. Laurent Gbagbo;

That for an efficient administration of justice, it was appropriate to disjoin the two proceedings: *Laurent Gbagbo* **v.** *Côte d'Ivoire* on one hand, and *Simone Ehivet et Michel Gbagbo* **v.** *Côte d'Ivoire* on the other hand.

It must be concluded from all that, that the ECOWAS Court of Justice is not only incompetent when adjudication on the dispute submitted before it is expressly entrusted to another court, under another legal order (that of the African Union or of UEMOA), but equally when, for reasons more expedient than actually legal, the Court exercising its jurisdiction would the risk of having zero impact or would lead to a direct judicial conflict or vexatious rulings vis-à-vis other courts. It is the principle of appropriateness which thus dictates that it declines its jurisdiction[17].

But even where there is possibly no factor capable of challenging its power to adjudicate on a case, the Court does not, to any less degree, remain subjugated by the obligation to assert its jurisdiction and justify its decision to adjudicate in a dispute.

Paragraph 2

In upholding the jurisdiction of the Court

Two significant ideas arise from the jurisprudence of the ECOWAS Court of Justice. The first is, in truth, problematic, in the sense that for a long time, its formulation was not satisfactory. It consisted, then, in stating that (A) "Merely citing the occurrence of human rights violation on the territory of a Member State suffices, for the purposes of upholding the jurisdiction of the Court". It is not the most fortunate of statements, as we are going to see.

The second idea has never been concisely formulated, it was born out of diverse case laws and may be represented as (B) the idea that there is no case over which the Court automatically has no jurisdiction to adjudicate; that the "nature" of a case – be it "political" or "military" – cannot constitute an obstacle to the Community judge in upholding the jurisdiction of the Court.

A. - "Merely citing the occurrence of human rights violation on the territory of a Member State suffices, for the purposes of upholding the jurisdiction of the Court": revisiting a formula now fortunately discarded

For a long time, to uphold its jurisdiction, the Court had recourse to that form of statement, according to which it was simply sufficient, for

---

17 It is not forbidden, either, to see in such prudent withdrawal, a form of judicial courtesy characteristic of the desire of the judges to show at least considerable regard for each other, even where they may not be seen to be "dialoguing" with each other. See, concerning this subject-matter, the article entitled: **"The ECOWAS Court of Justice and the other legal or judicial orders. The dialogue of judges as seen from Abuja"**, infra, Part II of this work.

the applicant, to allege human rights violation in the Defendant State. Buttressing this point of view, among others, are the following decisions:

- **Judgment of 8 November 2010, *Mamadou Tandja* v. *Republic of Niger* (ECW/CCJ/JUD/05/10):**

  §18.1(b): "(…) The mere invocation of the violations over which the Court has jurisdiction only suffices for the Court to establish its jurisdiction (…)."

- **Judgment of 8 February 2011, *Sidi Amar Ibrahim and Others* v. *Republic of Niger* (ECW/CCJ/JUD/02/11):**

  §30: "The Application brought before the Court, by the heirs of Sidi Amar and of Ousmane Sidi Ali is not anonymous, and it had not been taken before another international court; it is on issues of human rights violations, and recounts incidents that are alleged to have taken place on the territory of the Republic of Niger, an ECOWAS Member State; while all this is pursuant to the provisions of Articles 10(d) and 9(4) of the 2005 Supplementary Protocol on the Court. Thus, it behoves the Court to declare it admissible."

- **Judgment of 8 February 2011, *El Hadji Tidjani Aboubacar v. BCEAO and Republic of Niger* (ECW/CCJ/JUD/01/11) :**

  §25: "(…) for an application to be admissible, in matters of human rights, the mere citing of such facts connected with such description suffices to confer competence on the Court."

- **Judgment of 17 March 2011, *Bakary Sarré and 28 Others* v. *Republic of Mali* (ECW/CCJ/JUD/03/11):**

  §34: "The Court equally reaffirms that in accordance with its consistently held case law, once human rights violations constituting international or Community obligations of a Member State are brought against any Member State, the Court declares its jurisdiction to examine such violations."

For a long time, this formula became a ritual in the judgments delivered by the Court. For some time, that formula has disappeared and it is commendable that such inadvertence came to a halt. Indeed, the said formula clearly implied that the jurisdiction of the Court was upheld, mechanically, or one should rather say "magically", by virtue of the sole claim by the applicant that there is an occurrence of human rights violation. One might as well say that it is thus the person pleading his case before the Court who establishes such competence, and this then "binds" the Court, by the sole will of the applicant to bring the proceedings on the terrain of human rights.

Such supposed power of the applicant is obviously diametrically opposed to the elementary rules of judicial procedure, which demands that a court be the judge of its own jurisdiction. Consequently, it has occurred that after putting forth the formula a little bit too hurriedly, the Court realises, a little further in its analysis, that it is at least partially incompetent to adjudicate on certain issues raised by the application. One was therefore confronted with the unfortunate situation where a court affirms one thing, and then the contrary, its competence and incompetence. This is very clearly portrayed in the judgment on *El Hadji Tidjani Aboubacar* **v.** *BCEAO and Republic of Niger,* delivered on 8 February 2011. After clearly affirming its competence, in the terms recalled above, the Court clearly rules in the operative part of the Judgment, that: "The Court declines its rationae materiae jurisdiction." (§35). And in *Case Concerning Bakary Sarré and 28 Others* **v.** *Republic of Mali*, after stating the principle of its jurisdiction (§34), the Court ends up restraining that affirmation in regard to at least one issue : its lack of jurisdiction to re-examine the national judicial decisions. At the end of the judgment, it has to admit that: "... it has no jurisdiction to adjudicate on aspects of the Application seeking a reversal of the judgments delivered by the Supreme Court of Mali." (§41).

The truth however compels us to acknowledge that the idea which was behind the formula was not heretic. There is every indication that through the formula, the Court simply sought to indicate that from the moment an applicant alleges human rights violation, the Court may, and even shall, analyse the allegation made; that there isn't, in principle, any foreclosure on the subject-matter, and that in bringing a case before the Court, an applicant does not need to give further proof, further demonstration. In other words, much less in terms of establishing jurisdiction per se, the allegation of human rights violation simply "brings" the case before the Court, seals the capacity of the Court to entertain the case, pending its subsequent declaration of lack of jurisdiction over the case. It can be seen – and the subsequent declarations of partial or total incompetence prove so – that the application "seises" the Court with the case but does not necessarily render the Court "competent" to adjudicate in the matter brought.

The point can be stated in another way: the jurisdiction of the Court in matters of human rights violation is simply "general" – it is asserted in terms of principle or on the basis of contingency – it may not be upheld in certain cases. The function of the formula therefore appears on the red-letter day, it plays out in a manner similar to an exemption on the address of the applicant, and may be expressed in the following way: to lodge a case before the Court, there will be no need for the applicant to go beyond the allegation of violation of human rights. The Court will "take hold" of the case, but the automatic nature of "taking hold" of the case shall neither prevent the Court from declaring in due course that it lacks jurisdiction to adjudicate on the case nor on the merits therein, the applicant having failed, for instance, to adduce evidence to the allegations made.

It thus appears that the scope of the formula under discussion finally turns out to be significantly reduced. Since it does not in reality establish the "jurisdiction" of the Court in any way, it proves to be of limited benefit, and its omission, from quite a recent date, has procured at least the advantage of dispelling the misunderstandings. It should be a fortunate event, it must be said, that the Court has parted ways with such a formula, even if, of course, the idea contained therein must continue to be canvassed.

There is another front where the ECOWAS Court does not allow itself to be easily influenced by an argument regarding lack of jurisdiction: according to which certain cases should naturally be considered as outside the purview of the Court, on account of their particular "nature".

B.- Where the "nature" of the case is deemed immaterial

A general survey of the jurisprudence of the Court provides us with the hint that it is particularly in two areas that the hypothesis of *rationae materiae* is expressed: the "political" arena and the military or security domain. That would suppose that in those areas, the Court would be congenitally, constitutionally incompetent; that there would be cases whose very "nature" would not permit them to be brought before the Community judge[18].

---

18 One's mind goes of course, at this stage, to what had been the practice in certain States before the International Court of Justice at The Hague, which consisted of raising the predominantly "political" nature of the issues the judge could be confronted with, as a means of recusing the court as a forum for resolving the dispute. This attitude owes a lot to the popular distinction between "legal disputes" and "political disputes", which Article 36(3) of the United Nations Charter restored, in as much as the said Article 36 talks of "*legal disputes*" which may be "*referred by the parties to the International Court of*

The preponderance of political considerations in disputes on human rights violation before the ECOWAS Court however remains an undeniable fact. Apart from the fact that it translates an inadequate "citizenship appropriation" of those rights, and a form of dramatisation of the dispute – the State and its ministries and departments would be behind all the transgressions – that fact has the consequence of springing up a scenario of confrontation between the judge and the State, and to put the judge in a posture of an opponent in principle, an essential adversary of the State. These two consequences are both regrettable, and they hardly enhance the development of the international judicial protection of human rights. It would be healthy to abandon such approach and render "common", somehow, the safeguard of human rights. It is true that the realisation of that wish is largely dependent on the democratic nature of the States and their political regimes. That being the case, for the time being, the Court is devoted to a systematic rejection of that form of recusal of its jurisdiction, as is apparent in its case law:

- **In Judgment of 8 November 2010, *Mamadou Tandja* v. *Salou Djibo and Republic of Niger* (ECW/CCJ/JUD/05/10), the Court ruled:**

§17.1(b): That the authorities of the Republic of Niger maintained that the political nature of the case justifies the detention of Mr. Mamadou Tandja, and that the political detention does not require the formality required by a judicial detention.

That Article 9(4) of the 2005 Supplementary Protocol on the Court provides that the Court has jurisdiction to determine cases of violation of human rights that occur in any Member State.

That as worded, the Article does not make any distinction between jurisdiction over violation of human rights in political matters and other

---

Justice". Now, every time this argument had been raised before the Court, it had been set aside, to the extent that it shall not be illegitimate to ask, today, and in terms of the very practice obtaining at the said ICJ, if such distinction still entails any practical scope. The ICJ affirms not only its competence to adjudicate on disputes submitted before it, but bears a message more significant, much more symbolic: the Court affirms, by so doing, a sort of substantial capacity of a case being triable or not as arising from the postures of the States, and thereby, the possibility of the prevalence of law in a society infamous for anarchy and rebellion in regard to the conduct of their subjects. Such jurisprudence which promotes the integrity of the judicial function thus carries the promise of legal regulation within the international society. Concerning this issue, see our article published in 2012 on the online journal *Afrilex,* from which we apologise having repeated some lines here: "The international judge and politics. Reflexions on the incidence of the political factor in the Court of The Hague".

kinds of human rights violation; that whatever the case may be, merely citing human rights violation, which falls within the powers of the Court, suffices for the Court to uphold its jurisdiction.

That it must equally be noted that the violations of the rights in question were committed on the territory of Niger, a Member State of ECOWAS.

That the Court is thereby competent to adjudicate on the case brought.

- **In Judgment of 23 March 2012, *Barthélémy Dias* v. *Republic of Senegal* (ECW/CCJ/JUD/05/12), the Court held:**

> §16: That Barthélémy Dias alleges that his arrest and detention were dictated by political motives, and were thus arbitrary; he equally maintains that the court trying the case against him was, and continues to be, under the influence of the highest political authorities of the Republic of Senegal, namely the President of the Republic, the Prime Minister, the Minister of Interior; and as a result, the court trying him was not independent and impartial;
>
> §21: That the Court also observes that the statements made by the political authorities of the Republic of Senegal, on the facts underlying the proceedings instituted against the Applicant are personal opinions binding only on those who made the statements, and not constituting acts of authority made within the official framework of the functions exercised by the said authorities.
>
> §22: That the Court is of the view that such opinions, even coming from the top level authorities, as in the case at hand, are not of such nature as to compromise the independence and impartiality of the judge handling the case of the Applicant, outside any unequivocal and overriding indications which may guide it on the path of justice.

- **In Judgment of 22 February 2013, *Simone Ehivet and Michel Gbagbo* v. *Republic of Côte d'Ivoire* (ECW/CCJ/JUD/03/13):**

The Republic of Côte d'Ivoire cited the existence of "exceptional circumstances" and a breakdown of institutions during the period under consideration. The Court responds by referring to the International Covenant on Civil and Political Rights (ICCPR), whose Articles 4 and 12(3) are related to cases of "emergency" ; as well as General Observation No. 29 (72nd Session of the Committee on Human Rights). Besides, the Court engages in quite a meticulous analysis of the relevant case law of the European Court of Human Rights (§66 to 69), so as to conclude upon violation of the Applicants' rights by the Republic of Côte d'Ivoire.

The Court further decided in that same judgment:

§70: That in the light of the foregoing principles, it is of the view that the Republic of Côte d'Ivoire, even in invoking exceptional circumstances, did not act in conformity with the provisions of Article 4 of the ICCPR and Article 48 of the Constitution of Côte d'Ivoire;

§77: That it is of the view that the spectrum of factors solidly established are of such nature as to urge the Court to conclude that the copy of the decree produced by the Republic of Côte d'Ivoire cannot in any case be admitted as a legal instrument adopted upon the basis invoked and for the purpose of producing the legal effects claimed by the Defendant;

§78: That it finds that the Republic of Côte d'Ivoire does not show at any rate that in its attempt to act in conformity with the law, it could not have attained the ultimate purposes dictated by the management of a political crisis of the nature it referred to, i.e. safeguarding public interest and restoring peace and security in Côte d'Ivoire. That indeed, even under exceptional circumstances, a relaxation in the principle of legality is done in strict adherence to the national laws; that incidentally, since Article 6 of the Charter (African Charter on Human and Peoples' Rights), absolutely forbids arbitrary arrest and detention, the Republic of Côte d'Ivoire cannot arbitrarily detain a citizen of the nation.

- **Judgment of 23 April 2015, *Convention Démocratique et Sociale Rahama (CDS-Rahama)* v. *Republic of Niger* (ECW/CCJ/JUD/03/15):**

The Applicant is a political party bringing a case before the Court, for various acts alleged to have been committed by the authorities of Niger, and alleged to be contrary to certain rights claimed by the Applicant.

§ 33, 34, 35, 37 and 38: "It can equally be found in the application for expedited procedure, and in the request for stay of execution of judgment, as filed by CDS Rahama, references to allegations of a predominantly political trial of the case. One thus reads in application for expedited procedure, that: "...in order to reward these anti-party activities against CDS Rahama, some were appointed Ministers and Advisers in the Government for a job well done." (Page 1 of French version), and in the request for stay of execution, that: "...there is urgency, danger and very serious risk of malfunction of the Party" (Page 2 of the French version).

In its written pleadings, CDS Rahama equally invokes, in support of its claim of unfair trial and impartiality of the State judiciary, that the Chairman of the Superior Council of Judicature postponed the promotion of two (2) judges of the Court on grounds of "... questionable moral character...". It finally avers that the judge rapporteur of the first decision of the appeal proceedings was "... relieved of his duties and transferred to the Ministry of Justice to carry out administrative duties.

The Court is well aware that once it is seised with a matter from a political body, the case will necessarily depict a political landscape. The Court shall however recall, as it has done in other decisions, that the political intents or declarations of one party or the other have no relevance to its legal mandate. More precisely, its mandate, in regard to disputes on human rights violation, is limited to examining, in reality and in concrete terms, whether there is violation of a well-defined right, and the Court does not unnecessarily entangle itself with political motives and statements.

In other words, the mandate and actions of the Court shall not in any way whatsoever be questioned by the fact that a political party, CDS Rahama, has filed a case before it, or by the fact that the judgment of the Court may have objective consequences on the political scene of the Republic of Niger. The Court shall not seek to derive any consequences whatsoever from the very fact that the exercise of its mandate in connection with the instant case could have repercussions on the political or electoral scene.

As a result, the Court shall not entertain the considerations made by CDS Rahama in this instance; and as well, those considerations cannot be entertained by the Court for the purposes of finding out whether human rights violations have been committed or not."

- **Judgment of 24 April 2015, *Pascal A. Bodjona* v. *Republic of Togo* (ECW/CCJ/JUD/06/15):**

§ 35 to 36 "(...) the Court must first of all recall its own framework of analysis, so as to set aside, first and foremost, a number of considerations either alluded to or raised by the Parties.

In that regard, one may first of all refer to certain political considerations, like the reasons why Mr. Bodjona was removed from the Government of Togo following the reshuffle carried out on 31 July 2012. The Applicant wrote that the dismissal was decided upon "... **with the sole aim of circumventing Article 422 of the Code of Criminal Procedure of Togo**

and the enforcement Judgment No. 48/12 of the Supreme Court…." (Page 4 of the Application in French). Further on, one reads that "… **in truth, the Hounourable Minister Bodjona Akoussoulélou Pascal is simply being persecuted for unexpressed political reasons** …" (Page 38 of the Application in French). Finally, the Applicant makes mention of **"… loss of opportunity"**, in terms of harms suffered by him, by virtue of the fact that "… **he was destined for a long and brilliant political career, seriously compromised today**… " (Page 25 of the Application in French).

There shall be no ground for the Court to be drawn into conducting its analysis upon such a political terrain. The Court shall reaffirm its view, as corroborated by its well established case law, that it shall not examine in any manner whatsoever, the political considerations or allusions contained in the pleadings brought before the Court, and that its mandate is simply to find, upon factual grounds, whether there have been occurrences of violation of the rights of the applicants coming before the Court. Consequently, the Court shall not countenance in the instant proceedings any of the purely political points raised by Mr. Bodjona in his Application."

- Judgment of **23 October 2015, *Mamadou Baba Diawara* v. *Republic Mali,* (ECW/CCJ/JUD/22/15):**

§ 32, 33, 34, 35 : "The Applicant, in his written pleadings, regularly refers to statements allegedly made by the President of the Republic of Mali himself, a day after the delivery of the decision (i.e. Judgment of 27 May 2009) releasing Messrs. Diawara and Haïdara, the two accused persons. The Applicant even produced the cassette containing the statements made by the President, according to which (in the terms of the Application) the President resolved "… to use all means to maintain the Applicant in prison." According to the Applicant, "… all these factors form a combination of serious indications of unjustified intervention of the Executive power in the functioning of the Judiciary, exercise of undue pressure on judges, and partiality of the courts of justice."

In support of that argument, he once again cites the Supreme Court Judgment of 13 September 2012 annulling the Presidential Decrees which relieved the Director of Public Prosecutions (Procureur Général) and the Avocat Général (Advocate General) of their functions. That according to the Supreme Court: "… the two judges were dismissed from office in response to a judgement delivered by the Criminal Chamber of the Supreme Court which instantly quashed the judgments sentencing Messrs. Mamadou Baba Diawara et Ismael Haïdara, in the case between them and the Office of Public Prosecutions and BHM, as proved by press statements attributed to the President of the Republic."

It should not occur to the Court to deny the probable political backdrop of the criminal trial proceedings which were held before the Malian courts, not to mention the fact that the trials concerned embezzlement of public funds, and worse still, involving colossal sums of money (more than six billion CFA Francs). The intervention of the President of the Republic of Mali and the involvement of the Malian public authorities undoubtedly fit into that context.

Such engagement by the political powers is undeniable, but the Court must recall that its mandate consists of making pronouncements on concrete acts of human rights violation, on measures which affect the individuals in the exercise of their rights or the rights they are entitled to. The Court cannot pay undue attention to mere declarations, with all the likelihood of contradicting the principle of independence of the judiciary; the Court does not make declarations in regard to assertions or intentions, but indeed in regard to legal acts or concrete actions which cause prejudice to human rights. As such, it cannot infer transgression of rights from mere statements; the Court expects from every party submitting an application before it, to establish that the violation of the right being claimed is real, concrete and actual. In a word, any averment concerning rights violation must be accompanied by facts, and must be corroborated by precise indications of violations pertaining directly to recognised human rights."

- **In Judgment of 1 July 2016, *Hama Amadou* v. *Republic of Niger* (ECW/CCJ/JUD/21/16), the Court declared:**

Pages 6 and 7(French Version): That first of all, a claim is made that the reasons for the court action instituted against Mr. Hama Amadou find their basis in the internal politics of Niger;

That the Court has always dismissed, however, the argument concerning the political factor. As a judicial institution mandated to deal solely with the legal aspects of the cases it handles, even if it is not unaware of neither the political context nor the possible political knock-on effects from such cases, the Court has always refused to pay attention to those political aspects, a decisive factor in the exercise of its jurisdiction;

That in the Application submitted before the Court, the Applicant, Mr. Hama Amadou, makes reference, at least twice, to the "political" nature of the case and therefore, to the blameable nature of the procedure instituted against him;

That on page 9 of the Application, it is stated that upon reading the facts, one can attempt finding out the reason behind the action taken by the Bureau of the National Assembly, in the sovereign decision of the party of which the Applicant is the Chairman, to leave the coalition of the parties in power. That further, on page 20, the Application makes mention of a declaration by the Minister of the Interior, as reported in the 7 September 2015 edition of the magazine *Paris Match*, according to which: "*as soon as Hama Amadou sets foot in Niger, he will be arrested*". That finally, the argumentation of the Applicant reposes, in great measure, on the fact that it is allegedly for the purpose of eliminating a political opponent or preventing him from presenting himself for election, that he was sued before court;

That it is certainly always regrettable that declarations issued by political authorities may give the impression that the authorities in the political arena are interfering with the judicial procedure. That the Court makes it a duty to recall that every time such arguments have been wielded before it, it has always responded that political considerations neither obstructs the principle of its jurisdiction nor its traditional methodological approach.

The hypothesis of incompetence of the Court on the basis of the "military" nature of a case has been maintained – and dismissed – in the following cases:

- **Judgment of 28 January 2014, *Alimu Akeem* v. *Federal Republic of Nigeria* (ECW/CCJ/JUD/01/14)**

§31: "On the other hand, the Federal Republic of Nigeria avers lack of jurisdiction of the Court on the grounds that the Applicant, by virtue of his status as a soldier of the Nigerian Army, is bound to follow the procedure provided under Sections 148, 178 and 183 of the Armed Forces Act. The Federal Republic of Nigeria further contends that Alimu Akeem must exhaust the remedies provided for by the said law before taking any other step, and that as a public officer he had three months at his disposal to appeal the decision, under Section 2(a) of the Public Officers Protection Act."

§33: "In line with its consistently held case law, the Court has jurisdiction in a matter, once the case brought before it substantially seeks to ask the Court to find that there is an occurrence of human rights violation. To that end, it suffices that a human rights violation be contained in the application. (...) Consequently, the Court declares that it has jurisdiction to adjudicate on the Application of Mr. Alimu Akeem."

- **Judgment of 1 July 2016, Judgment of 1 April 2016, *Djibril Yipéné Bassolé* v. *Burkina Faso* (ECW/CCJ/JUD/22/16):**

Page 11-12: "This last point, at any rate, urges the Court to consider another aspect of the argument put forth by Burkina Faso, equally canvassed in the course of the hearing of 7 June 2016. That argument consists of particular emphasis being placed on the peculiar nature of the procedure in question – as having been initiated on the basis of the Martial Code of Justice, as applied to a military person and for offences relating to "State security" – so as to advance the claim that normal procedural rules may not apply in the case at hand; simply put, that the 'military' and 'political' nature of the case precludes the application of the ordinary criminal procedure, and does justify restrictions placed on the rights of a defence. It was by virtue of that narrowly-defined standpoint, founded upon the exceptional nature of the context within which the events unfolded, that Burkina Faso, the Defendant State, was thus able to affirm that certain instruments invoked by the Applicant "... did not contain provisions relating to martial courts."

On the other hand, the case law of the ECOWAS Court of Justice itself has always held that the peculiar nature of a procedure, notably in regard to political considerations, does not in any way constitute a factor which could on its own render the Court incompetent to adjudicate on a case or 'justify' an occurrence of human rights violation. It is therefore erroneous for Burkina Faso to invoke the exceptional nature of the political context which prevailed at that material time, as a ground for justifying the acts it engaged in."

Finally, in another case, it is the peculiar nature of the economic sector in cause – the cocoa-coffee sector – which was advanced as an argument, to void the ECOWS Court of its jurisdiction over the case. But, in ruling against the Ivorian Government, which was of the view that the Court could not examine the legitimacy of the legal measures in cause – fiscal measures, to be precise – as adopted by Côte d'Ivoire in the cocoa-coffee sector, the Court declares:

- **In Judgment of 17 December 2009, *National Co-ordinating Group of Departmental Representatives of the Cocoa-Coffee Sector* (CNDD) v. *Republic of Côte d'Ivoire* (ECW/CCJ/JUD/05/09):**

> §41: "The Court cannot agree with such a stance, which tends to exclude from the jurisdiction of the Court, human rights violation which may occur in any sector governed by the national law, be it on taxation law or otherwise."

SECTION 2

ADMISSIBILITY

In relation to the admissibility of applications for human rights violation, it is apparent that the rules in force are sub-divided into two categories. Some of the rules find their source in the texts themselves, whereas others are the fruit of judicial "discoveries". One must therefore make a distinction between what is (Paragraph 1) "given", and what is (Paragraph 2) "derived".

Paragraph 1

Given for a fact

This has to do with (A) all that concerns the formal nature of the application – including identification of the applicant, which refers to the non-anonymous nature of the originating application, and (B) *lis pendens*, a possible cause of inadmissibility.

A.- A formal application procedure

In principle, access to the Court is by way of application. Addressed to the Court Registry, this court process shall, in the terms of Article 11 of Protocol A/P1/7/91, set out the subject-matter of the dispute, the parties involved, *and "a summary of the argument put forward as well as the plea of the plaintiff"*. According to Article 33 of the Rules of Procedure of the Court, on the application must feature "... the name and address of the applicant; the designation of the party against whom the application is made; the subject-matter of the proceedings and a summary of the pleas in law on which the application is based; the form of order sought; and where appropriate, the nature of any evidence offered in support." It is equally required that the application state an address for service "*... in the place where the Court has its seat*", and the name of the person who is authorised and has expressed willingness to accept service. It is provided that if an application does not comply with the formal requirements made therein, the defect may be "*cured*" upon a request by the Court Registry, and if the applicant fails to put the application in order or produce the required documents within the prescribed period, "... the Court shall, after hearing the Judge Rapporteur, decide whether the non-compliance with these conditions renders the application formally inadmissible."

Generally speaking, the jurisprudence of the Court on compliance of the applications coming before the Court is rather marked by liberalism, the Court not being inclined towards adopting an extremely formalised approach. It is only when an application is filed with quite serious flaws that the Court decides to rule that it is inadmissible, as is apparent in certain judgments:

- **Judgment of 17 February 2010, *Daouda Garba* v. *Republic of Benin* (ECW/CCJ/JUD/01/10):**

The Republic of Benin raised two objections on the formality of the application: absence of indication of address for service in the application – in its stead, a mere office address – and absence of the applicant's signature, which, according to the Republic of Benin, rendered the application "anonymous".

> §26: "On these two points, the Court considers, on its part, that the mere absence of the citation of the Applicant's address on his Application cannot constitute an obstacle to the admissibility of the Application, and that in that respect, the Court dismisses that Argument."
>
> §28: "Article 10 (d) of the Supplementary Protocol on the Court certainly requires that for an application to be admissible it must not be anonymous; but the anonymity of an application presupposes that the author is not identified ; that implies that neither the name nor status nor profession or nationality of the Applicant are known."
>
> §29: "But, the Court finds that the Application of Mr. Daouda Garba contains all these indications for his identification. Besides, the Court finds that Mr. Daouda Garba, having engaged the services of a lawyer for his defence, has fulfilled all the conditions required for the representation in issue."

- **Judgment of 8 November 2010, *Mamadou Tandja* v. *Salou Djibo and Republic of Niger* (ECW/CCJ/JUD/05/10):**

The Defendant relied on the fact that the main application was not lodged in tandem with the application for expedited procedure, as required by Article 59(2) of the Rules of the Court. But the Court responded that the said Article does not make mention of lodging them in tandem but rather as

> "A separate document". It must be recalled that the Article provides that: "An application for a case to be decided under an expedited procedure shall be made by a separate document lodged at the same time as the application initiating the proceedings or the defence, as the case may be."

For the Court:

> §18 (c): "Whereas the main requirement of Article 59(2) is the lodgment of a pleading seeking expedited proceedings, separate from the main application, it is not necessary that the lodgment of the two applications must be simultaneous, the concept of simultaneity being absent from Article 59(2) and not corresponding to the spirit of that article (…)."

- **Judgment of 31 January 2014, *Georges Constant Amoussou* v. *Republic of Benin* (ECW/CCJ/JUD/02/14):**

In a case where it was still an issue of omission of signature at the bottom of the application, the Court once again makes known its liberal and hardly formal approach:

§25: The Court equally rules that the Applicant, Constant Amoussou, is sufficiently identified in the application, and that the absence of his signature at the bottom of the application does not render his application anonymous, within the meaning of Article 10 (d)(i) of the Supplementary Protocol.

- **In Judgment of 23 April 2015, *Georges Constant Amoussou* v. *Republic of Benin* (ECW/CCJ/JUD/05/15) the Court rules that:**

Article 33(2) of the Rules of the Court requires that the applicant indicates an address for service at the seat of the Court. That the memorial of the Republic of Benin indicates an address for service at the Embassy of Benin in Nigeria, at Abuja, and that the lawyer of Benin consents to receiving the processes by mail or telefax (Article 33(3) of the Rules); hence, the Court concludes thus:

> § IV.9: "It follows then that the requirement of the article has been satisfied."

- **Judgment of 30 June 2015, *Association of Voluntarily Retired Workers (ATVR)* v. *Republic of Mali* (ECW/CCJ/JUD/14/15):**

As regards the unfortunate omission of a word, the Court does the rectification and decides not to attach any importance to such error:

> Page 6: "The Court notes that by the expression "human violation", as contained in the said application, ATVR meant "human rights violation", as could be deduced from the ensuing submissions it had made;
>
> At any rate, it is a case of obvious slip, which has no effect on the powers conferred on the Court for adjudicating on the matter submitted before it, pursuant to the provisions of Article 9 (4) of the Supplementary Protocol of 2005 (...)."

The liberalism of the Court however has limits. When the application omits certain essential requirements, the application is declared inadmissible.

- **Judgment of 30 June 2015, 167 Former Workers of SONIDEP Represented by Eli Haggar and B. Kanfideni v. Republic of Niger and SONIDEP (ECW/CCJ/JUD/15/15):**

In that case, the Court declares the application inadmissible for anonymity and lack of locus standi – the mandate for acting is supposed to reveal the identity of the applicants:

§IV.12: That the 167 former workers of SONIDEP who lodged their case before the Court were not formally identified in the application;

That the list entitled "list of beneficiaries of voluntary departure from SONIDEP" attached as annexed document depicts only forty-five (45) names without any other additional information;

That till the day of the judgment, no other pleading in the case-file enabled the jury to identify the applicants on an individual basis;

That an application which does not contain the essential elements required by Article 33(1)(a) of the Rules of the Community Court of Justice, ECOWAS, namely the name(s) and address(es) of the applicant or applicants, shall be considered as anonymous.

B.- Lis pendens: ups and downs in the use of a concept

The operation of the concept of lis pendens by the ECOWAS Court of Justice has for a long time posed a problem, in the sense that the understanding which had been attached to it by the judge had always remained debatable. Rather fortunately, for some time, the understanding of the concept seems to have stabilised, and the recourse the Court has had to it, to us, appears in conformity with the orthodox stand. To understand the issue raised, all the various facets of the concept of lis pendens must be outlined.

First of all, the rule in question is stated by Article 10(c) and (d) of Supplementary Protocol A/SP.1/01/05 of 2005. The said Supplementary Protocol provides that:

> "Access to the Court is open to the following: individuals on application for relief for violation of human rights; the submission of the application for which shall (i) not be anonymous; nor (ii) be made whilst the same matter has been instituted before another International Court for adjudication."

The provision is clear. It states two traditional conditions regarding filing cases before judicial and semi-judicial bodies in matters on human rights. The first rule, which is the prohibition of anonymity, is somewhat a matter of course, for it is clear that to adjudicate on the merits of an application, one must first of all know who lodged the application, but one must also know the one who claims to be the victim – for the applicant will often be the one who has suffered the violation alleged. The second rule reposes on less factual considerations, more systemic, in so far as it translates constraints pertaining to the international system itself. The system is characterised indeed to a very large extent, by the absence of a central tutelary authority, which is true for States – essentially constituted by the members of that society – just as it is for the international courts, since there is no relation of hierarchy, in principle, amongst the international courts.

It is precisely the absence of that unifying authority of the jurisprudence of courts and tribunals, which explains the maximal avoidance of conflicts in jurisprudence. In case of divergent rulings among the judicial bodies, one could thus have easily found oneself confronted with an unresolvable situation. It is to avoid such unfortunate extreme ends that the rule on prohibition of parallel or simultaneous lodgment of cases before courts was devised.

Several observations may be made from the manner in which the said Article 10 has been applied by the ECOWAS Community Court of Justice.

The first, is that, in a number of cases, the Court correctly interpreted the text by dismissing the objections regarding inadmissibility on grounds of concomitance in lodgment of application before a semi-international court or a domestic court. The first instance occurred in *Hissène Habré* **v.** *Republic of Senegal.* In that dispute, the Defendant State raised an objection concerning inadmissibility on the ground that the case at hand was pending before the United Nations Committee against Torture, as at the time the Court was to make a pronouncement on the same case. By a Ruling of 14 May 2010, the Court dismissed the objection in Judgment of 18 November 2010, *Hissène Habré* **v.** *Republic of Senegal* (ECW/CCJ/JUD/06/10) (§5 and 6).

It is worthwhile to approve of that judgment because the idea of lis pendens could be contested on two fronts: not only does Article 10 of the above-cited Protocol of 2005 make mention of "… instituted before another International Court for adjudication" – and the United Nations Committee not even a "Court", – but the matters for determination in the dispute were far from being the same, in as much as the concept of lis pendens makes reference to similitude in the matters for determination and in the proceedings instituted, which we shall revisit. In one instance, what was at stake was the blame laid against a signatory State of the Convention against Torture, bound by the obligation to organise trial proceedings in that regard, and in another instance, a blame made against a State in respect of a private person complaining of violation of his rights by the State, thereby requesting monetary compensation.

Similarly, the ECOWAS Court of Justice must be applauded, when in a series of cases, it sets aside an objection brought for lis pendens on the basis that the cases in question had already been filed before the judge in a domestic court. Once again, a literal interpretation of the text would lead to the solution, since a domestic court is not an "International Court".

- **In Judgment of 26 January 2012, *El Hadji Mame Abdou Gaye* v. *Republic of Senegal* (ECW/CCJ/JUD/03/12), the Court declared that:**

§28: The Republic of Senegal raised an objection regarding incompetence of the Court, arguing that the case in the trial instituted against the Applicant was pending before the Senegalese courts, and that court decisions had already been made in regard to that cause.

In that regard, the Court indeed did point out that it had no jurisdiction to adjudicate on decisions made by the local courts of the Member States, but noted that the fact that a case had already been filed before a domestic court of a Member State could not have any influence on its jurisdiction, in matters concerning human rights violation, and recalled that the only limit on its jurisdiction was stipulated in Article 10(d)(ii) of the Supplementary Protocol on the Court, barring it from trying a case already lodged before another International Court for adjudication;

§29: The Court equally recalled, regarding its jurisdiction that allegations of human rights violation contained in an application brought before it, suffice, in formal terms, to engage the Court's power to admit the case without prejudging the truth of the facts alleged.

In two other cases it sat on some years ago, the Court however brought forth quite a debatable understanding of the concept of lis pendens as a ground for inadmissibility of application.

The first was the *Aziablévi and Others* case. In that dispute, the Applicants complained of the impossibility of enforcement of a judgment delivered on 21 April 2001 by the Labour Tribunal of Lome on 10 July 2003, asking the Togo Telecom company to pay to them various sums of money as monetary compensation. The reason given was that it was impossible to execute the judgment because the said company had immunity to that effect.

They filed their case before the *Cour Commune de Justice et d'Arbitrage* (CCJA) of OHADA, and the latter dismissed their application, after several other court decisions of Togo had recognised the said immunity of Togo Telecom.

The Court will then criticise the immunity at stake, in the light of equality before the law and equal protection by the law (Article 3 of the African Charter on Human and Peoples' Rights), but it does not make a pronouncement as to the merits, for the reason that the case was pending before the CCJA:

- **In Judgment of 31 January 2012, *Aziablévi Yovo and 31 Others* v. *Société Togo Telecom et Etat Togolais* (ECW/CCJ/JUD/04/12), the Court held that:**

§18: The Defendants argued that since the Applicants had already seised the *Cour Commune de Justice et d'Arbitrage de l'OHADA,* and the latter had already adjudicated, Article 10(d)(ii) of the Supplementary Protocol essentially provides that must be applied.:

> "Access to the Court is open to individuals on application for relief for violation of their human rights; the submission of application for which shall not be anonymous nor be made whilst the same matter has been instituted before another International Court for adjudication".

This resulted in the Application filed by Aziablévi Yovo and her Co-Applicants being declared inadmissible by the Court.

§19: Indeed *la Cour Commune de Justice et d'Arbitrage de l'OHADA*, which is an International Court, was seised by the Applicants for the purposes of enforcement of Judgment No. 27 of 10 July 2003 delivered by the Court of Appeal of Lome;

§20: *La Cour Commune de Justice et d'Arbitrage de l'OHADA* had already upheld its jurisdiction to determine on the case and had already adjudicated on it;

§22: In finding that those were the facts, and in recalling the points it had made beforehand, it found on the other hand that the conditions for the application of Article 10(d)(ii) of the Supplementary Protocol were met and therefore declined jurisdiction to adjudicate on the merits of the case brought before it by Aziablévi Yovo and her Co-Applicants.

In the second case, the Court equally decided upon a form of impossibility to adjudicate on the dispute, in as much as the International Criminal Court (ICC) was in a position to adjudicate on the individual liability of Mrs. Simone Ehivet Gbagbo. The Court avoids every reference to objection regarding inadmissibility for lis pendens, and contents itself in talking of "stay of adjudication", for the purposes of "serving the interest of justice", but the resultant effect, in our opinion, is the same: the Court considers that since the case is filed before another International Court for adjudication, it prevents it from adjudicating on that same case, at least for the time being. If not for any reason at all, because the Court gives the impression that the judgment it delivered had been overshadowed by the notion of lis pendens, it is important to juxtapose that case law with the ones which were previously cited:

- **In Judgment of 22 February 2013, *Simone Ehivet and Michel Gbagbo* v. *Republic of Côte d'Ivoire* (ECW/CCJ/JUD/03/13):**

§25 and 26: The Court notes that the matter concerning Mrs. Simone Gbagbo had been filed before the International Criminal Court (ICC) and that by virtue of the issuing of an arrest warrant against her, her situation becomes akin to that of Mr. Laurent Gbagbo, in which case the Court had decided that the transfer of Mr. Laurent Gbagbo's case before the ICC implied a "change of circumstances", which demanded, "in the interest of justice", suspension of the procedure, pending the determination of the proceedings before the ICC (Judgment of 23 March 2012, *Laurent Gbagbo* v. *Republic of Côte d'Ivoire*.)

The Court found that regarding the case in question, it had no reason to depart from its former position, and consequently, adjudged that there was a ground to suspend the procedure against Mrs. Simone Ehivet Gbagbo till the case before the ICC had been settled.

Without doubt, it would be somewhat out of place to assign to the Court statements it has not made, as much in its Judgment of 23 March 2012 as in the one we have just cited, of 22 February 2013. The Court does not talk of, we need to say that again, lis pendens per se as a ground for staying adjudication. There is every indication, at any rate, that it is for practical purposes ("serving the purposes of justice", "change of circumstances", etc.) that the Court declines to sit on the two cases.

Nevertheless, it shall be appropriate, at least from the standpoint of the other judgment cited (*Aziablévi Yovo and 31 Others*), to say a word on the concept of lis pendens, as it appears to manifest itself from the decisions of the Court. It has to do with, we have said, a fairly debatable understanding of the notion. It will be worthwhile for us to ask ourselves whether the position adopted by the Court in the case does not veer towards reverence, or if it does not exhibit a misplaced obsequiousness. In the case in point, indeed several points could make us doubt the existence of a lis pendens, and thus, the applicability of Article 10(d)-ii of the 2005 Protocol, expressly cited by the Community judge.

Lis pendens indeed pre-supposes cases being lodged simultaneously. If it poses a problem, to the extent of making one of the courts decline its jurisdiction, it is precisely because it introduces a form of *suspense,* of a potential misfortune which must quickly be averted. It is therefore at a preliminary stage, at the competence or admissibility stage, that such outcome must be made to take place. But, in the instant case, it is said, by the ECOWAS Court itself, that CCJA had upheld its jurisdiction and already adjudicated on the case. Therefore the simultaneity of lodgment of the cases was lacking, whereas such simultaneity of lodgment of the cases constitutes an essential component for the occurrence of lis pendens. Let us recall the definition of the concept in *Dictionnaire de droit international public* by J. Salmon, as:

> "State of a dispute already practically lodged before a court, which, though not yet settled (it is pending), has been lodged before another court equally competent to adjudicate on the case."[19]

[19] Brussels, Bruylant, p 670; the underlining is ours.

A second debatable issue still concerns the understanding of the notion of lis pendens. Actually, the concept does not only pre-suppose simultaneous lodgments, it also refers to the identity of the parties. Now, in the instant case, if the dispute before CCJA is between the applicants and the company called *Togo Telecom*, the dispute in cause before the ECOWAS Court cannot but be between the applicants and the Republic of Togo, the consistently held case law of the Court clearly stating that in matters of human rights violation, only the State, and no other person, may come before the Court as a defendant. We therefore do not have, in principle, the same persons pleading before the two Courts. From that standpoint, one may doubt the existence of lis pendens, and thus the relevance of the application of Article 10(d)-ii of the 2005 Protocol. Let us recall, equally, that it is the Permanent Court of International Justice (PCIJ), in its judgment of 25 August 1925, *Case Concerning Certain German Interests in Upper Silesia,* which indicates to us that for lis pendens to occur, apart from two identical applications – we shall return to that – the applicants must be the same[20].

Finally, the doubt on lis pendens resurfaces when it is matter of taking a look at the very subject-matter of the two applications. We have just seen, according to PCIJ itself, that where there is lis pendens, the two rival applications must be seeking the same object, or have the same purpose. Now, before CCJA, it is only a question of execution of a national court decision, which the court in question is specifically competent to handle, apart from its power to quash decisions in general. But before the ECOWAS Court, the application seeks relief for "a human right" violation. The object pursued, from the point of view of the *principles*, is therefore not the same on either side. Surely, one may always say *in actual fact*, that both requests seek execution of a judgement, but the discussion here is particularly an argument on principles. When we make mention of the identical nature of the purpose of two trials, we indeed seek to advance the hypothesis where two applications are *strictly* the same. Once before one judicial body, it is an issue of "execution" (jurisdictional provision specifically set out in the governing instruments), and before the other, "human rights violation" (competence assigned by an ECOWAS instrument, and applying norms of public international law binding exclusively on States), it becomes permissible to wonder whether one is dealing with the same proceedings, whether the issues at stake, from either party, are the same. For this third

[20] Ibid, p 671.

reason, also, it becomes permissible to doubt the relevance of having recourse to the concept of lis pendens and the subsequent application of Article 10 (d)-ii) of the 2005 Protocol.

Besides the explicit rules, constituted by the formal provisions on applications and objections regarding admissibility, on grounds of lis pendens, there are principles "devised" by the judge, which must now be examined.

Paragraph 2

Inferred or derived

These rules on admissibility are made either from nothing – or, if one will prefer, from logical inference or common sense – as in the case of (A) res judicata, or (B) from the texts themselves, in the light of the principle of non-exhaustion of local remedies.

A.- A rule derived or inferred *ex-nihilo* : objections raised on the strength of res judicata

It may occur – and has already occurred – that a case which is already tried, either by a national judge or, more scarcely, by the Court itself, be filed afresh before the Court.

It is difficult, theoretically speaking, to give one and a single reason for this phenomenon, quite curious. One can imagine, first of all, that the emergence of this new mode of application stems from the difficulties of enforcement of court decisions; such that an applicant thus imagines that it is by succeeding in suing the State again that it will be able to overcome the indifference or inertia of the State, by way of engaging in a more or less avowed bet that the pronouncement of an international court "will have greater weight" than that of a domestic court. It is equally imaginable that an applicant desire by such means, "to obtain double victory", over the same trial, and for example be compensated as much before the national judge as the Court, that approach remaining of course "unfair". But whatever the motivation behind the "application upon application" may be, is immaterial: the Court systematically declares such applications inadmissible, irrespective of the circumstances of the case.

In any case, whether it is a matter of refusing to assume the status of a court of appeal or trying a case which has already been settled, the attitude of the ECOWAS Court of Justice is firmly established on the same rationale: respecting the judgments made at the national level, carefully avoiding "touching" it. That is why this position can be seen as the basis for various creeds of the Community Court: refusal to constitute itself into a body for re-examining national decisions, respecting the national legal and judicial orders, or quite simply, observance of a more general rule of procedure, *non bis in idem*, according to which no legal action can be instituted twice for the same cause of action. The response of the Court is reasonable and beyond reproach. The Court always objects, ruling on the basis of res judicata:

- **In Judgment of 12 June 2012, *Aliyu Tasheku* v. *Federal Republic of Nigeria* (ECW/CCJ/RUL/12/12):**

The Applicant complained of being under arbitrary arrest and detention from 20 September, regardless of the order by the presiding judge of the Abuja Magistrate Court, according to which he was to be released.

The issue is that the same case had been tried by the national courts, and the requests of the Applicant had been fully granted. The Court will therefore declare as inadmissible, the application brought before it (on authority of res judicata at the national level), but not without posing the problem first of all.

> §15: "One may ask whether an application seeking to safeguard fundamental human rights constitutionally recognised and guaranteed before a judge at the domestic court may be considered as analogous with another application seeking to safeguard human rights internationally recognised and guaranteed before the Court of Justice of the Economic Community of West African States (ECOWAS)."

The Court will then respond:

> §11: "The Court notes that from the exhibits filed in the case-file by Counsel to the Federal Republic of Nigeria, notably with reference to the Judgment of 19 May 2011 cited above, it can be observed that the reliefs sought by the Applicant were granted when the High Court judge (…) ordered that the Nigeria Police authorities must send Mr. Aliyu Tasheku before the High Court on 23 May 2011 at 2 p.m. and granted him a compensation of Five Million Naira (N5,000,000) for unlawful detention …"

> §19: "The Court therefore deduces from the foregoing, that the Application brought by Mr. Aliyu Tasheku is essentially the same as the

one filed before the Nigerian judge, which subject-matter has already been dealt with and which outcome the Applicant neither contested nor considered to be dissatisfactory since he did not appeal the judgment before any Nigerian court. The Applicant did not also indicate that the Nigerian authorities refused to implement the decisions made by the judge at the High Court. Equally, he brought forth no new complaint or new application that may be entertained by the Honourable Court. The Court cannot retry a case on which a judgment of the domestic court of a Member State has already been delivered and against which no consideration has been raised. Consequently, the Court declares that the Application brought by Mr. Aliyu Tasheku is inadmissible."

- **Judgment of 14 December 2012, *Sa'adatu Umar* v. *Federal Republic of Nigeria* (ECW/CCJ/JUD/17/12):**

As in the above-cited *Aliyu Tasheku* case, the Applicant seeks to have his case, which has already been determined by the Nigerian judge, retried by the Court:

§20 : "The Court therefore concludes that, the instant case brought before it, is essential the same as the one earlier taken before the Nigerian judge, which was adjudicated upon, and whose settlement, if unsatisfactory, could have led Applicant to file an appeal ; but, this was not the case"

§22: "Consequently, the Court declares that there is no need to consider the case brought before it by Mrs Sa'adatu Umar on its merit".

If the Court brandishes res judicata objections before the national courts, much more so, does it do the same, when it is the ECOWAS Court itself which has already tried a case, as in the following two instances:

- **Judgment of 23 April 2015, *Georges Constant Amoussou* v. *Republic of Benin* (ECW/CCJ/JUD/05/15):**

The Applicant brought his case before the Court once, in the course of the year 2014, and files the case again, asking the Court to adjudge and declare that the restraint on his person in 2010 was an arbitrary arrest.

The Defendant State raises an objection on the ground that the ECOWAS Court had already adjudicated upon the issue of arrest, via a judgment delivered on 6 March 2014.

The Court ruled, as it had done before:

In §19, 21, 22, 23 p.14 (French version) of the Judgment, the Court found that the requests made by the Applicant in the second procedure were not new for the Court; that they formed part of the requests the Court had examined in 2014, and upon which it delivered a judgment on 6 March 2014.

The Court asked whether it was legitimately possible for the Court to sit on a case it has already decided, and that the general rules require that the answer shall not but be in the negative; that the action brought by the Applicant is not provided for in any of the texts.

The Court further decided that in that instance, the rule of res judicata indisputably applied, and the said principle prohibited parties from bringing before the judge a dispute he has already settled.

Thus, the Court declared the action brought by Mr. Amoussou inadmissible.

- **Judgment of 24 April 2015, *Gnassingbe Kpatcha and Others* v. *Republic of Togo* (ECW/CCJ/JUD/08/15):**

The Applicants complained that a judgment already declared by the Court (Judgment of 3 July 2013) had not changed their situation, and that they still remained in detention, whereas the Court had ordered their release.

The application was declared inadmissible. For the Court:

§IV.13, 18, 19, 20: "The Court (…) finds that the heads of claim applied for by the Applicants do appear among those already adjudicated upon by the Court and which yielded Judgment No. ECW/CCJ/JUD/06/13 of 3 July 2013.

It is finally established that the facts invoked are those arising from the events of April 2009 and their aftermath (…).

Again, the Court will have to ask the following question and draw conclusions from the legal effects which derive from the answer to the question – Can the Court adjudicate on a case it has already tried, having heard both parties? (…)

The Court addressed such issue in a previous decision (Judgment No. ECW/CCJ/JUD/05/15 of 23 April 2015: Case Concerning Georges Constant Amoussou **v.** Republic of Benin) (…)

It follows therefore that the Applicants in the procedure which resulted in Judgment No. ECW/CCJ/JUD/06/13 of 3 July 2013 cannot legitimately drag the Republic of Togo before this Honourable Court for the same cause and on the same subject-matter."

The two cases which have just been cited are peculiar in nature. The Court raised the issue of res judicata – automatically, in one of the cases – for the purpose of declaring the matter inadmissible. But it could have situated the matter within the context of enforcement of a court decision, and thus end up with a declaration of incompetence of the Community Court. Indeed, in seising the Community Court anew, the Applicants simply sought to bring to the notice of the Court that the judgment which had already been delivered, had not been enforced, or had been unsatisfactorily executed. Nothing obviously prevented the Court from entering upon the terrain of judgment execution; but the end product, for the Applicants, would have been the same in any case – they stood no chance of getting the Court to entertain their application.

Inadmissibility or incompetence, an application which revisits an already decided case shall not be examined the judges on its merits.

B.- A rule derived or inferred from the texts: non-exhaustion of local remedies

This is indeed a rule deduced from the texts, for, as it stands, it does not feature anywhere, it is not stated in written form in the texts. It is rather because the 2005 Protocol notably does not require in any instance whatsoever, exhaustion of local remedies as a condition for lodging a case before the Court that, reasonably, the Court regularly affirms that bringing cases before it is not in any way linked to procedures which may possibly be pending before the domestic courts. The judgments of the Court regularly state this distinctive feature of applications for human rights violation before the ECOWAS Court. Against a background where there was no well-established tradition of legal protection of human rights, not even a direct access of individuals before international courts – the 1998 Protocol adopted within the framework of the Organisation of African Unity and related to the African Court on Human and Peoples' Rights, providing for the possibility for private individuals of accessing it only on the condition of prior acceptance by their States of origin – leaving out the rule of exhaustion of local remedies came with a somewhat revolutionary outlook.

In regular fashion, counsel for the States dragged before the Court invoke the rule – either because they consider it as a kind of fundamental principle relevant to international human rights disputes, and thus provide a proof of the extent of ignorance of the rules in force before the ECOWAS Court, or because in in certain instances, notably in a scenario where a case, or aspects of a case, are pending before the domestic courts – exhausting the possibilities for seeking redress before the national judge appears to them as a rule of efficient judicial administration or a means of averting possible jurisprudential conflicts, always unpleasant when they occur.

No matter the motives of those who invoke it, the rule of exhaustion of local remedies is always dismissed by the Court:

- **Judgment of 27 October 2008, *Hadijatou Mani Koraou* v. *Republic of Niger* (ECW/CCJ/JUD/06/08):**

The Republic of Niger, though conscious of the fact that the condition of exhaustion of local remedies does not feature in the texts, requested the Court all the same, to '*fill in the lacuna*', by restoring that condition. The Court replied thus:

> §41: "In refraining from making the rule of preliminary exhaustion of local remedies a condition for admissibility of applications filed before the Court, the Community lawmaker of ECOWAS has undoubtedly responded to this call. The renunciation of such a rule is binding on all the Member States of ECOWAS, and the Republic of Niger cannot claim to be an exception in that regard."

> §45: "In the final analysis, there are no grounds for considering the absence of preliminary exhaustion of local remedies as a lacuna which must be filled within the practice of the Community Court of Justice, for the Court cannot impose on individuals more onerous conditions and formalities than those provided for by the Community texts without violating the rights of such individuals."

- **Judgment of 8 July 2011, *Ocean King Nigeria Ltd.* v. *Republic of Senegal* (ECW/CCJ/JUD/07/11):**

Senegal raised a preliminary objection related to exhaustion of local remedies, in arguing that the Court lacked jurisdiction; the Applicant had set off a judicial machinery in motion at the national level, and had not exhausted the procedure.

> §41: "That being the position of the law, this Court has decided in a plethora of cases including Prof. Etim Moses Essien v. Republic of The Gambia (Suit No. ECW/CCJ/APP/05/05, judgment delivered on 29 October 2007), Musa Saidykhan v. Republic of the Gambia (Suit No. ECW/CCJ/APP/11/07, judgment delivered on 19 December 2010) and Hadijatou Mani Koraou v. Republic of Niger (supra) that the exhaustion

of local remedies is not a condition precedent for the institution of an action for the relief of violation of human rights before it. Therefore, a plaintiff is not obliged to exhaust local remedies in order to have access to this Court."

- **Judgment of 28 January 2014, *Alimu Akeem* v. *Federal Republic of Nigeria* (ECW/CCJ/JUD/01/14):**

> §35: "The Federal Republic of Nigeria relies essentially on the provisions of Sections 148, 178 and 183 of the Armed Forces Act. Section 148 sanctions a criminal procedure before the military courts. Section 183 complements it and provides for appeal mechanisms (…)"
>
> §39: "(…) it is consistently held that exhaustion of local remedies is not a condition for the admissibility of applications for human rights violation before the instant Court."

- **Judgment of 23 April 2015, *Abla Azali and Anor* v. *Republic of Benin* (ECW/CCJ/JUD/01/15):**

The Applicants, whose case-file got "lost" in the courts of Benin, asked that charges be brought against the Republic of Benin, for the negligence and inaction of its judiciary. The Defendant State maintained that it was appropriate for the national judges to make a pronouncement before the case could be lodged before the Court, and the Court responded in the following terms:

> Page 7: "A further and more precise objection is that the Court is of the view that the issue of exhaustion of local remedies does not arise before it. That preliminary measure is neither prescribed in any of its texts in force nor in its case law. The Court has clearly stated the law in regard to arguments attempting, through various interpretations, to reintroduce exhaustion of local remedies as a condition precedent, all of which had no legal text upon which to base their arguments."

- **Judgment of 20 April 2016, *Samba Barry* v. *Republic of Côte d'Ivoire* (ECW/CCJ/JUD/06/16) :**

As a Burkina Faso national, the Applicant was established in Côte d'Ivoire. He sued Côte d'Ivoire before the Court for inaction of the State administrative and judicial authorities, in failing to take action against some alleged perpetrators of offences (theft of a herd of cows and acts of violence), himself becoming a victim in the process – the local courts before which the case went failed to act. The Republic of Côte d'Ivoire argued that one needed to wait for the national courts to make a ruling on the matter before bringing it before the ECOWAS Court of Justice:

In paragraph §IV-6, p.10 (French version), the Court reiterated that position, stating that the principle of exhausting local remedies before coming before international courts was not operative before the Community Court of Justice;

Besides, the Court stressed that specifically concerning the case submitted before it, the non-expiration of the period for the lapsing of the time-bar on public proceedings, was also not capable of preventing the Court from adjudicating on the matter brought before it;

Again, the Court stated that Mr. Samba Barry was not in any way whatsoever bound by the periods of time-bar for public proceedings in bringing matters of human rights violations wherein he may have been a victim, before the Court;

Then the Court finally ruled that the Republic of Côte d'Ivoire's application, seeking a declaration that Mr. Monsieur Barry's action before the Court was premature, was doomed to fail.

- **Judgment of 1 July 2016, Judgment of 1 April 2016, *Djibril Yipéné Bassolé* v. *Burkina Faso* (ECW/CCJ/JUD/22/16):**

Page 7: "In another instance, the Defendant State raised an objection concerning lis pendens, in claiming that the Community Court of Justice, ECOWAS shall decline its jurisdiction in so far as the local courts of Burkina Faso had already been seised with the same case at the time it came before the said Community Court of Justice.

With regard to this point, and judged against the circumstances of the instant case, it remains permissible for the Court to examine the scope within which to adjudicate over the matter brought before it. The truth remains that in principle, where a case is lodged before the local judge under the domestic court system of a Member State, there is no bar on the Community Court preventing it from entertaining the same case. In the terms of Article 10 of the 2005 Supplementary Protocol on the Community Court of Justice, ECOWAS access to the Court is only impracticable where the same matter is instituted before "**another International Court**" for adjudication.

Hence, the fact that the Burkinabe courts may have been seised with the case, whether in part or in whole, does not constitute an obstacle for the Court to entertain that same case. In the same vein, it must be recalled that the rule of exhaustion of local remedies is not applicable before the ECOWAS Court of Justice."

CHAPTER 3

HOW THE COURT HANDLES THE CASES

Right at the time he has to adjudicate on a case, the judge is situated within a particular context, his intervention takes place within a circumscribed environment. The context is necessarily taken into account (Section 1), before the actual unfolding of the judge's assignment, against the background of the case (Section 2).

SECTION 1

THE CONTEXT

Judicial activity remains a predominantly contextual act. Beyond the hard cold rules of law, the judge has the duty of paying attention to the factual environment, the general context within which his intervention is going to take place. Court activity is never carried out *in abstracto*; it must always respond to a necessity, in terms of the relevance of the decision made, the overriding need for it to be in tune with current events and matters, its suitability to the circumstances it comes to meet when judgment is delivered. The decision made by the judge must be opportune, that is to say appropriate for the circumstances, of time in particular. Under such conditions, the judge will be expected to quicken his pace for the case brought before the court demands promptness, or, on the contrary, discreetness, in declining the *juris dictio* of the court, because the circumstances may have ceased to be appropriate to the case at hand. In the first instance, it is a question of urgency (Paragraph 1), in the second, "want of prosecution" or "stay of proceedings" (Paragraph 2); the Court thus finds itself either before a necessity to adjudicate or not to adjudicate.

Paragraph 1

The necessity of adjudication: urgency

The notion of urgency before the ECOWAS Court of Justice will be found applicable principally in connection with (A) expedited procedure, and (B) applications for provisional measures[21].

A.- Expedited procedure

This is contained in Article 59 of the Rules of the Court. In the terms of the said Rules,

> "1.On application by the applicant or the defendant, the President may exceptionally decide, on the basis of the facts before him and after hearing the other party, that a case is to be determined pursuant to an expedited procedure derogating from the provisions of these Rules, where the particular urgency of the case requires the Court shall give its ruling with the minimum of delay."

The following provisions state that an application for a case to be decided under an expedited procedure shall be made by a separate document lodged at the same time as the application initiating the proceedings or the defence, as the case may be. According to the provisions, a reply or rejoinder may not be necessary, just as an intervention.

In its case law, the Court has occasionally rejected or accepted applications for expedited procedure submitted before it. Beyond that initial differentiation, we observe that generally speaking, the case law amply provides justification for it, but not in equal terms, explaining why there was an urgency, if founded, but gleefully omitting to offer such explanation in other cases, as is apparent in the statements of the judgments delivered.

---

[21] These are, in truth, the only instances of urgency. There is a third scenario, that of stay of proceedings, provided for under Article 85 of the Rules of the Court, thus: "*The provisions of this chapter shall apply to applications to suspend the execution of a decision of the Court or of any measure adopted by another institution, submitted pursuant to these rules. The order granting the application shall fix, where appropriate, a date on which the interim measure is to lapse.*"

1.- Cases where the Court did not grant the request of the applicant

- **Judgment of 7 October 2011, *Cheikh Abdoulaye Mbengue* v. *Republic of Mali* (ECW/CCJ/JUD/08/11):**

§28: "The Court states that such request must satisfy formally determined conditions laid down in Article 59 of the Rules of Procedure of the Court. The Court notes however, that the arguments raised by the Applicant to justify the particular urgency of his personal situation or that of his family, and the facts submitted for the consideration of the Court, are irrelevant for granting the request he made.

The Court therefore dismisses the application for expedited procedure as requested by the Applicant, pursuant to Article 59 of the Rules of Procedure of the Court. "

- **Judgment of 7 October 2011, *Ameganvi Manavi Isabelle and Others* v. *Republic of Togo* (ECW/CCJ/JUD/09/11):**

§51: "(…) the Court notes that Applicants respected the form of submission as provided under Article 59, however, the Court views that the particular urgency contained in the said Article 59 is not established, because the mere reference to the next election date to renew the mandate of the MPs, which is slated for September 2012, is not pertinent, since nothing debars Applicants to still present themselves at the next election, either as private candidates or within the framework of their new political party; thus the Court is of the opinion that it behoves it to reject the request to submit the Application to an expedited procedure."

- **Judgment of 11 June 2013, *Sow Bertin Agba* v. *Republic of Togo* (ECW/CCJ/JUD/05/13):**

§ 20: "A request for expedited procedure is granted when the particular urgency of a case requires that the Court adjudicates within the shortest possible time. The Applicant applied for the said measure, considering, himself, that his detention is arbitrary and illegal. But as the time the Court is pronouncing judgment on this case, the detention of the Applicant has ceased, since he was released on 16 April 2013.

Therefore, the urgency which warranted the expedited procedure is no more existent; and there is no ground to adjudicate on that issue."

- **Judgment of 23 April 2015, *Tidjani Abdoukarim, Amadou Aly Djibo, Saidou Bakari, Boubacar Mossi* v. *Republic of Niger* (ECW/CCJ/JUD/02/15):**

§ 24: In the case cited above, the Court ruled that the Applicants do not justify in any way any urgency which may require that the Court bring the case under expedited procedure; that the argument based on the absence of the President of the National Assembly does not constitute a situation which represents a particular urgency; that what was at stake was not a serious and irremediable danger likely to jeopardise the rights of the Applicants.

- **Judgment of 17 May 2016, *Yao N'Guessan* v. *Republic of Côte d'Ivoire* (ECW/CCJ/JUD/15/16):**

> Page 3: "By Order No. ECW/CC/CCJ/ORD/03/16 of 15 February 2016, the Presiding Judge rejected the said application for expedited procedure on the ground that the situation was not urgent, while reserving costs."

2.- Cases where the Court granted the applicants' requests

- **Judgment of 8 November 2010, *Monsieur Mamadou Tandja* v. *Gen. Salou Djibo and Republic of Niger* (ECW/CCJ/JUD/05/10) :**

> §18(b): "Whereas Mr. Mamadou Tandja, despite indicating that his conditions of detention were satisfactory, he indicated that his health problems would require a visit outside Niger (…)
>
> Whereas this urgency is related materially to the state of health of the Applicant, independently of whether he should be treated in Niger or outside Niger;
>
> Whereas in this sense, the existence of health problems on the part of Mr. Mamadou Tandja justifies the application of expedited procedure, and the Court approves of it."

- **In Judgment of 26 January 2012, *El Hadji Mame Abdou Gaye* v. *Republic of Senegal* (ECW/CCJ/JUD/03/12), the Court decided as follows:**

§3: That at the external court session held on14 November 2011 at Porto Novo in the Republic of Benin, the Court, after hearing Counsel for the Applicant on the benefits of the expedited procedure; and the Republic of Senegal, on its written observations, regarding the same question, made the ruling whose operative statement was to the effect that:

- Hearing the case under the measure of expedited procedure be granted, and the Court ordered the Parties to reappear in court on 1 December 2011 at Abuja at 10 a.m. for hearing;

That:

- The Parties lodge all orders sought, and exchange written pleadings at the latest on Friday, 25 November 2011;
- Proceedings were adjourned to the said date;
- Costs were reserved.

- **Judgment of 13 July 2015, *Congrès pour la Démocratie et le Progrès (CDP) and Others* v. *Burkina Faso* (ECW/CCJ/JUD/16/15):**

> § 15, 16, 17, 18: "As regards the allegation by Burkina Faso that the Court lacks jurisdiction to adjudicate on the case before it, as a result of the non-concrete nature of the claims of violation brought by Burkina Faso, the Court has always held that it only makes rulings, in principle, on cases of human rights violation which are concrete, real and proven, and not on violations claimed to be possible, contingent or potential. One may thus be tempted, in the instant case, to question whether or not the matter before the Court is indeed well grounded, because as at the time the Court was seised with the case, no violation had as yet been committed, nor had any case of actual rejection of candidature been brought before the Court, and no individual candidature had been set aside in accordance with the new provisions; that, in a word, there is no real prejudice caused.
>
> It would amount to consigning its own time-held case law to oblivion if the Court should rule that it may legitimately entertain violations which have not yet occurred, but are very imminent. In the instant case, the alleged violation has not yet been committed, but could very soon be. Going by the indications provided to the Court, the electoral process is to open seventy (70) days before the scheduled date for voting (i.e. 11 October 2015), on the fateful day of 1 August 2015. The Court was therefore seised with the case on grounds of urgency. In the present circumstances of the case, if the Court were to wait for the applications of candidature to be possibly rejected before acting, if it had to wait for the exhaustion of the effects of any transgression before stating the law, its jurisdiction in a context of urgency would have no sense, because the electoral rights of the presumed victims for participating in the electoral race would inexorably be breached."

From these different case laws, there is an apparent feeling of contrast, or even of an impressionable outlook of the work of the Court. The specific cases are numerous and diverse. At times, the Court grants that an applicant benefit from the virtues of the expedited procedure without stating the reasons for the decision, on other occasions, it dwells a little more on the analysis of its judgment, and still at other times, it evades the reasoning by putting forth a sort of presumption of existence of urgency (*Case Concerning Mamadou Tandja* **v.** *Republic of Niger,* as to invoking ill-health) or its non-existence (*Madam Ameganvi and Others Case*, as to resources available to the applicants in the event of a rejection of their application). It would be desirable, in all the cases, that the processing of the expedited procedure be not subjected to gains and losses, and that the Court take care to amply justify the recourse to it, whenever it decides to apply it. The judgment delivered in *Case Concerning CDP and Others* **v.** *Burkina Faso* represents however, an exception to the tendency to evade demonstration of the urgency at stake.

B.- Provisional instructions or orders

Urgency is still present when, in considering given circumstances, the Court decides, before ruling on the merits, to order provisional "instructions" or "orders".

The applicable provisions thus find their source in Protocol A/P1/7/91 and in the Rules of the Court. In terms of the first instrument, one needs to refer to Article 20, entitled "Provisional Measures and Instructions", which stipulates that: "

> The Court, each time a case is brought before it, may order any provisional measures or issue any provisional instructions which it may consider necessary or desirable".

But it is in the Rules of the Court that one can actually find the references to urgency, with Article 79 §1 stating that: "

> An application under Article 20 of the Protocol shall state the subject-matter of the proceedings, the circumstances giving rise to urgency and the pleas of fact and law establishing a prima facie case for the interim measures applied for".

Then follow the various practical steps the Court – and especially the President of the Court – shall take consequently. Till date, three judgments delivered by the Court under provisional measures may be cited:

- **Judgment of 22 February 2013, *Simone Ehivet and Michel Gbagbo* v. *Republic of Côte d'Ivoire* (ECW/CCJ/JUD/03/13), the Court ruled that:**

> §3 and 4: Upon the request of the Applicants and after hearing the Parties at the court session of 22 November 2011 held at Porto Novo, the Court decided to bring the case under expedited proceedings, in compliance with Article 59 of its Rules.

On 23 March 2012, upon the request of Mr. Michel Gbagbo, claiming objective threat to his life, notably to his health, and considering the urgency of the circumstances, the Court, in an interim judgment, ordered the Republic of Côte d'Ivoire to take all the necessary and appropriate measures required to safeguard his life and physical health.[22]

- **Judgment of 19 July 2013, *Karim Meissa Wade* v. *Republic of Senegal* (ECW/CCJ/JUD/09/13) :**

The Applicant, who was part of the group that lodged its case before the Court in Case *Concerning Abdoulaye Baldé and Others* **v.** *Republic of Senegal*, once again came before the Community judge for the reason that the Senegalese authorities had allegedly not enforced the judgment of 22 February 2013, regarding prevention of the Applicant from leaving the national territory, of which he had been made a victim by the Senegalese authorities as he was preparing to travel outside the country. It must be recalled that in the first instance, the Court ordered Senegal to remove the measure of prohibition from leaving the country. During the hearing of the case, Senegal considered that it has restored legality by serving on the Applicants the measure of prohibition from leaving the national territory (§48).

The Applicant, who averred that Senegal had disregarded its Community obligations, asked for suspension of Senegal from all ECOWAS activities, among others, as well as an indication by the Court of "(…) any appropriate measure to ensure that Senegal executes the judgment delivered by the ECOWAS Court of Justice." (§54-ii).

---

[22] Indeed, these two paragraphs portray two modalities by which the Court addresses such urgency. One is by employing the expedited procedure, in accordance with Article 59 of the Court. Naturally, the determining ground for such a measure remains the urgency of the matter, as expressly stated by the said article: "… *where the particular urgency of the case requires the Court shall give its ruling with the minimum of delay*". The Applicants, in the instant case, took advantage of the expedited procedure. But the urgency may translate into the indication of stated measures – "emergency measures", to be precise. With the case in point, the Applicants equally benefited from the above-cited provisions since an order was issued to the Ivorian authorities to take urgent steps to preserve the physical integrity of the lives of Simone Ehivet and Michel Gbagbo.

On the ground that an action brought by a private individual for failure by a Member State to fulfil its obligations is inadmissible, the Court will not have the opportunity to make a pronouncement on the measures requested by the Applicant. The Court will therefore make mention of the issue only in a veiled manner, in recalling the principles, even if the style of formulation chosen could have been more agreeable[23]:

> § 34: "The Court finds that granting provisional measures in accordance with the provisions of Article 79 and the related provisions of the Rules of Procedure, and in line with the case law of the Court, is conditioned as much by an emergence of a serious and irremediable harm resulting from the circumstances relating to the purpose of the dispute, as by the urgency to adjudicate upon it on a provisional basis."

- **Judgment of 31 January 2014, *Avocats sans frontières - France and ThankGod Ebohs* v. *Federal Republic of Nigeria and Edo State Government* (ECW/CCJ/JUD/18/14):**

Mr. ThankGod is a Nigerian national. He was sentenced to death by a special tribunal which was set up in 1995 by the Military Government of that time, and found himself, at the time the cause of action arose, on "death row". Whereas he had not exhausted all the channels available to him, since he had exercised one before the Appeal Court of Kaduna, he was threatened with execution (on 24 June 2013, to be precise). He argued by insisting on existing resolutions of the African Commission of Human Rights and of the United Nations General Assembly, asking the States to observe a moratorium of the implementation of the death sentence. He asks the Court for "a provisional instruction" suspending the execution of the sentence imposed on him.

The Court declared as follows:

> §41: That it is well-established in law that regarding the application of provisional instructions, certain factors must be taken into account, for the purposes of granting such measures. First of all, it is up to the court in question to examine whether the reasons given indicate that the situation in which the Applicant found himself was urgent and

[23] Truly, the statement is not quite satisfactorily couched. It is first of all clear that the indication of provisional measures or instructions is not "*conditioned ... by an emergence of a serious and irremediable harm ...*" On the contrary, it is indeed for the purpose of preventing the occurrence of such harm that the provisional measures are taken by the Court. It is that looming risk which creates the need for adjudication on grounds of emergency. The urgency is therefore no other factor than the risk of harm occurring; the two blend somehow. The extract we just quoted may equally be criticised in that respect, it presents the urgency as a separate factor, besides the risk of occurrence of harm.

extremely serious, to the extent that, to prevent irreparable damage, it be necessary to grant the provisional measure.

§45: That there was an urgent need for the Court to make a pronouncement on the Applicant's request; that his execution would imply violation of his right to file an appeal as guaranteed under Article 7 of the African Charter.

§53: The Court ordered stay execution of the death penalty and withdrawal of the name of the second Applicant from the list of prisoners on death row. [24]

Paragraph 2

Where it is necessary not to ADJUDICATE : want of prosecution or void of proceedings

The Court, like many other international courts, may consider it necessary not to try a case, and declare that there is no point in settling the claims submitted before it. That situation, *a priori* curious, may take place in two contexts: (A) when the circumstances which brought the dispute into being have disappeared, to the extent that if there should be any judgment at all, it would have no effect in real terms, and (B) when an amicable settlement has been made in the meantime, rendering any form of judicial intervention out of question. We can see, in the two instances, we are dealing with the social dimension of a court decision, as well as its rationale – it entails putting an end to the distress of any form of court proceedings, and returning to the peaceful situation which existed prior to the opening of the trial at stake. [25]

---

[24] This case indeed turns our minds to the *Lagrand* case before the International Court of Justice, where the issue also concerned the imminent nature of the enforcement of capital punishment. See request for the indication of provisional measures by the ICJ, dated 3 March 1999 and Judgment of 27 June 2001.

[25] See, in relation to this subject, the article entitled: *Le non-lieu à statuer devant la Cour de justice de la CEDEAO*, infra, (Want of Prosecution before the ECOWAS Court of Justice), Part II of our work.

A.- If prevailing circumstances make it pointless to proceed further

When the factual situation which gave rise to the cause of action disappears, there is no reason left for trying the case. This opportune approach to the job of the judge was at play at the Court in several cases:

- **Judgment of 9 May 2011, *Center for Democracy and Development, and Center for Defence of Human Rights and Democracy* v. *Mamadou Tandja and Republic of Niger* (ECW/CCJ/JUD/05/11):**

The Court received a case from an association claiming to sue President Tandja for human rights violation, as a result of his intention to amend the Constitution and stay in power. Considering however the changes which had occurred in the political situation in Niger at the time the Court was to make a decision – coup d'état against President Tandja, a transitional political programme and restoration of democracy, adoption of a new Constitution – the Republic of Niger asked the Court to bring an end to the proceedings. It is worthy to note that despite the developing trend in the political situation of Niger, the Applicants maintained their requests "on the grounds that the decision of the Court will contribute towards dissuading other leaders who may have the intention of tampering with the constitutions of their country, so as to perpetuate themselves in power." (§34).

After describing the various developments of the national political situation, the Court concludes:

> §37: "With regard to these latter events which occurred, and as exposed above, the Court concludes that the Applicants' claims seeking various orders of injunction to restrain Mr. Mamadou Tandja from organising the criticised referendum and quelling protestation marches have become devoid of purpose, pursuant to Article 88(2) of its Rules cited above."

The Court therefore on its own decided to void the proceedings[26].

---

[26] Article 88(2) of the Rules of the Court, which was referred to by the Court in that decision, is thus worded: "*The Court may at any time of its own motion consider whether there exists any absolute bar to proceeding with a case or declare, after hearing the parties, that the action has become devoid of purpose and that there is no need to adjudicate on it; it shall give its decision in accordance with Article 87(4) and (5) of these Rules.*" This provision seems indeed to give full rein to the Court to decide on the necessity or otherwise to proceed with the trial of a case, to adjudge whether the facts submitted before it have become outdated. It is obvious that sovereign power does not negate in any way whatsoever the right of the parties to apply for or subsequently contest a request on lack of prosecution.

- **Judgment of 23 March 2012, *Laurent, Simone and Michel Gbagbo* v. *Republic of Côte d'Ivoire and Alassane Ouattara* (ECW/CCJ/RUL/07/12)**

The Applicants came before the Court to contest the validity of their arrest and detention following the political crisis which shook Côte d'Ivoire in 2010-2011.

The Application was lodged on 20 July 2011, a first hearing which was held at Porto Novo on 22 November 2011, ordered a joinder of the two proceedings (that of Laurent Gbagbo on one hand, and that of Simone and Michel Gbagbo on the other hand); but on 30 November 2011, Côte d'Ivoire, in compliance with an international arrest warrant issued against Laurent Gbagbo by a Chamber of the International Criminal Court (ICC), decided to transfer the former Head of State to The Hague.

By virtue of what the Court calls a "new fact", it will then disjoin the two proceedings and order a suspension of the procedure in *Case Concerning Laurent Gbagbo* **v.** *Côte d'Ivoire* pending determination of the proceedings before the ICC.

Here, "to suspend the procedure" is understood somehow as "to void the proceedings". The Court:

§36: Orders suspension of the procedure, pending the determination of the matter before the ICC;

Reserves the applicability of the new Article 10(ii) of the Protocol on the Court for trial and decision pending resumption of the procedure in *Laurent Gbagbo* **v.** *Côte d'Ivoire.*

- **Judgment of 11 June 2013, *Sow Bertin Agba* v. *Republic of Togo* (ECW/CCJ/JUD/05/13):**

> § 20: "A request for expedited procedure is granted when the particular urgency of a case requires that the Court adjudicates within the shortest possible time. The Applicant applied for the said measure, considering, himself, that his detention is arbitrary and illegal. But as the time the Court is pronouncing judgment on this case, the detention of the Applicant has ceased, since he was released on 16 April 2013.
>
> Therefore, the urgency which warranted the expedited procedure is no more existent; and there is no ground to adjudicate on that issue."

Incidentally, it is required that the Court hears the parties before pronouncing such a measure and one may reasonably suppose that the applicants will make their case heard on that point.

- **Judgment of 24 April 2015, *Gnassingbe Kpatcha and Others* v. *Republic of Togo* (ECW/CCJ/JUD/08/15):**

At the time the case is filed before the ECOWAS Court of Justice, the Criminal Chamber of the Supreme Court of Togo delivered a judgment of 15 September 2010, bringing charges against the Applicants, but the National Commission of Human Rights, before which the matter was referred by the Government, confirmed that acts of violence, cruel, inhuman or degrading treatment were committed on the persons of the Applicants. The Republic of Togo thereafter admitted that these acts of violence were committed but contested violation of human rights like the right to visit, healthcare, etc.

> §42: "Here again, the Court upholds the acknowledgment by the Defendant State, that acts of torture were committed by its officers. The Court recalls that the Republic of Togo acknowledged that the Applicants were tortured and that a process of compensation has even been put in place. The Court concludes thereby that such acknowledgement implies that the Republic of Togo is fully and totally liable for the acts of torture and other inhuman and degrading treatment the Applicants were victims of. However, the Court is of the view that the Republic of Togo cannot cite the fact that steps have been taken towards compensating the Applicants, as a ground for maintaining that the requests brought forth by them are without purpose."

> Page 27: The Court "Upholds the stand taken by the Republic of Togo to repair the damage caused the victims of those acts of torture (…)"

- **Judgment of 19 July 2013, *Karim Meissa Wade* v. *Republic of Senegal* (ECW/CCJ/JUD/09/13):**

> §35: "The Court further finds that in connection with the substantive case before it, the provisional measures applied for have become devoid of purpose. Consequently, the Court adjudges that at this stage of the procedure, there are no more grounds to adjudicate on the provisional measures sought and the Court sets aside all arguments, prayers and requests made by the Applicant relating to that issue."[27]

---

[27] One would certainly have liked to see the Court being more informative, at the time of making this ruling, regarding the measures in question and the context of the dispute. But one notices, once again, the liberty with which the Court appreciates an opportunity regarding its own *juris dictio*. One may even go further: it is undoubtedly because the Court considers that there is no purpose in talking of the past that it does not even give any more details to the reader, on the measures initially requested and on the nature of such measures, now inappropriate.

- **Judgment of 14 October 2015, *Hope Democratic Party* v. *Federal Republic of Nigeria* (ECW/CCJ/JUD/19/15) :**

The Applicant, a political party, files a case before the Court in the course of the electoral process of Nigeria, which saw the defeat of President Goodluck Jonathan and the triumph of Mohammed Buhari. The Applicant criticises the conditions under which the party of the ex-President may have been financed. But at the time the Court has to examine the case, the election period was already over. The Court then adjudges that there was no point trying the case, in spite of the persistent demands by the Applicant to have the case tried, so as to "dissuade", in future, other political leaders.

As in *Center For Democracy and Development and Others* **v.** *Republic of Niger*, cited earlier, in which the Applicants maintained their requests "… on the grounds that the decision of the Court will contribute towards dissuading other leaders who may have the intention of tampering with the institutions of their country, so as to perpetuate themselves in power." (§34), the Applicant, in the instant case, also urged the Court to make a declaration on their case, at all cost, for the same reason. But, unmoved in its estimation of what the facts held, and in considering whether it was appropriate or not to try the case, the Court finally concludes that there was indeed no purpose to sit on the case[28] :

> p.33 (French version): "As for the Plaintiffs, they declared that they wanted their applications to be maintained, on the grounds that the decision of the Court will contribute towards dissuading others leaders who may have the intention of tampering with the Constitution of their country, so as to perpetuate themselves in power".
>
> p.34 (French version): "Therefore, just as this Court determined in the Mamadou Tandja case, this present case is devoid of purpose since President Goodluck Jonathan and his PDP did not win the elections, hence this instant case has lost its meaning and is hereby ruled to be devoid of purpose, and hence dismissible"

- **Judgment of 20 October 2015, *La Rencontre Africaine pour la Défense des Droits de l'Homme (RADDHO)* v. *Republic of Senegal* (ECW/CCJ/JUD/20/15):**

RADDHO brought a case before the Court for the Court to order various measures against the Republic of Senegal on the eve of the 2012 presidential elections, marked by violence (notably after the candidacy

---

[28] Indeed, it is permissible to wonder whether the Court could have simply declined jurisdiction, for that seemed rather obvious, and a reading through the judgment makes it abundantly clear.

of President Wade was validated by the Constitutional Council). Among others, the Court is asked to order suspension of the elections.

But at the time the Court is still adjudicating on the case, the elections come to a close and President Wade is beaten. Moreover, some of the measures sought had already been adopted by the new authorities.

The Court then decided that there was no ground anymore to pursue the case further, that:[29]

> §33: The Court notes that the question of whether or not Mr. Abdoulaye Wade's candidacy is valid, and whether the request for suspension of the presidential election of 26 February 2012 could be suspended, were of no current relevance;
>
> §40: The actions taken by the Republic of Senegal were consistent with the measures requested by the Applicant;
>
> §41: In the light of the above, the Court finds that the action of RADDHO had become devoid of purpose, and consequently that it was ripe and appropriate to adjudge that there was no purpose in any further sitting on the case.

B.- Amicable settlement

It is the second instance where the Community Court considers that further adjudication becomes pointless. Such conclusion is natural. The Court did adopt it in the following cases:

- **Judgment of 9 October 2012, *Harouna Warkani, Dr. Gueye Abdoulat* v. *President of ECOWAS Commission and ECOWAS Commission* (ECW/CCJ/JUD/12/12):**

Since an amicable settlement had been concluded among the parties – withdrawal of the Applicants' complaint against the Defendants, re-admission of the Applicants, with removal of sanctions and restoration of the entitlements existing before the disciplinary procedure – and the Court acknowledges it[30]:

---

[29] One may however wonder if the Court could not have determined the case on the basis of lack of jurisdiction or inadmissibility of application, not only in view of the fact that one does not know the category of claims under which RAAHO was bringing its case (human rights violation or failure to fulfil obligation?) but, supposing it was for human rights violation, RADDHO could not argue that it had "personally" suffered any harm.

[30] The signatures of the judges – unique – and that of the registrar, are written at the bottom of the document. In the annex, the amicable settlement, signed by the lawyers and the two parties. It is however curious that the decision made by the Court does not cite any text

In the written decision of the Court, the Court orders that the cases lodged by the Applicants against the Defendant be struck off the cause list. That the decision was taken in line with the terms of an amicable settlement deposited on 3 October 2012 at the public hearing, by Plaintiff Counsel, and approved by both Plaintiff Counsel and Defence Counsel. That the terms of the amicable settlement were annexed to the principal document. That the judgment was thus considered as duly rendered by the Court in a public hearing on Tuesday, 9 October 2012.

- **Judgment of 30 June 2015, *Association of Voluntarily Retired Workers (ATVR)* v. *Republic of Mali* (ECW/CCJ/JUD/14/15):**

With the World Bank, the Republic of Mali had put in place a programme for voluntarily retired civil servants and the State undertook certain commitments towards the workers involved (payment of various sums of money). In the year 2000, ATVR dragged the Republic of Mali before the Industrial Court, and thereafter, before the Bamako Court of Appeal. Each of these courts ordered the Republic of Mali to produce the framework agreement which was signed between the World Bank and the Republic of Mali, but to no avail.

The Court will declare the case inadmissible on the ground of an amicable settlement already having been reached:

> p.5 (French version): "Whereas the Republic of Mali raised the issue of inadmissibility of the Application on the strength of an agreement reached between the Parties (...) that indeed (...) it was decided through a mutual agreement, that the dispute shall be terminated, through a Memorandum of Understanding dated 18 July 2007 and signed by the Parties. (...) Therefore, the provisions of the Malian Civil Code are to be applied, to the extent that the transactions made between the Parties must be viewed in the light of those provisions, as a way by the Republic of Mali to fulfil the obligations binding on it."

---

relating to the procedure which had just unfolded. Indeed, two provisions of the Rules of the Court were relevant, both, to "discontinuance": Article 72 : *If, before the Court has given its decision, the parties reach a settlement of their dispute and intimate to the Court the abandonment of their claims, the President shall order the case to be removed from the register and shall give a decision as to costs in accordance with Article 66(8), having regard to any proposals made by the parties on the matter.»*, and Article 73: "*If the applicant informs the Court in writing that he wishes to discontinue the proceedings, the President shall order the case to be removed from the register and shall give a decision as to costs in accordance with Article 66(8) of these Rules.*"

The Court even goes much further, for in its analysis, it conducts a check on the content of the agreement and its mode of execution. It thus notes that the memorandum of understanding is indeed:

> "... as a result of a tripartite negotiation between the Government of the Republic of Mali, the Employers' Council of Mali and the Labour Union of Mali, with the latter playing the role of legal representatives of ATVR, so as to terminate the claims made by ATVR."

Then, that some sums of money had already been paid by the Government initially to 1,073 of the voluntarily retired workers. The Court equally finds that from letters of discontinuance of the ATVR Council dated 31 January 2007, and filed among the pleadings of the proceedings:

> "... the Republic of Mali did carry out its commitments and that 1,206 Voluntarily Retired Workers from the Civil Service and the Military were paid their due pension funds, representing a total of 1, 208, 227,572 CFA Francs."

- **Judgment of 16 February 2016, *Kagbara Bassabi and Babale Philomène* v. *Republic of Togo* (ECW/CCJ/JUD/04/16):**

The Applicants had brought their case before the Court for violation of their right to property and arbitrary arrest. But before the Court adjudicates on the case, an amicable settlement was reached, and brought to the notice of the Court; the Parties confirmed it at a subsequent court hearing. Consequently, the case was struck off the cause list, in accordance with the request of the Parties and by virtue of Article 72 of the Rules of the Court.

The Court thus ruled as follows:

> §5 to 11: That by a correspondence received at the Court Registry on 21 January 2016, the Parties requested that their case be removed from the register, in accordance with Article 72 of the Rules of the Court, and to adjudge and declare that the Parties will bear the costs;

That Article 72 of the Rules of the Court provide:

> "If, before the Court has given a decision, the parties reach a settlement of their dispute and intimate to the Court the abandonment of their claims, the President shall order the case to be removed from the register and shall give a decision as to costs in accordance Article 66 (8), having regard to any proposals made by the parties on the matter";

That the Parties, by their correspondence dated 11 January 2016, notified the Court that in connection with their dispute, an amicable settlement had been reached among them;

That the settlement was concretised by the signing of a notification of agreement certified the President of the *Tribunal de première instance de première classe* (Lome Court of First Instance) on 3 December 2015, thus terminating the claims brought by the Applicants;

That the said notification of agreement indicates that the Parties have agreed as follows: "For the resolution of the case between the parties, the *Caisse Nationale de Sécurité Sociale* (CNSS) (National Social Security Fund) accepts to pay to Mr. Kagbara Bassabi and Madam Babale Philomène, alias Kagbara, a total balance sum of Twenty Million CFA Francs (CFA F 20,000,000), upon the signing of the present notification…";

That at the court hearing of 16 April 2016, Counsel for CNSS and for the Republic of Togo confirmed the terms of the correspondence cited;

That it was therefore ripe and appropriate, and in accordance with Article 72 of the Rules of the Court, to order removal of the case from the Court's register.

After examining the context within which cases are brought before the Court, which now and then may call for the necessity, either to speed up the determination of the case, or on the contrary, to prune it, we must now turn our attention to the subject-matter itself, of the case filed before the Court.

SECTION 2

THE SUBJECT-MATTER

At the stage where the Court sets out to examine the merits of the case, the judge notably ensures that the application submitted before him does not mix up the legal genres, and transform itself into an application brought against a State that may have violated its commitments as a Member of the Community of States. It is one thing indeed to have disregarded a right that can be invoked by an individual – pursuant to a wide range of international texts – and another thing, to sue a State for transgression of a rule laid down by ECOWAS. Proceedings for human rights violation equally differ, with regard to what the trial puts at stake and what is constituted by the purpose of the request, from proceedings on the national plane. From this twin viewpoint, (Paragraph 1) the specific nature of the case must be recalled by the Court. Once this basis is established, (Paragraph 2) the Community Court could then make a declaration on the merits of the requests, and gradually, build up a stock of jurisprudence, some of the most pre-eminent features of which may already have to be depicted.

Paragraph 1

A two-sided autonomy of the trial proceedings: the specific nature of the application and the subject-matter of the dispute

The ECOWAS Court of Justice, when examining an application for human rights violation, devotes itself to upholding two principles, which converge, in as much as the two of them put a premium on the autonomy of the specific nature of the trial proceedings for human rights violations. The principles may be subsumed in two assertions: (A) an application brought for human rights violation is a specific suit, which particularly not be confused with an application for default by a Member State to fulfil its obligations; moreover, (B) the trial proceedings before the municipal courts of the Member States, and that before the ECOWAS Court do not have the same purpose. It is these two statements that must be re-examined.

A.- An application for human rights violation is not an application for failure to fulfil an obligation

We stated it above: a suit for human rights violation, within the context of the ECOWAS Court, is a dispute with high political content. So it is, first of all, for obvious reasons. Indeed, in so far as, *by principle,* only States are in a position to assume the status of defendants – for they alone are bound by the international rules, in that instance, applied by the judge – the proceedings may very quickly transform itself into a political trial, especially if the applicant is, for example, a political opponent, as is regularly the case. Such politicisation unquestionably generates tension, even personalisation of the dispute submitted before the Court.[31].

[31] One point may be made in that regard: the applications target at times the Head of State himself, cited thus as defendant, in cases concerning Niger or Côte d'Ivoire, for example,

It also has another effect on the conduct of the proceedings. Since the State and its departments, even the Head of State, are perceived as responsible for the complaints brought, or even the organisers of the human rights violation, the trial is going to assume the shape of questioning the good faith – in general – of the State in question. The transgression complained of, as brought before the Court, is no more going to take the form of a case brought against a State observing the minimum level of the rules it is bound to observe, with the complaint being a single pathological occurrence, a transient anomaly, but rather as a demonstrable habit of an inclination towards delinquency, the sign of a psychological frame of mind essentially synonymous with indiscipline. Such bias on the part of the applicant becomes pronounced when – as has already occurred – the unsuccessful State in the case shows reluctance in enforcing the judgment. What the applicant thus seems to request from the Court, in such situations, in general, is a form of stigmatisation of the State, an acknowledgement by the Court that the State in question "is not fulfilling" or "is refusing to fulfil" its obligations as a member of the Community in general. We indeed see the change there is from evaluating the act or the action – which is in principle what is in cause at the trial – to blacklisting the State itself.

If there is no doubt that a State which persists in violating human rights necessarily ends up entangling itself with the serious issue of its very membership of the Community, as may be demonstrated by the possibility of sanctions being imposed on that State, the Court always insists on recalling the autonomy surrounding proceedings instituted for human rights violation, by recalling that an application for human rights violation is not an application for failure by a Member State to fulfil its obligation, and that whatever the case may be, private individuals are not admissible to proceedings for default of States concerning their Community obligations:

---

which of course constitutes legal heresy in the light of the principles the Court has unceasingly drawn our attention to. Such a subjective approach to the dispute provides a picture, of course, of the sub-conscious thoughts of the applicants: it should indeed be the first judge of the country who should, closely or remotely, be behind the violations committed by the ministries and State departments. Also, the personalisation of the stakes in the trial equally portrays the very "presidential" nature of many of the political regimes.

- **Judgment of 18 November 2010, *Hissène Habré* v. *Republic of Senegal* (ECW/CCJ/JUD/06/10):**

§33: "On this point, the Court observes that, as an individual, the Applicant lacks the legal status to bring this allegation before the Court, in regard to Article 10 of the Supplementary Protocol, since this has to do with the failure by a Member State to carry out its Community obligation; it therefore behoves the Court to reject this grievance formulated by Mr. Hissène Habré."

- **Judgment of 6 July 2012, *Kemi Pinheiro v. Republic of Ghana* (ECW/CCJ/JUD/11/12):**

The Applicant, a Nigerian national, intended to open a second law firm at Accra but was barred on grounds of nationality. He sues Ghana before the Court, for violation of freedom of movement and establishment:

§55: "The Court, after hearing the parties in an open hearing, holds that the Applicant has no legal capacity to file an action against a Member State for failure to honour its obligations arising from Community texts. Therefore, the action is dismissed."

The case does illustrate at any rate the difficulty which may confront an individual when injured by a default in obligations as may be caused by a State, where such individual cannot bring such State conduct before court, precisely because the door to the proceedings for default through State acts, instantly on our minds, is closed against him. In the instant case, and for the purposes of a commendable educational approach, the Court is going to attempt outlining solutions to such instances when they occur:

§49: "Therefore, the Community citizen who has been a victim of an alleged violation of a right enshrined in the Community Protocol by a Member State is provided with only two alternatives:

a) To ask his own State to take on the defence of his interest and file an action before the Community Court of Justice against the defaulting Member State, pursuant to Article 10(a);

Or

b) To decide to file an action against the defaulting Member State, addressing the domestic jurisdiction of the State where the alleged violation of his rights has occurred."

§50: "At this point, one should bear in mind that national courts are also Community courts as they have competence to apply the Community law which forms part of the internal order."

That being so, the matter proved more complex than it appeared to be and contained within itself daunting and stimulating questions[32].

---

32 We first of all need to begin by a commendation, that the Court, in this dispute, is led to make a pronouncement on norms which find their basis, authentically, in integration. We often complain that matters on economic integration, its original mandate, are not directly filed before the Court. That the Court should therefore more often make decisions with economic bearings, like freedom of movement and establishment of persons and economic actors. Certainly, such issues may have been raised before the Court, but truly, they were raised behind the generally bigger and more attractive screen of human rights violation. Such that the Community judge did not actually rule on that aspect of the applications submitted before him. One can accordingly cite cases like *Afolabi* v. *Nigeria* (2004) – first judgment delivered by the Court, but the application was inadmissible; *Laurent Gbagbo* v. *Côte d'Ivoire* (2012), or *Baldé and Others* v. *Senegal* (2013). In the matter at hand, we are dealing with a case which truly and directly stands against freedom of movement and establishment in the Community space, a Nigerian lawyer being challenged on grounds of nationality by the authorities of Ghana, the latter thus refusing to allow the Nigerian to establish himself in Ghana.

The other aspect of the decision, we have said, concerns the procedural options available to Mr. Pinheiro for seeking redress. The response of the Court, we have seen, hinges on the matter being brought under failure by a Member State to fulfil its obligations and the implementation of such obligations. It was then said that the application will be doomed to failure, such complaints being actionable only by a Member State or the President of the ECOWAS Commission. The Court does not merely dismiss the application however, it mentions in passing, the options available to a private individual desirous of seeking sanctions against a State which does not respect its Community obligations, outside bringing the matter under disputes on human rights violation, for which the person can come directly before the Court. In paragraph 49 of the above-cited judgment, the Court shows two ways out. These two ways must both be stressed a little further and nuanced as well.

There is no doubt, as the Court has said, that a private person seeking to sue a defaulting State in respect of failure to fulfil Community obligations, may bring the matter before the national judge. This reminder is no more than a truism, but it is essential. We tend to forget that the first judge of Community legality, and international legality at any rate – from a more general standpoint – is indeed the national judge. As indicated by the Court, the Community law forms an integral part of the domestic legal order of the Member States, under conditions incidentally facilitated, in relation to the rules of general international law, since the traditional mechanisms of admitting the ECOWAS norms into the general body of laws does not in principle exist here – subject to the issue not being one where notably, treaties have been concluded within the framework of the Community. The instruments of subsidiary law in particular, manifestations of the unilateral will of the international organisation, enter directly upon the legal order of the Member States, under certain provisos. Every law officer pleading a case before court is therefore entitled to claim the application of such derivative instruments of the treaties. A Member opposing the application of the Community law shall thus be held accountable for its commitments.

In the prevailing circumstances, and failing to bring his case before the national judge – but wouldn't he have objected, even wrongly, on the requirement of Ghanaian nationality? The

Therefore, we need to note, regarding this case, that once more, the Court rules on the impossibility of an individual to initiate an application for default in State obligations. It will do so in other judgments:

- **Judgment of 19 July 2013, *Karim Meissa Wade* v. *Republic of Senegal* (ECW/CCJ/JUD/09/13):**

§83: "(...) the Court finds that in the terms of the Article 10 referred to above, actions for failure by a Member State to fulfil its obligation may only be brought by a Member State or by the President of the ECOWAS Commission. Consequently, an application lodged on such subject-matter by an individual or corporate body other than a Member State and/or the President of the Commission, shall be declared inadmissible, for lack of locus standi."

- **Judgment of 23 October 2015, *Alternative citoyenne et Roch Gnaoui David* v. *Republic of Benin* (ECW/CCJ/JUD/21/15):**

The Applicant brought his case before the Court seeking a declaration that Benin had violated the provisions of the 2001 Protocol on

---

issue remains as to the category of pleadings in law under which the case should be filed before the ECOWAS Court.

Clearly, filing the case under failure to fulfil obligation is excluded, for the reasons mentioned above.

One will first of all be tempted to consult the texts on freedom of movement and establishment. But there again, two questions arise immediately: do these texts exist, that is to say, are they made for the legal profession, which is at stake here? That comes as our first point of interrogation, for, we know, if the freedoms in cause are matters which are consubstantial with the process of integration, if there is even no doubt that some of the texts exist at ECOWAS – Protocols of 1979, 1986, 1990, without forgetting the Protocol of 1982 on citizenship – we know that the regulation of certain specific professions, often the liberal professions, may be deferred and my come in later. At the time the case comes before the Court, does such a regulation exist for lawyers? The second question is that, supposing even that these special texts exist, do they grant access to individuals to come before the Court? Today, that individual right to come directly before he ECOWAS Court only exists, in clear terms, in matters of human rights violation. If the texts in question do not provide for that, it will obviously be impossible to come before the Court within the context we have presented.

If this first avenue proves, for one reason or the other, a fertile ground to explore, we are not left with any other choice than to file the case under human rights violation. The question which then comes up at once is the following: is the freedom in question capable of being described as a "human right"? The discussion, however it may appear, is neither theoretical nor philosophical. What we mean by that is that the answer to this puzzle is a purely factual one: the applicant only needs to see if, in a relevant text, adopted within or outside the framework of ECOWAS, there is a provision which provides that right for the individual. It is, in our opinion, the text which should resolve the case. If the freedom in question is contained in a catalogue of rights which may be invoked before the Court, there is no doubt, we think, that the applicant will be able to invoke it, without prejudice to the final decision of the Court of course.

Democracy and Good Governance, in failing to take measures relating to the computerised electoral roll for local elections. The Applicant equally blames the Constitutional Court for delivering a judgment which violated the principle of prohibition of maintenance of all forms of non-democratic government (Articles 1 and 22 of the said Protocol). Other complaints are filed against the Government and the Parliament.

The Court will declare the Application inadmissible for lack of locus standi (for bringing an application for default of a State to fulfil its obligations), ruling that:

> §15 and16: In that particular case, the application lodged by the Applicants seeks a declaration from the Court to the effect that the Republic of Benin defaulted in its obligations arising from the Protocol on Democracy and Good Governance; that it was therefore an application complaining about a Member State failing to fulfil its obligations;
>
> That by virtue of Article 10 of the 19 January 2005 Protocol, only a Member State or the President of the ECOWAS Commission may bring such complaints before the Court;
>
> That in compliance with the above-cited Article 10, it was ripe and appropriate to declare the Application inadmissible for lack of locus standi.

- **Judgment of 24 April 2015, *Pascal A. Bodjona* v. *Republic of Togo* (ECW/CCJ/JUD/06/15):**

The Applicant, who was successful in an earlier judgment delivered in 2015 by the Court, comes before the Court once again to complaint about the bureaucracy of Togo in enforcing the judgment of 24 April 2015. The Application could lead the Court onto the path of having to examine the execution of judgments it had delivered. The matter also raised between the lines, we can imagine, the issue of setting in motion proceedings on default on the part of the Member State to fulfil its Community obligations.

§23: The Court refers to the judgment of 24 April 2015, delivered in *Case Concerning Gnassingbe Kpatcha and Others* **v.** *Republic of Togo* (ECW/CCJ/APP/15/14), and that of 19 July 2013, made in *Case Concerning Karim Meissa Wade* **v.** *Republic of Senegal* (ECW/CCJ/JUD/09/13). Both judgments decided that it was beyond the powers of a private person to initiate proceedings for failure of States to perform their Community obligations.

B.- The purpose of a trial before the domestic court of a Member State is not the same as that before the Court

This has to do with a very important doctrinal point, which has numerous dimensions and implications we shall attempt to outline. But it is appropriate that we avoid any dogmatic or rigid understanding of this significant rule, for, as we shall see, even if we should rule out every form of vertical hierarchical relationship between the international court and the national court, a situation may arise where that the national court will take account of a judgment delivered by the international court. That form of intrusion will be discussed when we tackle the issue relating to the independence of the two trial processes (Chapter 3, section 2, § 2, A). For the time being, we will only concern ourselves with varying patterns of the principle according which the ECOWAS Court is neither an appeal court nor a *cour de cassation* (court of cassation or cassation court).

The case at stake goes beyond the scenario, already looked at, where the applicant sought, directly speaking, to obtain the retrial of a case which has already been determined by the municipal courts of a Member State. Here, we find ourselves in a broader and more subtle context, one where the applicant is after a reproduction of the national procedural pattern, in urging the Court, for example, to source its analysis from the personal case of the applicant rather than from the relevant question at stake: observance of the international commitments made by a State. It is quite rare, it must be acknowledged, that applications may follow only that line of discussion. It is no doubt the reason why the reminder on the difference of purpose between the national trial, and the trial before the ECOWAS Court, is revisited, as in the same old song, in the case law:

- **Judgment of 28 January 2014, *Alimu Akeem* v. *Federal Republic of Nigeria* (ECW/CCJ/JUD/01/14):**

§40: "The Court notes that it is within the jurisdiction of the criminal martial court before which Alimu Akeem appeared, to determine whether he is guilty or not for the incidents which occurred in the performance of his functions. The instant Court is not seised with the same facts. The Court is rather seised in regard to the detention imposed on him in the course of the procedure for the determination of that case, which he considers long, illegal, a violation of human dignity, and notably a violation of Article 6 of the African Charter on Human and Peoples' Rights. On the other hand, he brings his Application in regard to alleged physical torture amounting to violation of Article 5 of the said Charter (...)"

§41: "Similarly, it is the view of the instant Court that under such circumstances, the findings or conclusions established or yet to be established by the martial courts of Nigeria seised to determine whether Alimu Akeem is guilty or not, and to sentence him, do not have any determining effect on the Court's adjudication upon the grievances and requests brought by the Applicant. At any rate, the Application before the instant Court has no criminal connotation. As such, the criminal nature of the action instituted against Alimu Akeem in Nigeria cannot be admitted as a ground for declaring the Application which the instant Court is seised with as inadmissible (...)"

§42 : "(...) in the instant case, the Court is not asked to re-examine the judgments of the General Court-Martial which determined the culpability of Alimu Akeem; the Court is rather seised with a case on the human rights violations which allegedly occurred in the course of the procedure at the domestic court."

- **Judgment of 23 April 2015, *Georges Constant Amoussou* v. *Republic of Benin* (ECW/CCJ/JUD/05/15):**

The Applicant was arrested in connection with a financial scandal, and incarcerated. He initially brought his case before the Court in the year 2014; he comes before the Court again asking it to adjudge and declare that the restraint exercised on his person in 2010 was an arbitrary arrest. Beforehand, he had lodged the case before the Constitutional Court of Benin (September 2010). The Court declared in:

§ IV.20, p.14 (French version) that the rulings made by a national court, be it a constitutional court, regarding facts on which the Honourable Court may have already made a ruling, are not binding on that national court, to the extent of challenging the domestic court's case law.

- **Judgment of 30 June 2015, *Bourama Sininta and 119 Others* v. *Republic of Mali* (ECW/CCJ/JUD/13/15):**

IV.13, p.10 (French version): Mali argues that the abrogation of the national law upon which the Application was based must constitute, for the Court, a ground for the inadmissibility of the Application, but the Court found that:

The admissibility of an application before it is not determined by the national rules of the Member States;

The conditions of admissibility of an application for human rights violation before the Community Court of Justice, ECOWAS are fixed by the provisions of Article 10(d) of Supplementary Protocol A/SP.1/01/05.

- **Judgment of 30 June 2015, *167 Former Workers of SONIDEP Represented by Eli Haggar and B. Kanfideni* v. *Republic of Niger and SONIDEP* (ECW/CCJ/JUD/15/15):**

The Applicants had agreed to a retirement package brokered by SONIDEP, but considering that they had been abused by SONIDEP, and upon being unsuccessful in their suit before the national judge, decided to bring their case before the ECOWAS Court, and the latter ruled by asking:

§IV.4, 6, 7: Whether the fact that a case was lodged before the national courts, was a ground for inadmissibility of the application before it;

In answering, it ruled that previously accessing the national court cannot constitute a ground for inadmissibility of an application before the Community Court of Justice;

That incidentally, the Court had always received applications and upheld its jurisdiction where a national court had been seised with the case beforehand, for instance in *El Hadji Mame Abdou Gaye* **v.** *Republic of Senegal*.

- **Judgment of 13 July 2015, *Congrès pour la Démocratie et le Progrès (CDP) and Others* v. *Burkina Faso* » (ECW/CCJ/JUD/16/15):**

§27: "The Court (...) still holds that, neither in the instant case nor in the ones which preceded it, will its function consist of seeking to discover the intention of the national lawmaker, or of competing with the domestic courts, within their own scope of jurisdiction, which, precisely, consists of interpreting their own national texts. But the Court assumes its rightful powers where the interpretation or application of the national text aims at depriving the citizens of rights embedded in international instruments to which Burkina Faso is a party."

- **Judgment of 6 October 2015, *Djelou Kodjovi, Akumani Koffi and Alipui Ablavi v. Republic of Togo*(ECW/CCJ/JUD/17/15):**

§22 : "In this respect, the Court recalls that if by principle, the Court has no powers to review the reasoning for a decision made at the level of a Member State of ECOWAS, whereas the Court neither assumes the role of a national judge in a broader sense, nor that of an Appeal Court or a Cassation Court, it nevertheless remains important that it is the responsibility of the Court to derive (from the application of the domestic law) all the consequences arising from human rights cases brought before it."

- **Judgment of 30 November 2015, *Stella Ifeoma Nnalue and 20 Others* v. *Federal Republic of Nigeria* (ECW/CCJ/JUD/24/15):**

Pages 5 and 6: "In its written pleadings dated 18 December 2012 and lodged before the Court on 19 December 2012, the Defendant, namely the Federal Republic of Nigeria, raised a preliminary objection wherein it argued that the action brought before the ECOWAS Court of Justice should be inadmissible since the Plaintiff had already filed the same suit before the Nigerian courts (Federal High Court), and that in the event that it is determined that the suit before the Federal High Court was decided against them, the Plaintiff cannot come to re-litigate the same issue before the Community Court. On their part, the Plaintiff maintained that the issues, subject-matter, claims and parties in the suits before the High Court of Benin (subsequently struck out), before the Edo State High Court (re-filed and still pending), and before the ECOWAS Court of Justice, are substantially different, and that based on the same set of facts, the Plaintiff can maintain separate and different suits against different Defendants for different reliefs and in different courts, and as such, their action before the ECOWAS Court of Justice does not amount to abuse of court process or estoppel res judicata.

The Court therefore considers that its duty is to examine whether the two suits have the same subject-matter. It is apparent, in that regard, that if the facts in issue remain incontrovertibly the same, the substance of the actions filed before court greatly differ. The Plaintiff's action before the judge in the domestic courts of Nigeria was to seek criminal investigation and prosecution of the alleged killers and compensation for the loss of their breadwinners, whereas the object of matter before the ECOWAS Community Court of Justice is to ask the Court to find that there is an occurrence of human rights violation, and to seek reparation for the harm done, if the Court should so find.

The texts relied on in pleading the two cases are equally different. Before the national courts of Nigeria, the request sought application of the provisions of the domestic criminal law of Nigeria, whereas before the ECOWAS Court, the request was to urge the Court to find an occurrence of the alleged human rights violation, essentially derived from the African Charter on Human and Peoples' Rights, which Nigeria is party to.

The two proceedings thus instituted are therefore independent of each other; they do not overlap, and one cannot be confused for the other. Similarly, the Court is of the view that in entertaining the instant case, the Community Court of Justice, ECOWAS is not acting as an appellate court, since the case filed before it does not have the same substance as the suit filed before the judge in the domestic court of Nigeria. The concept of "appeal" presupposes that the same case is transferred to a higher court, so as to adjudicate on the same facts and to examine the same arguments of the parties; but such is not the case here.

The Court thus holds that the thesis that the two suits are totally identical, cannot be upheld; and hence, the Court holds that the Plaintiff's right to bring their case before the ECOWAS Court of Justice cannot be contested. For that reason, the Court rules that the preliminary objection thus raised by the Federal Republic of Nigeria is ill-founded, and the Court receives the action brought by the Plaintiff as admissible."

- **Judgment of 4 October 2016, *Col. Mohammed Sambo Dasuki (RTD)* v. *Federal Republic of Nigeria* (ECW/CCJ/JUD/23/16):**

The Applicant, former Security Adviser to President Goodluck Jonathan, defeated in the 2015 elections, was arrested for "corruption". For lack of sufficient legal charges against him, the national courts ordered his release.

The Court decided along the same lines:

Page 23: "It is a well-established fact that this Court does not have criminal jurisdiction as has been held in a plethora of its decisions. The allegation of misappropriation of funds and unlawful possession of ammunition is not before this Court and even it is, the Court lacks jurisdiction to entertain same.

We are therefore not deciding on the guilty or otherwise of the Applicant on the charges before the National Court and has only assumed jurisdiction based on the facts before it to establish whether the human rights of the Applicant as alleged has been violated."

That being the case, it is appropriate that we make a very important point concerning the independence of the international trial in relation to the trial at the national level. It will certainly be out of proportions indeed to view the trial proceedings at the national level as compared to the international level, as two parallel zones doomed to stay completely out of each other's way, as two spheres of activity, separated like watertight compartments. By the operation of the rule, already mentioned, of non-exhaustion of local remedies, a decision of the ECOWAS Court may indeed be intended to interfere with an ongoing or future national judicial procedure – an overlap which the classical system of exhaustion of local remedies, as a condition precedent for access to the international court, by its very nature, does not envisage.

Given such a scenario, the independence of the respective two trial processes subsists, but their independence must be qualified by two reserved instances.

First of all, from a *legislative* point of view, nothing debars a national authority from considering that a decision made by the ECOWAS Court necessitates a streamlining of the national law, precisely where it is the national law which constitutes the source of the violation found, and where, if such national law should subsist, there will be a high probability of further violations in future. This was the typical situation which justified recourse to the recent technique of "pilot judgments" well known in the European human rights protection system. We thus find ourselves in a situation where the desirable legislative amendments derive directly from the international case law. We have even put forth an advocacy, for the purpose that, eventually, the Court may make determinations on problematic national laws, – which is not the case for now.

Again, from a *judicial or jurisprudential* point of view, a judgment of the Community Court may influence the decision of a national court in a decisive manner, in the sense that the judge at the domestic court of the Member State of ECOWAS may choose to take full account of the judgment made by the Community Court. The principle of independence of the national trial proceedings, from the international trial process, is not opposed to this other mode of recognising the case law of the Community Court, far from it. Such recognition of the Community law brings about radical effects, in so far as, hinged upon a sort of theory of maximisation of the virtues of the international court decision, the national court makes full use of the fruits obtainable from the international court. Such radical approach is also prophylactic in nature – and that is its principal virtue – in neutralizing the toxins of the violation complained of by the supra national Court, this approach purges the proceedings at the national level of its vices and weaknesses and, in the final analysis, sanitises the legal order, in the same way as it demonstrates the will of the State and its organs, to raise the quality of safeguard of human rights to a particular standard of requirements.

From the points thus made so far, one does realize that the doctrine of separating the national proceedings from the international trial must be considered in a relative light. It must be all the more so, when applied to the ECOWAS Court, where the absence of exhaustion of local remedies as a precondition for access to the Court creates a greater likelihood for the occurrence of such overlaps and interference at the two different levels of the proceedings.

So there is a radical way to avoid such interactions that can be deleterious for the principle of separation of roles of the national judge and the international one. It would be the establishment of the principle of exhaustion of the local remedies, well-known principle in international human rights protection systems.

Paragraph 2

An outline of recurring features

At the end of a number of years of practice, as an international court mandated to sanction human rights violation, it is possible to portray some significant lines of action in the jurisdiction of the ECOWAS Court. Truly, the points selected for discussion on the case law of the Court are the product of a personal choice –which, however, we intended as much as possible not to be arbitrary. Incidentally, this review exercise remains "historically biased" therefore, subject to modification, considering the potential situations which may be born out of an evolving jurisprudence. It is possible – it is even desirable – that some other significant jurisprudential lines of action would see the light of day, which would be the most eloquent proof that the judicial protection of human rights is advancing, and that, having conquered certain grounds already, the safeguarding of human rights by judicial means has assigned new tasks to itself, and turned to look towards other horizons. We did mention, in our introductory remark to this book, some marks of progress, and potentialities of conquest, which could be credited to the Community Court. That being so, it shall be appropriate to point out that in a relatively young case law, what has been achieved – not necessarily in the form of revolutionary or very original contributions – but which may all the same not be ignored, within the context of a nascent court, could, all things being equal,[33] be grouped into two categories: those considered from a formal point of view, and those looked at in terms of substance, those classified under a sort of (A) certain essentials at stake before the Court, which litigants would do better to be aware of, and on the hand, (B) certain rights proclaimed for litigants, a very interesting development, before which one must all the same remain clear-sighted and avoid, for the time being, any illusions as to their being either permanent or irreversible in nature.

A.- Prologue to a discourse on judicial method

Three aspects may be looked at under this point: the affirmation of a judicial power to reclassify the facts and complaints brought, to assess the purpose or proportionality of restrictive measures placed on rights, and the necessity to clarify the grievances made on human rights violation.

The power to reclassify the facts and complaints was made manifest in the following decisions:

- **Judgment of 13 March 2012, *Isabelle Manavi Ameganvi and Others* v. *Republic of Togo* (ECW/CCJ/JUD/06/12):**

The suit followed from a judgment which had already been delivered by the ECOWAS Court on 7 October 2011. The case was submitted as "an application for revision", because the Applicants maintained that the Court had omitted to adjudicate on their application for reinstatement to the National Assembly of Togo. The Court begins with a correction:

> §10: The Court describes the application thus made as "asking the Court to adjudicate on an omission in adjudication" and not "an application for revision".
>
> §19: "Consequently, the Court declares that the presumed omission to adjudicate on the issue of reinstatement, as brought by the Applicants, has no grounds, and must therefore be dismissed."

33 The segmentation is, we must admit, somewhat debatable, in as much as what is featured under "discourse on method" may well be under "acquired rights" or rights in the process of being acquired. It is clear, for example, that an evaluation of the end-product or the proportionality may now and then be described as a methodological rule (of the judge) or as inseparable from the rights of human beings (since it is always a matter of having to reduce the power or freedom of the perpetrator of the disputed measure). We therefore apologise for the limits of the proposed distinction.

- **Judgment of 23 April 2015, *Georges Constant Amoussou* v. *Republic of Benin* (ECW/CCJ/JUD/05/15):**

This was an application for interpretation, but the Court, in employing its sovereign power of reclassification, declared the application ill-founded, declaring:

§ IV.5, 8,11: That it was with the intention of circumventing the time bar stipulated under Article 63 of the Rules of the Court that the Applicant adopted the ploy of initiating a procedure for interpretation of judgment;

That the reasons for the judgment of the Court are clear and precise;

That Mr. Amoussou may not have been convinced by the reasons of the Court, and that the reasons cannot carry any other import than they did;

That in any case, the Court is not bound to have the same appreciation of the facts as would Mr. Amoussou;

That the Applicant did not indicate any specific portion of the operative part of judgment that called for interpretation;

That Mr. Amoussou's Application sought to urge the Court to go back on the reasons for the Judgment of 6 March 2014, adopt his own, and thereby call into question the already made decision;

That such shall not be the purpose of an application for interpretation.

The Court could be seen exercising checks and controls or a proportionality on contentious measures in the following judgments:

- **Judgment of 31 October 2012, *Baldini Salfo* v. *Burkina Faso* (ECW/CCJ/JUD/13/12):**

§21: False imprisonment is any form of denial of freedom carried out without legitimate or reasonable grounds and in violation of the conditions provided for under the law. One or all of the criteria may be lacking when a detention measure, non-arbitrary in the beginning, becomes unduly prolonged. It culminates in an abusive detention.

- **Judgment of 22 February 2013, *Simone Ehivet and Michel Gbagbo* v. *Republic of Côte d'Ivoire* (ECW/CCJ/JUD/03/13):**

The Republic of Côte d'Ivoire pleaded 'exceptional circumstances' and breakdown of institutions in the course of the period in question. The Court responds by relying on the International Covenant on Civil and Political Rights (ICCPR), whose Articles 4 and 12(3) relate to 'exceptional circumstances', as well as the General Observation No. 29

(72nd Session of the Human Rights Committee) concerning exemptions in emergency situations. The Court declares:

> §70: In the light of those principles, that the Court was of the opinion that the Republic of Côte d'Ivoire, even in invoking 'exceptional circumstances', had not acted in accordance with the provisions of Article 4 of the ICCPR and Article 48 of the Constitution of Côte d'Ivoire;
>
> §77: That the combination of these well-established factors are of such nature as to lead the Court to conclude that the copy of the decree produced by the Republic of Côte d'Ivoire cannot in any case be admitted as a legal act adopted on the basis invoked, and purportedly meant to produce the legal effects the Republic of Côte d'Ivoire was claiming;
>
> §78: That the Republic of Côte d'Ivoire does not, at any rate, demonstrate that in abiding by legality, it could not have attained the legitimate political ends required by a political crisis of that nature, namely: safeguarding public interest and restoring peace and security in Côte d'Ivoire. Indeed, even in exceptional circumstances, a relaxation of the principle of legality is done within the confines of respect for the national laws; that considering the case at hand, pursuant to Article 6 of the African Charter of Human and Peoples' Rights, the prohibition of arbitrary arrest and detention being absolute, the Republic of Côte d'Ivoire cannot hold a citizen arbitrarily.

- **Judgment of 22 February 2013, *Abdoulaye Baldé and Others* v. *Republic of Senegal* (ECW/CCJ/JUD/04/13):**

The Applicants, dignitaries of a regime voted out of power in March 2012, were subsequently brought under prosecution, with a measure of prohibition banning them from travelling outside the national territory. They challenge those measures before the ECOWAS Court, as well as the application of a law regarding an Anti Illegal-Wealth Court, to which the ECOWAS Court responds thus:

> §58 : "(...) On this issue, the Court holds that even if the said measure were to prove necessary, it shall be adopted within the dictates of the law or in compliance with a court decision. Even so, the measure must not be disproportionate in terms of the objective pursued (...)"

- **Judgment of 6 November 2013, *Chude Mba* v. *Republic of Ghana* (ECW/CCJ/JUD/10/13) :**

The Applicant, possessing Nigerian and British nationality, files a case before the Court to complain of injury arising from injunction to stop work on a certain twin tower, the injunction having been issued by the Ghana Civil Aviation Authority whereas the job had been executed by almost 80%. The Ghanaian authorities will later arrest the Applicant for "money laundering". For the Court,

> §89: "The object of detention for questioning is to further a criminal investigation by confirming or discounting suspicions which provide the grounds for detention. The suspicion however must be based on reasonable grounds in order to safeguard against arbitrary arrest and detention."

- **Judgment of 24 April 2015, *Pascal A. Bodjona* v. *Republic of Togo* (ECW/CCJ/JUD/06/15):**

> § 45, 46, 47 et 50 : "The Court is fully conscious that a complaint has been lodged against Mr. Bodjona for complicity of fraud and that in connection with the investigations necessitated by that complaint, he may well have his freedom curtailed or be detained himself. But it is imperative that such unpleasant measures be carried out in strict compliance with the legal procedures, and in guaranteeing the rights of the litigant. Of fundamental importance is that the procedure be conducted in such manner as to reduce the trial time, and to determine once and for all the fate of the accused or suspect. In that regard, the Court finds that no precise or decisive pleading exists in the case file capable of justifying the extension in M. Bodjona's time of detention. Throughout its written pleadings, the Republic of Togo simply contents itself with statements such as: "... an accusation was made against the Applicant and the criminal investigation was based on serious and consistent indications of guilt… (Page 8 of the Defence in French), or yet still, that there were "…reasonable grounds for affirming that he had committed an offence…" (Page 9 of the Defence in French), without ever stating precisely the "indications" or "reasons" in question.
>
> The Court cannot, months after the Applicant has been detained, be satisfied with such imprecise accounts, for the purposes of justifying his prolonged detention. The Court must at this stage recall its case law on such matters.
>
> In Case Concerning Mr. Chude Mba **v.** Republic of Ghana (Judgment of 6 November 2013), the Court, which held that the Applicant's rights had been violated, noted that "… The object of detention for questioning is to further a criminal investigation by confirming or discontinuing suspicions which provide the grounds for detention. The suspicion however must be based on reasonable grounds in order to safeguard against arbitrary arrest and detention…" (§88 and 89). In referring to the

case law of the European Court of Human Rights, as to the notion of "reasonable grounds for suspicion", the Court further held as follows: "... at least some facts or information capable of satisfying it that the arrested person was reasonably suspected of having committed the alleged offence..." (§90). Finally, the Court, in making further reference to the jurisprudence of the said European Court, again held that: "..."reasonable suspicion" meant the existence of facts or information which would satisfy an objective observer that the persons concerned might have committed the offence..." (§91).

But when an inquiry stagnates unduly, when the procedures occur one after the other, without the incriminating evidence being pleaded in the case file, and on the merits of the case, there is a serious risk of the initially lawful detention finally becoming an arbitrary detention (...)"

- **Judgment of 16 February 2016, *Konso Kokou Parounam* v. *Republic of Togo* (ECW/CCJ/JUD/02/16):**

The Applicant, a former military personnel, was summoned for questioning in connection with two units of arms following a handover ceremony. He explained in vain, that at least one of the units of the arms which had disappeared was the personal property of a senior officer; he was transferred and detained at the National Intelligence Agency (SRI) and interrogated. For two years (December 2009 – December 2011), he remained under detention. For the judges of the ECOWAS Court:

§40: It appeared manifest that the detention of the Applicant on the premises of the SRI was abusive in the sense that the Republic of Togo provided no ground to justify that the gendarmerie could, on the basis of a mere suspicion of having committed an offence, hold a person on such premises for several months before deciding to bring him before a judge.

It is certainly not out of place to see in the manner in which the ECOWAS Court of Justice has handled the laws of amnesty, an additional manifestation of a check on the ends and proportionality of amnesty measures. The judges, in effect, did put curbs on the power pertaining to amnesty, in the hands of those governing, as they sought to abolish the past in their decision to grant amnesty on certain given incidents. The Court exercised such checks on proportionality in two judgments, the second one being more systematic and more detailed than the first:

- **Judgment of 8 February 2011, *Sidi Amar Ibrahim and Others* v. *Republic of Niger* (ECW/CCJ/JUD/02/11):**

The Court was asked to order the Republic of Niger to find and try the perpetrators of the acts in cause. The Republic of Niger countered that request by invoking the amnesty law deriving from the Order of 23 October 2009 (notably Articles 1, 2 and 3). The judicial response was as follows:

§51: "It is however the duty of the Court to reiterate that international doctrine and case law on such matters exceptionally admit that for serious and widespread violations of fundamental human rights such as those endorsed by international custom and relevant human rights instruments, the application of the amnesty law in such circumstances amounts to forgoing the right to effective remedy before the competent courts. (Appeal Chamber, Special Court of Sierra Leone, Judgment of 14 March 2004 in the case concerning Kallon v. Kamara (SCLS-04-15-060-SCSL-04-15-PT-060-II), 14 March 2004); In the Barious Altos case - Inter-American Court of Human Rights, judgment of 30th November 2002 (Series C No. 87 case concerning Barious Altos v. Peru)."

§52: "The Court thus holds that even though the facts of this case constitute serious human rights violations, they are far from being widespread violations and do not therefore fulfil the applicable criteria set out in international doctrine and case law. The Court equally concurs in adjudging that the amnesty law cited by the Republic of Niger is applicable to the facts of this case, and the Court consequently rejects the application by the Plaintiff seeking an order from the Court to compel the Republic of Niger to find, prosecute and sentence the masterminds, accessories and accomplices of the incidents leading to the deaths of Sidi Amar Ibrahim and Ousmane Sidi Ali on 9th December 2007 in the Agadez region."

- **Judgment of 23 October 2015, *Heirs of Mainassara Baré* v. *Republic of Niger* (ECW/CCJ/JUD/16/15):**

The Applicants were swept off by several claims of foreclosure – or by outright lack of response – in every attempt they made to seek clear information from the political or judicial authorities of Niger, as to the conditions in which the late Ibrahim Baré Mainassara, (former Head of State, victim of a coup d'état) was assassinated. Invariably, the authorities cited in defence, the laws of amnesty whose effects were always presented as having wiped off and "abolished" the matters in contention. The Court will then clearly spell out the effects of a law of amnesty:

§51 to 58: "In as much as in every instance a response was given to the heirs of Mainassara Baré, it consisted of invoking the effects of the amnesty law, the Court is of the view that it is precisely upon this very point that the determination of the case must be anchored. The issue before the Court to determine is therefore quite simple and may be formulated as follows:

Does a legally instituted amnesty shut the door to every form of judicial investigation?

Does it foreclose or constitute an estoppel to every form of attempt to seek information on a matter, purely speaking, – in terms of seeking the truth or enquiring about the facts thereon?

The Court cannot share such a tyrannical concept of effects of an amnesty measure. The Court recalls that it has had occasion in the past to consider, regarding the same State – Niger –, the scope of such a law. Indeed, in Case Concerning Sidi Amar Ibrahim and Others v. Republic of Niger (Judgment of 8 February 2011), the Court was called upon to examine the effects of Order No. 2009-19 of 23 October 2009 on amnesty, concerning events which had occurred between 2005 and 2009. Even if the Court had recognised the existence of the order, and accepted the decision taken by the authorities of Niger to set aside every form of judicial proceedings on the matters at stake, the Court nevertheless made a pronouncement as to the inefficacy of the amnesty law in situations of serious and widespread violation of fundamental human rights (§51).

The Court considers, today, that it shall be appropriate to raise the requirements of the law on amnesty, and prop up level of acceptability of amnesty laws.

Amnesty laws cannot constitute an unreasonable cover-up for the past, an estoppel which may automatically be invoked against every legitimately inquiring mind attempting to know the truth. An amnesty law shall leave intact a victim's right to know the truth, and this is so relevant in the instant case, where such right is held by persons with whom the deceased victim had particularly close bonds of relationship. The Mainassara Baré family did not see any of their numerous requests for inquiry being taken into account. The Court deplores the fact that their pain and desire for legitimate information – which should be the same for any other victim in similar circumstances – were not properly handled.

It shall be appropriate therefore, in such context, to affirm victims' right to the truth. In concrete terms, it translates into an obligation on State authorities to conduct inquiries and investigations into incidents and events in cause, and to guarantee, even if not a publication of findings thereon, at least free access to such findings. This is a minimal obligation, which the Republic of Niger completely defaulted on in the instant case. By so doing, the Defendant State trampled on the Applicants' right of access to justice. It is therefore in order that the Applicants cite, in support of their claims, the following provisions, all binding on the Republic of Niger:

- Article 2 (3) a, b, c of the International Covenant on Civil and Political Rights as cited above;
- Article 7(1) of the African Charter on Human and Peoples' Rights, equally cited above.

A very significant point must however be made at this stage.

The Court is of the view that if the necessity to forget or to forgive, on a massive scale, may be imperative and applicable to a society at a given time in its history, such necessity cannot imply that one must treat with scorn, the right to know, the right of access to the truth, which victims in a cause are entitled to. The Court is not ignorant in any way whatsoever of the sovereign right of a State to adopt, in a given situation, measures of amnesty. Equally, the Court is not seeking to cripple the effects deriving from amnesty provisions, but it holds that the scope of an amnesty measure is limited within the confines of the criminal issues at stake, and should not in any way affect the civil reparation for the victims of the incidents involved. In other words, the Court finds that amnesty laws do not wipe off criminal accusations, but they leave unimpaired victims' right to reparation, no matter the form such reparation may take. Before this Court therefore, amnesty laws must be properly situated within their exact confines, i.e. within the limits of incriminating charges and criminal proceedings, to the exclusion of individuals' civil rights.

This principled position respects the imperatives of pacification and social cohesion, the ultimate goal of amnesty measures, and it equally takes into account the fate of victims of facts surrounding amnesty measures. It would be very wrong and unfair to completely ignore the situation of persons who have suffered from the events in cause, under the pretext that State authorities have decreed that the events have been wiped out of existence just at the stroke of the pen, or that in fact they are deemed to have never existed. For the Court, amnesty does not justify inertia, and respect for victims' rights is not incompatible with the necessity of social reconciliation."

The third and last jurisprudential contribution, regarding methodology, is the necessity of backing up the complaints pleaded before the Court. The Court revisits the point in a long line-up of decisions among which:

- **Judgment of 17 February 2010, *Daouda Garba* v. *Republic of Benin* (ECW/CCJ/JUD/01/10):**

§34: "(...) The cases of violation of human rights must be backed by indications of evidence which enable the Court to find that such violation has occurred in order for it to prefer sanctions if need be."

§39: "(...) Indeed, to enable the Court find that violations have occurred, particularly in the instant case, the Applicant was expected to file sufficiently convincing, and not equivocal evidence."

§41: (...) The Court is of the view that the only point of evidence provided by the Applicant is neither sufficient nor compelling enough to convince the Court of the truth of the alleged attack committed by Benin Immigration Officers, in order for the Court to implicate the State in any offence."

- **Judgment of 7 October 2011, *Cheikh Abdoulaye Mbengue* v. *Republic of Mali* (ECW/CCJ/JUD/08/11):**

§32: "The Court notes that a close look at the complaints made in support of the allegations of human rights violations brought by Mr. Cheick Abdoulaye Mbengue reveals that none of them is relevant indeed."

§36: "The judiciary of Mali responded in reasonable time to the requests for withdrawal of the arrest warrant and recusal of the investigating judge (...)"

§37: "On the whole, since no human rights violation could be established against the Republic of Mali, the Court dismisses the requests for monetary reparation formulated by the Applicant, which he connects to human rights violations he has failed to establish before this Honourable Court."

- **Judgment of 26 January 2012, *El Hadji Mame Abdou Gaye* v. *Republic of Senegal* (ECW/CCJ/JUD/03/12):**

§34: The Court noted that the Applicant had not till then complained of any violence against his person nor of procedures of such nature as to violate his dignity or his physical integrity; and that the fact that the police officers investigating the case acted under the guise of workers of a telephone company, or that they made use of any other similar process for obvious reasons of discretion required by the nature of the inquiry, cannot constitute on its own, a transgression of the dignity of the person summoned for questioning;

§41: The Court equally found that the Applicant was assisted by his Counsel at all stages of the court proceedings and made use of various channels for seeking redress against the decisions taken by the judicial authorities, notably for appealing and asking for release;

§42: Again, the Court adjudged that in the light of the points made above, the arrest and detention of Mame Abdou Gaye had a legal basis and that he was not arbitrarily arrested and detained.

- **Judgment of 23 March 2012, *Barthélémy Dias* v. *Republic of Senegal* (ECW/CCJ/JUD/05/12):**

§19: The Court notes that the complaints of human rights violation brought against the Republic of Senegal are situated with the context of a criminal judicial procedure which had commenced and was ongoing in accordance with the legal principles in force in the Republic of Senegal;

§20: The Court finds that the judicial procedure in question – both at the preliminary investigation stage, which culminated in the opening of investigative proceedings by the Public Prosecutor for offences provided for and punished by the laws of Senegal, and at the trial conducted by the Dean of Investigating Judges – constitute a sufficient legal basis for the arrest and detention of the Applicant; the arrest and detention of the Applicant could hence not be arbitrary;

§27: The Court thus concluded that the Republic of Senegal did not commit any human rights violation that injures the Applicant.

- **Judgment of 31 October 2012, *Baldini Salfo* v. *Burkina Faso* (ECW/CCJ/JUD/13/12):**

The Applicant, accused of armed robbery in Burkina Faso and outside the country, complained of arbitrary arrest and detention, and in particular, abuse at the stage where he was being kept in custody.

§37: The Court finds that the Applicant does not support his allegation (of cruel, inhuman and degrading treatment) with any evidence. He does not even provide an enlightening description of the maltreatment he went through, the persons who may be implicated, the circumstances of time and place within which such persons may have acted. Again, he does not disclose the suffering he may have endured psychologically, or the bodily pains he may have experienced by virtue of the acts complained of.

- **Judgment of 21 February 2013, *Carmel Max Savi* v. *Republic of Togo* (ECW/CCJ/JUD/02/13):**

Page 7: "The Court (...) Finds that the summoning of Mr. Carmel Max Savi on 9 February 2012 to Lome and the despatch of the same Mr. Carmel Max Savi for interrogation at the camp of the Research and Investigations Department (SRI) occurred within the legal framework of the execution of a mandate assigned by authority to a criminal investigations police vested with the powers to do so, and therefore this does not constitute an arbitrary arrest and detention."

- **Judgment of 23 April 2015, *Georges Constant Amoussou* v. *Republic of Benin* (ECW/CCJ/JUD/05/15):**

§43, 44: The Court finds that in the course of the procedure, the Applicant was constantly assisted by Counsel who pleaded his defence and made submissions against the measures of detention issued against him, and upon which appeal bodies adjudicated, notably the Constitutional Court, the latter concluding that the procedure employed against the Applicant was in order;

Also, the Court concludes that the Applicant was detained upon a legal basis, and that his detention was not arbitrary.

- **Judgment of 23 April 2015, *Tidjani Abdoukarim, Amadou Aly Djibo, Saidou Bakari, Boubacar Mossi* v. *Republic of Niger* (ECW /CCJ/ JUD/02/15):**

The Applicants criticise the composition of Niger's Bureau of National Assembly, which allegedly did not respect the provisions of the Constitution (Article 89) and the case law of the Constitutional Court. The Court adjudges:

§ 37 and 38: That for the Applicants' application to succeed, he must state the specific human rights which may have been violated and provide evidence of violation of the rights in question;

That in examining the matter filed before the Court, the Applicants do not only fail to disclose specific human rights which may have been violated by the Republic of Niger, but they still do not prove violation; that the narration of the facts relating to the establishment of the Bureau of the National Assembly does not demonstrate human rights violation in anyway whatsoever.

- **Judgment of 30 June 2015, *Bourama Sininta and 119 Others* v. *Republic of Mali* (ECW/CCJ/JUD/13/15):**

The Applicants lay claim to their customary rights to land (Bozo fishermen established on the banks of the River Niger for a long time) in dragging the Republic of Mali before the Court, the Republic of Mali having leased the disputed land to a business entity, for the purposes of building a hotel complex. They invoke provisions from the 1986 Code Concerning State-Owned and Privately-Owned Lands.

§IV.20, pp.12-13 (French version): The Court notes that the Applicants could not produce any administrative document attesting to their right to the zone where the plot of land with Land Title No.16551 of Bamako is situated;

Whereas, it is trite that a claim brought by an applicant under human rights violation shall be backed by evidence.

- **Judgment of 6 October 2015, *Djelou Kodjovi, Akumani Koffi and Alipui Ablavi* v. *Republic of Togo*(ECW/CCJ/JUD/17/15):**

The Applicants were arrested and put before court for forgery and use of forged documents (registration of a building). They will be acquitted and discharged in first instance and appeal proceedings. Subsequently, they filed a case before the ECOWAS Court seeking a declaration that they were arbitrarily arrested, and also ask for a compensatory award. They equally claim to be victims of acts of torture:

§34: "In the instant case, the Applicants do not prove that they have suffered acts of torture or inhuman, cruel and degrading treatment, within the meaning of the International Convention Against Torture; they only limit themselves to pleading laconic medical certificates made in 2011 and 2013 which do not state precisely, at any rate, any causal link between their condition of health and the ill-treatment they allege."

- **In Judgment of 7 October 2015, *Wiayao Gnandakpa and Others* v. *Republic of Togo* (ECW/CCJ/JUD/18/15), the Court decided that:**

§10 and 11: In considering that as a general rule, it is up to the applicant to bring evidence for his claims, and that in compliance with that principle, the ECOWAS Court consistently upholds that all instances of human rights violation invoked before the Court by an applicant must be specifically supported with sufficiently convincing and unequivocal evidence;

With regard to the case at hand, the Court finds, at the end of the proceedings, and on the basis of the pleadings of the case, that the Applicants do not bring any proof of evidence regarding their arrest and detention by the judicial authorities of Togo;

§16: the Court finds at any rate that the Applicants invoke in support of their requests a number of national texts. The Court must instantly set aside however such references, in accordance with its case law which consists in asserting that the ECOWAS Court is not a judge over the constitutionality or legality of acts and actions undertaken by the States. The ECOWAS Court refers only to the international norms which bind the States, which signifies that before the Court, only the States may, in human rights violations, constitute the defendant in the case.

- **Judgment of 16 February 2016, *Konso Kokou Parounam* v. *Republic of Togo* (ECW/CCJ/JUD/02/16):**

§31: The Court finds that the Applicant never furnishes proof of the acts of torture he claims to have suffered. In the case file, there is neither testimony, nor, especially, written records of scientific or medical nature, to buttress the assertions contained in the Application. But, considering the case at hand, in many others, it is incumbent upon the applicant to submit before the Court, for assessment, material evidence attesting to the reality of the violation cited.

- **Judgment of 16 February 2016, *Ibrahim Sory Touré and Issiaga Bangoura* v. *Republic of Guinea* (ECW/CCJ/JUD/03/16):**

> §66 and 73: "Whereas in the instant case, the Applicant, Mr. Issiaga Bangoura does not produce any points of evidence which may support allegations of violation of his right to defence; whereas indeed he furnishes neither the decision sentencing him to a one-month imprisonment nor any other pleading of another nature which may attest, on one hand, that he was tried for desertion, and on the other hand, that he was a victim of violation of his rights to defence during the said judgment; whereas there is no pleading in the case-file which may attest to the statements made;
>
> Whereas whatever the case may be, the allegations of the Applicants, as to their arrest being arbitrary, are not based on any point of evidence; whereas no pleading in the case enables the Court to find an absence of notification of the grounds upon which they were summoned; whereas as noted above, the Court cannot establish human rights violation upon baseless allegations. Whereas whatever the case may be, the allegations of the Applicants, as to their arrest being arbitrary, are not based on any point of evidence; whereas no pleading in the case enables the Court to find an absence of notification of the grounds upon which they were summoned; whereas as noted above, the Court cannot establish human rights violation upon baseless allegations."

- **Judgment of 18 April 2016, *Dr Malachi Z. York* v. *Republic of Liberia* (ECW/CCJ/JUD/05/16):**

The Applicant, detained in the United States, complaints notably that his country of origin, Liberia, allegedly failed to "support" him, thus violating a "human right".

> p.26 (French version): "Similarly in Moussa Leo Keita **v.** Republic of Mali (2004), this Court also refused to assume jurisdiction where the Applicant did not identify the exact violation alleged or specified the particular right allegedly violated.

Applying the principles established in the above cases, this Court is of the view that the Plaintiff in the instant case, has not identified the specific right violated by the Defendant in relation to him".

- **Judgment of 17 May 2016, *Marie Molmou and 114 Others* v. *Republic of Guinea* (ECW/CCJ/JUD/16/16):**

The Applicants had initially brought their case before the Court, even if the name of the Applicants had changed in a subsequent proceeding before the Court; Their Application was declared inadmissible on grounds of absence of power of attorney to act on behalf of the concerned persons (Judgment of 25 March 2015). Again, they sue the Republic of Guinea and SOGUIPAH (Guinea Oil Palm and Rubber Company), for allegedly benefitting from expropriation of the lands which rendered them victims in the hands of the Republic of Guinea.

Pages 11 and 12 (English version): "Especially, the Court holds that irrespective of the litany of facts narrated in the Application, the request brought before it severely lacks the evidence to back up the allegations. No title to the land is produced; there is nothing, absolutely nothing in the case-file, which may compel one to think that the Applicants are holders of a title to the ownership of the disputed lands. Asking the Court to grant their requests under such conditions, implies that the Applicants are making a demand on the Court to take their word for the truth.

Certainly, the Applicants did advance, notably in the course of their pleadings, that the traditional land ownership system in Guinea does not require the production of a land title or a deed to serve as a proof of ownership. All the same, the Court is of the view that attempts at proving ownership of the occupied lands could have been submitted in the case file. Now, there is no land title, nor title deed of any kind whatsoever, nor even a testimonial to that effect. The Applicants only limit themselves to mere averments throughout the submission of their written pleadings, and they make no effort at producing any proofs for their statements. (…)

The same observation must be made concerning the violent incidents the security forces may have been guilty of. The facts alleged are extremely serious, since we are dealing with rape, despoilment, arbitrary arrests, and even murder. But in no instance, once again, was evidence produced to back up those allegations: no certificate of death, not even a medical certificate, nor statements capable of lending credence to the allegations made.

Whereas, the Court has always held that allegations of human rights violation must be buttressed by evidence. (…)

Re-invoking the reasoning inherent in this case law, founded upon the requirement of minimal proof, which, at any rate, stems from a general principle of procedural law, thus compels the Court to conclude that the allegations of human rights violation made against the Republic of Guinea do not have any basis."

- **Judgment of 17 May 2016, *Yao N'Guessan* v. *Republic of Côte d'Ivoire* (ECW/CCJ/JUD/15/16):**

The Applicant contests the rejection of his candidature for presidential election by CENI (Independent National Electoral Commission) of Côte d'Ivoire and by the Constitutional Council (which cited the incomplete nature of filed documents submitted for that purpose). He asserts that his right to eligibility was violated.

§17 and 18: "Whereas as a general rule, the onus lies on the Applicant to provide evidence, and whereas in applying that principle, the ECOWAS Court of Justice has consistently held (...) all cases of human rights violation brought before it shall be relevantly supported with sufficient, convincing and unequivocal evidence.

Whereas in the instant case, the Court finds, on the basis of the pleadings of the procedure, that the Applicant did not provide any concrete proof of any violation whatsoever of his right of candidacy to any elective office without discrimination, nor of his right to participate in the management of the public affairs of his community, within the meaning of the Articles cited above from the International Covenant on Civil and Political Rights, and the Universal Declaration of Human Rights."

- **Judgment of 1 July 2016, *Hama Amadou* v. *Republic of Niger* (ECW/CCJ/JUD/21/16):**

p.8 (French version): Relying on contents of the case file, the Court can hardly lay its finger on any concrete violation of rights to defence;

The Court finds that Mr. Amadou was never practically prevented from intervening in the procedure, through any formal act made by the judicial or political authorities. At no moment was his lawyers obstructed from appearing in court, and the court decisions were always reached after both parties had been heard (Judgment of the Correctional Court, 30 January 2015; Judgment of the Court of Appeal, 13 July 2015; various trial processes; Judgment of the Constitutional Court, 4 September 2014);

The Applicant, moreover, was at liberty to avail himself of the channels offered him for seeking redress. He thus wrote to the Prime Minister, to the First Vice- Speaker of the National Assembly, Member of the Bureau of the National Assembly, and particularly, was able to bring his case before the Constitutional Court through a letter dated 26 August 2014.

> Incidentally, it was during the intervention of the judge at the Constitutional Court that he always realised the guarantee of the respect for his rights, if one should go by the very terms of the very terms of the previously cited mails. The Constitutional Court, in that particular case, delivered two judgments dated the same day (4 September 2014), on the application of Mr. Hama Amadou on one hand, and that of the group of 14 Members of Parliament, but concerning, in the two instances, constitutional provisions on the immunity of a Member of Parliament. One cannot therefore claim that the right of access to justice or the right to appeal was disregarded.

Now, the Court has always adjudged, in such circumstances, that no charge of human rights violation may be made against the States. To go beyond that assertion would lead the Court towards assessing the legality or even the appropriateness or otherwise of the criminal proceedings, a competence the Court obviously does not have.

After painting the forerunner features of a discourse on the judicial method of the Court, it shall be appropriate to turn our attention to the rights specifically dedicated to litigants before the Court, in nursing the hope that they become permanently recognised.

B.- Gradual emergence of a regime of rights

Three strands of rights are equally recognisable here. There is the general right to protection and security – which is owed to the State – and, in the order of relations of the citizen with the State judicial system, the right of access to justice – understood in its broadest sense – as well as the rights to defence.

The right to protection and security was upheld in certain decisions of the Court. Truly – and the interrogative form of the title to this part translates that doubt – it is not certain that this right may be upheld, in the future, with the same force as in the judgments delivered till now. Without doubt, the cases in point marked a degree of audacity on the part of the Court, but one can surely bet that the judges may not, in future, consider that in absolute terms or systematically speaking, every violation of the citizen's security, occurring under any circumstance whatsoever, necessarily establishes State responsibility. In other terms, the idea of reasonable State diligence may set in, and with it, the State being absolved of every blame when it is demonstrated that the State did take the required minimum preventive measures to honour its minimum duty of protection. Such re-adjustment in State responsibility is at any rate dictated by a measure of realism which had better be taken into consideration by the judges, as a factor, in their reasoning. Modulation of the general duty of protection incumbent upon States becomes all the more required in situations where, without it being a question of abandoning the citizens to their own fate, it becomes easily noticeable that a State may be encountering objective constraints in fulfilling its obligations. One of the ways out may thus consist, indeed, of abstaining from laying down such duty of protection by the States as a general or absolute obligation, but rather to make it punishable only where non-fulfilment, taking the circumstances into consideration – and notably the foreseeability of a turmoil – the authorities would have had to take preventive or dissuasive measures.

Meanwhile, the Court has insisted on the right to security in some of its decisions.

- **Judgment of 10 June 2014, *Modupe Dorcas Afolalu* v. *Federal Republic of Nigeria* (ECW/CCJ/JUD/15/14):**

The Applicant brought her case before the Court, following the death of her husband, a victim of post-electoral riots at Zaria, in Kaduna State. The death of the husband plunged the family into penury. The Applicant complained that the Federal Republic of Nigeria did nothing about the situation afterwards: no act of compassion, and especially no implementation of the conclusions of the commission of enquiry put in place by the Republic of Nigeria itself.

The Court will declare Nigeria responsible (within the context of electoral tension), and enjoin it to conduct inquiries into the matter and award financial compensation to the Applicant:

> §50: "The Court recalls that this clearly stated obligation regarding protection of life, as enshrined in Article 4 of the African Charter on Human and Peoples' Rights, implies that the State shall put in place an administrative and legal framework specifically designed to deter violent acts from being committed against people; the framework must be anchored on a mechanism of application conceived to prevent, suppress and sanction violent acts.
>
> §51: Consequently, in the context of tension-packed elections, the Court is of the view that the State shall take the required security measures and make the utmost effort at ensuring maintenance of order. The State is under obligation to prevent all demonstrations with the likelihood of degenerating into violent acts which may cause loss of human lives."

- **Judgment of 17 May 2016, *Heirs of the late Aissata Cissé and Others* v. *Republic of Mali* (ECW/CCJ/JUD/13/16):**

The Applicants had directly suffered from violent incidents arising out of local elections in the year 1997. The explosion of a grenade at the home of the Applicants, also the home of the Vice Chairman of Independent Regional Electoral Commission, Mr. Bouréima Sidi Cissé, resulting notably in the death of two members of his family. Almost sixteen persons will subsequently be arrested by the police, and charged with violation of State security, but not long after, the matter was declared as a no case.

It is appropriate to indicate that in a previous judgment, dated 12 February 2014, the Court, seised by Mr. Bouréima Sidi Cissé alone, declared Mali blameable. In the succeeding case, the Court will equally find that Mali violated the Applicant's rights to protection, security and protection, particularly, his rights to security and justice within the particular context of pre- and post-election violence (as in the above-cited judgment of 10 June 2014, in the *Modupe Dorcas Afolalu* case.), in declaring that:

> §27: From the oral and written submissions on the case, it was apparent that in organising municipal elections in an atmosphere of social tension without any guarantee of protection of public order, for the masses of the people, and especially for the life of as Bouréima Sidi Cissé, Vice Chairman of Independent Regional Electoral Commission of Ségou, and the lives of the members of his family, the Republic of Mali defaulted in its obligations regarding protection.

- **Judgment of 15 June 2016, *SERAP, Nura Abdullahi and Others* v. *Federal Republic of Nigeria* (ECW/CCJ/JUD/19/16):**

It was a case of "collateral victims" of a "war" being waged by Government of the Federal Republic of Nigeria against "Boko Haram" rebels. The Applicants brought their case before the Court asking the Court to find that their rights to security and life were disregarded, and they requested monetary compensation, which was granted by the Court in line with its principle:

> p.6: "SERAP is seriously concerned about the policy of government that there will be no compensation paid to victims of Boko Haram attacks. This policy is clear violation of the Country's international human rights obligations and commitments to provide effective remedies, including compensation and reparation to victims of serious human rights abuses such as those perpetrated by Boko Haram".

The right of access to justice, which is the second right which we cited, must be understood in a wide sense, as incorporating its corollaries, which are, among others, the right to remedy – effective and efficacious remedy – the right to be tried in reasonable time or yet still the right to execution of court decisions.

- **Judgment of 8 February 2011, *Sidi Amar Ibrahim and Others* v. *Republic of Niger* (ECW/CCJ/JUD/02/11):**

The Applicants are heirs to two persons who had intended to go to the Agadez region, a zone of insecurity; for that purpose, they had taken the trouble to notify the high command of the security forces, but they all died all the same in the course of their journey, in circumstances quite obscure but related, it seemed, to the insecure environment. The heirs to the deceased persons attempted several times to obtain reliable information from the authorities, but in vain: two letters were addressed to the Minister of Defence, and to the Public Prosecutor, who only ended up informing them that the case had come to a dead end, apparently as a result of the martial law in force, according to the Public Prosecutor. It was under those circumstances that the ECOWAS Court of Justice received the case for adjudication, and made a pronouncement thus:

> §44 and 45: "The Court holds that in spite of repeated requests by the Plaintiff, amounting to complaints before the relevant authorities of the Republic of Niger, so as to enable them refer the case before a military court, for justice to be done, as demanded from the Minister of Defence by the heirs to Sidi Amar Ibrahim and Ousmane Sidi Ali, the Defendant failed to act and institute such a public proceeding.
>
> Also, the Court holds that this default on the part of the authorities of the Republic of Niger is a violation of right of the Plaintiff to effective remedy before the competent national courts of the Republic of Niger as provided for by Article 7 of the African Charter on Human and Peoples' Rights and Article 8 of the Universal Declaration of Human Rights."

- **Judgment of 31 January 2012, *Aziablévi Yovo and 31 Others* v. *Société Togo Telecom and Republic of Togo* (ECW/CCJ/JUD/04/12):**

> §21: The Court equally finds that the Application submitted before it by the Applicants precisely talks of non-enforcement of the judgment of the Court of Appeal, and thereby gives weight to the Applicants' allegations of human rights violation.

- **Judgment of 31 October 2012, *Baldini Salfo* v. *Burkina Faso* (ECW/CCJ/JUD/13/12):**

The Applicant, accused of armed robbery in Burkina Faso and abroad, complained of arbitrary arrest and detention, with particular complaints regarding abuse during the time he was held in custody. The Court was of the view that:

§40: The national judicial authorities are under obligation to act with all the diligence required, so that at all the phases of the criminal procedure (inquiry, trial and judgment), there will be no undue, prolonged or unjustified delay. Thus, any prolonged or unjustified delay occurring at any of the phases of the procedure unavoidably affects the right trial in reasonable time.

- **Judgment of 3 July 2013, *Aziagbede Kokou and 33 Others, Atsou Komlavi and 4 Others, Tomekpe A. Lanou and 29 Others* v. *Republic of Togo* (ECW/CCJ/JUD/07/13):**

§65: "(...) the Court is of the view that the inaction of the Togolese judicial authorities, in terms of investigating the complaints brought by the Applicants and examining their cause in accordance with Togolese law, during a period of 3 or 4 years for some, and 7 years for others, resulted in a situation where it had become clearly obvious that the Applicants' right to have their cause examined in reasonable time had been violated."

- **Judgment of 28 January 2014, *Alimu Akeem* v. *Federal Republic of Nigeria* (ECW/CCJ/JUD/01/14):**

§ 45 and 47: The Court was of the view that the inaction of the authorities of the Federal Republic of Nigeria "deprived Alimu Akeem of his right to trial within reasonable time."

- **Judgment of 10 June 2014, *Modupe Dorcas Afolalu v. Federal Republic of Nigeria* (ECW/CCJ/JUD/15/14):**

The Applicant filed her case before the Court, following the death of her husband, rendered victim of post-electoral violence at Zaria, in Kaduna State. The Applicant complained that the Federal Republic of Nigeria subsequently did nothing, in terms of implementing the findings of a commission of inquiry which it had instituted itself:

§64: "The Court finds that till today, three years after the murder of Mr. Felix Afolalu, the Defendant State has neither produced the report of the Commission of Inquiry which was set up, nor has it taken any steps towards trying before the courts of the Federal Republic of Nigeria, those responsible for the unlawful killing of Mr. Felix Afolalu; equally, the Federal Republic of Nigeria has not compensated the Applicant.

The Court holds therefore that the violation of the provisions of Articles 1, 2 and 4 of the African Charter on Human and Peoples' Rights is proven."

- **Judgment of 23 April 2015, *Abla Azali and Anor* v. *Republic of Benin* (ECW/CCJ/JUD/01/15):**

The Applicants, whose case file "got lost" in Benin's courts of law, asked the Court to charge Benin for negligence and inaction on the part of its judiciary. Both Applicants won their case in first instance proceedings but on appeal, their case files "were nowhere to be found":

Page 10: "Considering all the points made above, the Court finds that the judicial system of the Defendant State bears traces of deficiencies which unquestionably renders the Defendant State blameworthy in the instant case. At this juncture, the Court deems it appropriate to recall a number of judgments delivered on the issue of implementation of court decisions, on the right to trial in reasonable time, and on right of access before the judge."

Page 11: "In conclusion, the Court holds that the rights of the Applicants were disregarded and that it was rightful that Article 8 of the Universal Declaration of Rights and Articles 3 and 7 of the African Charter on Human and Peoples' Rights were invoked and relied on."

- **Judgment of 24 April 2015, *Pascal A. Bodjona* v. *Republic of Togo* (ECW/CCJ/JUD/06/15) :**

The Applicant, accused of having a hand in an attempted political destabilisation, was arrested, detained and made to go through numerous haphazard judicial procedures, whereas he had been released at a particular point in time. He files a case at the Court for false imprisonment. He emerges successful as to that specific point of pleading. In passing, the Court criticises the length of time and recurring nature of the procedures applied against the Applicant.

- **Judgment of 24 April 2015, *Bodjona A. Pascal v. Republic of Togo* (ECW/CCJ/JUD/06/15):**

§ 45, 46, 47 et 50 : "The Court is fully conscious that a complaint has been lodged against Mr. Bodjona for complicity of fraud and that in connection with the investigations necessitated by that complaint, he may well have his freedom curtailed or be detained himself. But it is imperative that such unpleasant measures be carried out in strict compliance with the legal procedures, and in guaranteeing the rights of the litigant. Of fundamental importance is that the procedure be conducted in such manner as to reduce the trial time, and to determine once and for all the fate of the accused or suspect. In that regard, the Court finds that no precise or decisive pleading exists in the case file capable of justifying the extension in M. Bodjona's time of detention. Throughout its written pleadings, the Republic of Togo simply contents itself with statements such as: "... an accusation was made against the Applicant and the criminal investigation was based on serious and consistent indications of guilt… (Page 8 of the Defence in French), or yet still, that there were "…reasonable grounds for affirming that he had committed an offence…" (Page 9 of the Defence in French), without ever stating precisely the "indications" or "reasons" in question.

The Court cannot, months after the Applicant has been detained, be satisfied with such imprecise accounts, for the purposes of justifying his prolonged detention. The Court must at this stage recall its case law on such matters.

In Case Concerning Mr. Chude Mba **v.** Republic of Ghana (Judgment of 6 November 2013), the Court, which held that the Applicant's rights had been violated, noted that "… The object of detention for questioning is to further a criminal investigation by confirming or discontinuing suspicions which provide the grounds for detention. The suspicion however must be based on reasonable grounds in order to safeguard against arbitrary arrest and detention…" (§88 and 89). In referring to the case law of the European Court of Human Rights, as to the notion of "reasonable grounds for suspicion", the Court further held as follows: "… at least some facts or information capable of satisfying it that the arrested person was reasonably suspected of having committed the alleged offence…" (§90). Finally, the Court, in making further reference to the jurisprudence of the said European Court, again held that: "…"reasonable suspicion" meant the existence of facts or information which would satisfy an objective observer that the persons concerned might have committed the offence…" (§91).

But when an inquiry stagnates unduly, when the procedures occur one after the other, without the incriminating evidence being pleaded in the case file, and on the merits of the case, there is a serious risk of the initially lawful detention finally becoming an arbitrary detention (…)"

Here, the Court recalls its ruling in Baldini Salfo **v.** Burkina Faso where it held that "… Arbitrary detention is any form deprivation of liberty which is carried out without a legitimate or reasonable ground and in violation of the conditions provided by law. One or all of these characteristics may be absent in an initially lawful detention, but when unduly prolonged, an initially lawful detention may end up becoming unlawful." (§21).

- **Judgment of 16 February 2016, *Ibrahim Sory Touré and Issiaga Bangoura* v. *Republic of Guinea* (ECW/CCJ/JUD/03/16):**

§87: "(...) in failing to respond to the applications seeking to annul the unfavourable judgment made against them and to bring the written procedure to a close, the Criminal Chamber of the Conakry Court of Appeal and the investigating judge (...) violated the Applicants' right to effective remedy."

- **Judgment of 20 April 2016, *Samba Barry* v. *Republic of Côte d'Ivoire* (ECW/CCJ/JUD/06/16) :**

The Applicant, established in Côte d'Ivoire, dragged the latter before the Court for inaction on the part of its administrative and judicial authorities against the alleged perpetrators of the offences (theft of a herd of cows and acts of violence), as a result of which they became victims, because the courts before which the case was lodged failed to act:

IV.22, p.14 (French version): The Court was of the view that the attitude of the public service of the Côte d'Ivoire judiciary in the handling of the complaint brought by Mr. Samba Barry was at variance with observance of the texts and norms which must govern every judicial procedure;

Whatever the case may be, the Court finds that the destination of the minutes of proceedings of a preliminary inquiry cannot be the office of a Minister of State even if he is in charge of the Judiciary;

By acting in that manner, the judiciary of the Defendant elongated the procedure by an additional phase not prescribed by law;

It thus prolonged the time of the procedure unfairly.

- **The Court decided in Judgment of 17 May 2016, *Heirs of the late Aissata Cissé and Others* v. *Republic of Mali* (ECW/CCJ/JUD/13/16) that:**

§29 and 30: It was established through the hearings that the judiciary of Mali became dysfunctional in the management of the cases filed by applicants, by depriving them of their right to appropriate and effective remedy, as well as fair trial, within the meaning of the rules of international law;

That it could not be contested in that instance that the case in question had been lodged before the Malian courts Malian since 1998 and that till date, the procedure was still pending before the Appeal Court of Bamako, thus depriving the Applicants of their right to fair hearing and hearing in reasonable time.

Finally, a randomness of the cases coming before the Court has led to the Court laying particular emphasis, on three occasions, on the right to defence, more precisely, in regard to the free choice of lawyers and counsel, which is available to every person pleading a case before the Court, and in regard to the principle of hearing both parties before delivery of a judgment, and as well, in regard to equality of arms, inseparable from the free choice of lawyers and counsel.

- **Judgment of 3 July 2013, *Kpatcha Gnassingbe and Others* v. *Republic of Togo* (ECW/CCJ/JUD/06/13):**

> §58: "The Court equally recalls that the State is under obligation to officially assign counsel to the Applicants who had none; thus, the Court adjudges that the right to defence must not merely be proclaimed, nor merely feature in the national law, but must be effectively implemented.
>
> §60: In the instant case, the oral proceedings of the hearing before the Honourable Court enabled the Court to note that the Defendant State, through its police and judicial officers, did not allow the Applicants to freely choose their counsel, and even in the event of the Applicants having refused to constitute counsel, the Defendant State did not go ahead to officially assign them counsel; and the Defendant State does not, at any rate, bring any evidence to prove that it assigned counsel to the Applicants."

- **Judgment of 16 February 2016, *Ibrahim Sory Touré and Issiaga Bangoura* v. *Republic of Guinea* (ECW/CCJ/JUD/03/16):**

> §96 and 101 : "(…) equality of arms is one of the inherent elements of the concept of fair trial (…) ; the concept of equality of arms requires that each party be availed a reasonable opportunity to plead its cause under conditions which do not put one party in an unfavourable situation with respect to the opposing party, and demands an arrangement of fairness and balance among the parties (…) the principle of adversarial proceedings signifies the possibility for the parties to take notice of, and comment on all the points of evidence produced, and on all the observations submitted, such as to direct the decision of the court (…),this principle is closely linked to equality of arms.

(…) in the light of the foregoing, it is ripe to conclude that the Republic of Guinea, through its judicial authorities, violated the principle of equality of arms and of adversarial proceedings in the procedure instituted against the Applicants."

- **Judgment of 1 July 2016, Judgment of 1 April 2016, *Djibril Yipéné Bassolé* v. *Burkina Faso* (ECW/CCJ/JUD/22/16):**

Pages 10 and 11: "Nevertheless, by a more general scope of principles, the right to choose one's lawyer constitutes today an undeniable component of the rights to defence, a prerogative which arises from "human rights". The unfettered right to choose one's representative or lawyer before a court is thus consecrated by:

- The African Commission of Human Rights, in its Communication No. 48/90, in Amnesty International v. Sudan: "The right to freely choose one's counsel is essential to the assurance of a fair trial. To give the tribunal the power to veto the choice of counsel of defendants is an unacceptable infringement of this right." (§64);
- The United Nations Human Rights Committee, while examining the meaning and scope of Article 14 of the International Covenant on Civil and Political Rights, was of the view that the right to choose one's counsel: "… **apply to all courts and tribunals within the scope of that article whether ordinary or specialised, civilian or military.**" (General Comment No. 32, Right to equality before the courts and tribunals and to a fair trial, 90th Session (2007) of the United Nations Human Rights Committee, Part III, paragraph 22)."

PART II

REFLECTIONS ON THE COURT FROM THE POINT OF VIEW OF DOCTRINE

ACCESS TO THE ECOWAS COURT OF JUSTICE IN MATTERS OF HUMAN RIGHTS VIOLATION : SOME REFLECTIONS ON THE STATUS OF THE APPLICANT

The process of establishment of the ECOWAS Court of Justice presents certain peculiarities, because, the facts do demonstrate that, the text on its organisation and functioning dates back to 1991[34], whereas the very principle of its establishment was enacted in a post-dated Treaty (1993)[35], which revised the Treaty of 28 May 1975, the founding treaty. It is known for a fact that subsequently, a Supplementary Protocol – dating back to 2005[36] – amended the 1991 Protocol, and that, one of the most important amendments made by the 2005 Protocol was the introduction of a new sphere of competence for the Court: the possibility for "individuals on application for relief for violation of their human rights" to come before the Community Court[37].

Originally, the Court had no mandate on human rights. Designed on the model of the Community Court of the European Union, as derived from the 1957 Treaty of Rome, the ECOWAS Court of Justice was required to see to the interpretation and application of norms devoted to economic integration, since ECOWAS had fixed for itself the objective for realising an economic and monetary union, in the terms of the preamble to the Revised Treaty. The organisation of the channels for seeking redress, and of the procedures enacted before the ECOWAS Court, was practically the same as the one before the Court of Luxembourg. Notably, one could find in either court, the following mechanisms: applications for default on obligation, and for annulment,

---

34 Namely, Protocol A/P.1/7/91, adopted on 6 July 1991 at Abuja by the Authority of Heads of State and Government of ECOWAS.

35 Namely, the Treaty of 24 July 1993, often described as the "Revised" Treaty, adopted at Cotonou by the Authority of Heads of State and Government of ECOWAS.

36 Supplementary Protocol A/SP.1/7/91 relating to the Community Court of Justice, adopted at Accra on 19 January 2005 by the Authority of Heads of State and Government of ECOWAS.

37 Article 10 of the 2005 Protocol

actions brought against Community institutions, and referrals for preliminary determination[38].

In those circumstances, the introduction of a new area of competence in 2005 constituted a non-negligible disruption. Not only was the Court not conceived to handle "human rights", but rather, other judicial or quasi-judicial bodies had been assigned that jurisdiction, and thus, the Court found itself not equipped with its own legal instrument which shall serve as a compass, and the Court had no specific text of reference on the basis of which it will try the cases submitted before it for adjudication. In principle, as at today, it does refer to any instrument binding on the Member States in question, which naturally thrusts upon the Court a huge judicial potential.

Every step of the Court was therefore being watched with expectation, under its new mandate as a human rights protection body. Among those expectations, the issue of access before the Court was not the least.

The notion of access to the Court may be understood in various ways.

It is possible, in the first instance, to accord the notion of *access*, quite a wide understanding. Access to the Court may thus concern, not only the actors in the trial (regarding notably the status of the plaintiff or applicant), but a set of formal conditions that must be met by the action filed before court, and which must revolve around the admissibility of the application brought before the court.

It is equally possible to delimit the notion of access to the Court, and thus restrict it to the first version mentioned above, which stays within the confines of the status of the plaintiff or applicant. The conditions of admissibility of applications, strictly within the meaning of Article 10 of the 2005 Protocol, would therefore be excluded from such an approach. It is known that the conditions for admissibility of applications are two in number: non-anonymity of the application and a bar on *lis pendens* of the application on the international scene. In the terms of the said Article 10(d)-ii, the application "… shall not be made whilst the same matter has been instituted before another International Court for adjudication."

The texts contain therefore some indications on the status of the applicant before the Court. One will have to admit however that such indications remain relatively meagre, relatively "vague", and that it was intended that the Court would lay down a number of judge-made rules on the status of an applicant in a proceedings for human rights violation.

---

38 These procedures are cited in Article 164 of the Treaty of Rome.

The present contribution deals precisely with this point. It indeed appears that after a decade of practice, the Court – which has virtually become a human rights court, if one should judge by the number of applications submitted before the Court during that period of time – has succeeded, in certain respects, in setting down clearly spelt out rules on the status of the applicant, whereas in other respects, it finds difficulty in fixing its doctrine, the case law even appearing somewhat hesitant, or even contradictory.

The analysis of an issue of that nature cannot obviously stop at statements of the relevant texts only. One may even assert that the core interest of the matter lies in the fact that apart from the texts, the Court has produced a flourishing jurisprudence, which is not always devoid of contradictions. In the light of the latter point, this study will attempt to propose solutions where it is observed that there have been instances of wavering, hesitation or contradiction in the jurisprudence of our Court.

One possible source of concern must however be gotten rid of. That the case law of the Court may be or may have been hesitant can easily be understood. All the similar courts of justice did experience, at one period or the other, ebbs and flows in their jurisprudence, regarding certain questions. It must even be considered to be normal in the case of the ECOWAS Court, which, we have seen, had no human rights mandate whatsoever, but did brace itself, one may say, "on the spur of the moment", towards assuming that jurisdiction. There is no doubt that, not too long from now, the areas which need to be clarified once and for all will be, and the rules concerning the status of applicants before the Court will be fixed for good.

From that perspective, a quick survey of the texts and case law reveals a reality of contrasts. In one instance, one finds categories of applicants whose access before the Court does not, or no more poses any problem, and in another instance, one notices that the Court either finds itself at crossroads, and thus realises the obligation to clarify its position, or else the Court advances hypotheses for cases it has never had to handle before, but which could perfectly be submitted before the Court.

It can therefore be said that regarding access to the Court for human rights violation, and in relation to the status of the applicant, there are (i) settled or undisputed cases, and (ii) debatable cases, open to argument, on which it is recommended to the Court to establish a doctrine.

I.- Undisputed cases

There are three of them: (a) individuals (natural persons) (b) the outsider, and (c) groups of individuals who come together to plead a cause in court. Special mention must be made of each of these cases.

A.- The Individual

If the ECOWAS Court of Justice remains somewhat peculiar as a human rights court, it is undoubtedly as a result of the fact that it has granted the access of its court to individuals, and also because it is not bound by the rule of exhaustion of local remedies.

Such was not originally the case, in the 1991 Protocol, which is the first text on the organisation and functioning of the Court. Article 9 §3 of the said Protocol, in following the age-old tradition of international law, did not envisage any other means for human-being applicants to appear on the international judicial scene, than through the instrumentality of their States of origin. The text of the 1991 Protocol stated indeed that:

> "A Member State may, on behalf of its nationals, institute proceedings against another Member State or Institution of the Community, relating to the interpretation and application of the provisions of the Treaty, after attempts to settle the dispute amicably have failed."

Thus, not only was the individual justice seeker excluded from immediacy in international adjudication, but also, any matter likely to concern him remained locked up behind the closed doors of inter-State communication, whose conciliatory phase was the most remarkable feature. As such, it will not be an exaggeration to say that the individual was not, strictly speaking, party to the procedure. As obtained in the mechanism of diplomatic protection, the natural-person litigant remained obscured behind the screens erected by the States.

Incidentally, the first case which was tried before the Court concerned that issue. Seised by a Nigerian businessman, Mr. Afolabi, who complained of the harm caused him by a measure of border closure between Nigeria and Benin, a measure adopted by the authorities of his country, he saw his application declared inadmissible. The judgment of 27 April 2004 ruled that:

> "By the examination of the said Protocol, the Applicant cannot bring proceedings other than as provided in Article 9(3) of the Protocol. This view proves the point that the Applicant in this case cannot bring the

proceedings against his Country or Member State which by law is saddled with the responsibility of instituting proceedings on his behalf."[39]

The first crack in the walls of State monopoly for bringing actions before the Court on behalf of individuals, was opened by the Protocol on Democracy and Good Governance.[40] It states in its Article 39 that the 1991 Protocol on the Court shall be reviewed to give the Court the power to hear human rights violations. That provision even ended by adding that: ".... after attempts to resolve the matter at the national level have failed", but we know that this reservation disappeared in the 2005 Protocol.

It is indeed the 2005 Protocol which will open the doors of the Court to individuals.[41] In the terms of its Article 10, on access to the Court:

> "Access to the Court is open to ... (d) individuals on application for relief for violation of their human rights; the submission of application for which shall (i) not be anonymous; nor (ii) be made whilst the same matter has been instituted before another International Court for adjudication."

Thus, the question of access of individuals to the Court for human rights violation no more arises. It had better be said that this procedure has turned out to be the most travelled road of access to the Court, the access road conveying the highest number of cases to the Court.

B.- A Non-Citizen of ECOWAS Member States

Can an "outsider", that is to say a non-citizen of an ECOWAS Member State, gain access to the Court?

The question is not a misplaced one when judged against the background of the habit adopted by the Court at the beginning of its activities, in making a systematic mention of the nationality of the litigants before it, in the terms of "a Community citizen", or "a national of a Member State of ECOWAS". Those traits of identification were undoubted references to the 1982 ECOWAS Protocol on Citizenship. Such descriptions could give the impression that the Court first of all carried out checks on the nationality of those bringing cases before it

---

39 Judgment No. ECW/CCJ/JUD/01/04 §62

40 Protocol A/SP1/12/01 on Democracy and Good Governance, signed at Dakar on 21 December 2001

41 Protocol A/SP.1/01/05 of 19 January 2005 amending the 1991 Protocol

before examining their case, since statements on litigants' nationality appeared in the early lines of the decisions made by the Court.

The question is whether such references are justified. Indeed, from both the spirit and the letter of the texts, brandishing nationality as a condition for access to the Court could pose problem. From the standpoint of the very philosophy of human rights – a philosophy heavily influenced by *jus naturalism*, that is to say the idea that human rights shall not be tied to nationality but remain indissolubly attached to the human person, and not to the "citizen" – the practice of mentioning nationality lends itself to criticism. Furthermore, nowhere in the texts setting out rights or the organisation of the functions of the Court, does it seem that the applicant is required to possess the nationality of a Member State.

Very fortunately, the practice before the Court has cleared that concern. It has indeed occurred that the Court was seised by persons who were not citizens of any of the Member States of ECOWAS, without the Court expressing any misgivings about it. One may cite the case which gave rise to the judgment of the Court dated 4 March 2010, in the case concerning *Dr. Mahamat Seid Abazene* **v.** *Republic of Mali.* The applicant in that case was a Chadian national employed in the position of Deputy Director-General at the Afro-Arab Cultural Institute, whose headquarters is at Bamako, and here again the Court did not devote any particular attention to the issue of nationality[42].

There was also the case concerning *Chude Mba* **v**. *Republic of Ghana*, which produced the judgment of 6 November 2013[43]. Here, the applicant possessed dual nationality: Nigerian and British. It is an interesting illustration because if the criteria for 'Community citizenship' were to be applied, as set out in the 1982 Protocol, Mr. Mba could not in effect have been considered as a 'Community citizen' since he still held the nationality of a non-Member State. Though not a Community citizen, within the meaning of the 1982 Protocol, his action was nevertheless declared admissible by the Court, and the Court, in that instance, made no further mention concerning the issue of nationality. One may finally cite the case – *Etablissements Vamo* **v.** *Republic of Benin* – settled in 2015 by the Court, where we find the two applicants, *Etablissements Vamo* itself, and Mr. Pascal Kuekia, a businessman of Cameroonian

42 Judgment No. ECW/CCJ/JUD/02/10

43 Judgment No. ECW/CCJ/JUD/10/13

origin and of British nationality, featuring in the action brought before the Court[44].

It must thus be said that, in our opinion, it shall be worthwhile to subscribe to the approach adopted by the Court. It would be a pity therefore if the ECOWAS Court of Justice should fall behind in the practice of similar international courts which take no account of nationality, as a condition for granting the access of their courts to litigants. The relevant legal instruments abstain, at any rate, from making any form of reference to any link of nationality, the notion of "person" being preferred. The universal values of human rights demand that such non-differentiation be placed above the requirements of nationality.

C.- Groups of Individuals

Is what is admissible for one human being equally admissible for several? The answer to the question may seem automatic, but that would imply forgetting that a procedure is an aggregate of formalities. When a text states that it admits one individual, it would amount to a somewhat 'warped' reading of the text if one should interpret it as meaning that "groups" of individuals shall equally be admitted. One can perfectly imagine a judge refusing to admit actions of that nature in a given instance. One may consider the judge's interpretation as unfortunate, but not necessarily absurd.

It was for that reason, without doubt, that the Committee on Human Rights instituted in connection with the 1966 United Nations Covenant on Civil and Political Rights expressed the need to provide, in a General Observation, the following details for precision purposes: That beneficiaries of rights recognised by the Covenant are human beings. That even though with the exception of Article 1, the Covenant does not mention the rights of corporate bodies, or entities or similar groups, a number of the rights recognised by the Covenant such as freedom of religion or freedom to manifest one's religion or beliefs (Article 18), freedom of association with others (Article 22), or the rights of minorities (Article 27), are jointly accessible, in union with other persons. That the fact that the competence of the Committee to receive and examine submissions may be restricted to submissions made by or on behalf of individuals (Article 1 of the Optional Protocol) does not prevent such individuals from equally asserting that actions or omissions affecting

---

44 Suit No. ECW/CCJ/APP/22/14

corporate bodies or similar entities constitute violation of their rights as well. Irrespective of this opening, it is known that the Committee does not admit cases filed by commercial companies and it firmly excludes every form of *actio popularis*[45].

The ECOWAS Court of Justice has, on its part, attempted to adopt a balanced position. When dealing with an action brought by a group of individuals, the Court does not reject the action, in principle, but requires that at least an authorisation must be issued to the representative(s) of the group intending to plead the case before the Court. While dwelling on the status of "victim" in its Judgment of 17 March 2011 on *Case Concerning Bakary Sarré and 28 Others* **v.** *Republic of Mali*, the Court held that:

> "... the applicant, acting on personal grounds as a result of a legally protected injured interest, reserves the right to come before a judge to have his claims examined; alternatively, an Applicant, **authorised to act by virtue of a power of attorney on behalf of another person or for a group of people** whose legally protected interests have been harmed, shall exercise the power of representation in the action…"[46]. Finding that the Applicant, Bakary Sarré, had no such authorisation, the Court then ruled that he had no "… legal title to act before the Court of Justice of ECOWAS on behalf of the said year-group…"[47].

In another case decided in 2015, *Saoro Victims of Human Rights Violation* **v.** *Republic of Guinea*[48], the Court equally required that the representative of the alleged victims produce an authorisation for representation which shall enable him to plead the case before the Court on behalf of all the others.

One may not say of course that the position of the Court on the matter is too demanding. One may even claim that the Court only asks for a minimum requirement: the production of the power to act. That

---

45 See for example: *A Newspaper Publishing Company* **v.** *Trinidad and Tobago*, Communication No. 360/1989, UN Doc.CCPR/C/36/D/360/1989 (1989). Diametrically opposed to this relative strictness is the European Convention on Human Rights whose Article 34 provides: "*The Court may receive applications from any person, nongovernmental organisation or group of individuals claiming to be the victim of a violation by one of the High Contracting Parties of the rights set forth in the Convention or the Protocols thereto. The High Contracting Parties undertake not to hinder in any way the effective exercise of this right.*"

46 Judgment No. ECW/CCJ/JUD/11 § 37 of the Judgment (the emphasis is ours)

47 §38 of the Judgment

48 Suit No. ECW/CCJ/APP/21/14

requirement should not, in principle, pose a problem. The Community Court does not therefore object to actions being instituted by a group of persons. The stand taken by the Court deserves, in our view, to be commended. In a context like that of Africa, in general, "the culture of human rights" is not always firmly implanted, and it is fortunate, without conceding to the excesses of *actio popularis*, that it be possible for human rights cases to be borne by individuals within a given group. One condition must however be fulfilled always: the applicants themselves must have suffered the injury; they shall, in the expression of Article 10 of the 2005 Supplementary Protocol, be the "*victim(s)*" of the human rights violations in cause. Fulfilling that condition is indeed fundamental. The Court cannot, by way of extravagant liberalism or generosity, open its precincts to the floodgates. Keeping to the afore-stated pre-requisite could constitute its distinctive feature as a court of justice, in contrast with other bodies that may want to appear more liberal in admitting applications for human rights violation.

Such are the various cases for which the Court has developed a doctrine and adopted a stance which may be considered as firm. There are however other points, still relating to the status of a victim of human rights violation, which need further clarification by the jurisprudence of the Court. They may be considered as the debatable cases.

II.- Debatable cases

They are equally three in number: (a) "potential" victims, (b) corporate bodies, and (c) States.

A.- "Potential" Victims

The question raised here is whether an individual, who is not yet a victim of human rights violation, but who risks becoming one, can gain acccss to the ECOWAS Court of Justice.

On three occasions, at least, the Court has had to deal with this issue. Initially, the jurisprudential responses from the Court fluctuated, but it must be said that the overall position of the Community Court seems to have stabilised today.

The first was in *Case Concerning Hissène Habré* **v.** *Republic of Senegal*, whose judgment was delivered on 18 November 2010[49]. The

[49] Judgment No. ECW/CCJ/JUD/06/10

known fact is that the Applicant, Mr. Habré, was of the opinion that the Republic of Senegal was getting things underway towards the violation of his rights, by way of adoption of a number of constitutional and legislative reforms. According to him, those reforms were made to appear as if Senegal was taking appropriate steps to bring its national law in line with the international obligations it has subscribed to, whereas, in his own estimation, the actions of Senegal were preparatory schemes towards bringing him to trial. He contended that such trial, if instituted against him, would be baseless. In short, he found himself in the situation of a potential victim of the acts undertaken by Senegal.

The Court was therefore required to make a pronouncement on his situation. The position held by the Court was truly not clear. Indeed, the Court began by stating that "*... the alleged violations by the Applicant are tied to a hypothesis*[50]*, thus the Court can state that they are but potential...*", and that it has no jurisdiction to examine human rights violation *in abstracto*, but only concrete cases[51]. Strangely enough however, almost immediately afterwards, the Court declares that a case law may somehow undergo mitigating circumstances, and that in invoking "utterly exceptional circumstances", one may be compelled to admit that the risk of a future violation confers on the applicant the status of a victim (...)[52]. In support of that shift, the Court cited the case law of the European Court of Human Rights[53].

In a judgment delivered on 3 July 2013 on *Aziagbede Kokou and 33 Others, Atsou Komlavi and 4 Others, Tomekpe A. Lanou and 29 Others* **v.** *Republic of Togo*[54], the Court seems to establish a connection with reality, and not the mere probability of an alleged violation. The Court thus rules that:

> "... an application on human rights violation which at the time of lodgement does not exhibit any international nature, and proves to be **premature or precocious,** may be declared inadmissible.[55]

Until recently, the ECOWAS Court of Justice has not put down any solid doctrine on the issue of "potential victim". We think it would be

---

50 §30 of the Judgment

51 §48 of the Judgment

52 §49 of the Judgment

53 Refer to the cases concerning *Noel Narü Tauira and 18 Others* **v.** *France ; Dudgeon* **v.** *United Kingdom,* 22 October 1989 *; Soering* **v.** *United Kingdom,* 7 July 1989

54 Suit No. ECW/CCJ/APP/21/22/23/11

55 § 20 of the Judgment (the emphasis is ours)

desirable if the Court would raise the level of probability of violation when a claim of potential violation is brought before it by an individual claiming the status of a potential victim. In the *Hissène Habré* case for instance, it is certain that it was difficult to accuse the Defendant of being on the verge of committing the violation of a right, whereas the said Defendant was indeed simply acting in fulfilment of an international commitment. The indecisiveness of the Court in this particular case undoubtedly explains the ambiguity in the operative statement of the judgment, which neither states the merits in the parties' claims, nor does it state clearly where each of the two parties are to be placed in the final ruling; the Court ultimately makes no clear-cut decision.

Conversely, the handling of the notion of probable or possible harm was without doubt better processed in a recent case, between the national authorities of the political transition of Burkina Faso and certain political parties and citizens of Burkina Faso, earmarked for exclusion from the electoral race (Judgment of 13 July 2015)[56]. The Defendant State, Burkina Faso, contested the very jurisdiction of the Court on the ground that the Court only entertains proven cases of violation, and not possible violations or those which may occur in the future. The Court admits the principle inherent in the affirmation made by the Defendant State, but immediately corrects the statement made by the latter. To follow the argumentation of Burkina Faso, according to the Court, would amount to "

> ... consigning its own time-held case law to oblivion if the Court should rule that it may legitimately entertain violations which have not yet occurred, but are very imminent. In the instant case, the alleged violation has not yet been committed, but could very soon be. Going by the indications provided to the Court, the electoral process is to open seventy (70) days before the scheduled date for voting (i.e. 11 October 2015), on the fateful day of 1 August 2015. The Court was therefore seised with the case on grounds of urgency. In the present circumstances of the case, if the Court were to wait for the applications of candidature to be possibly rejected before acting, if it had to wait for the exhaustion of the effects of any transgression before stating the law, its jurisdiction in a context of urgency would have no sense, because the electoral rights of the presumed victims for participating in the electoral race would inexorably be breached."

56 Judgment No. ECW/CCJ/JUD/16/15

B.- Corporate Bodies

Here, we are going to deal with a scenario different from the one we previously discussed, concerning a group of human beings who have decided to come together to plead their case before court, not as a truly structured formal body, and assigning to one of their lot the power to represent them all. The question at stake now is a more fundamental one. Does the human rights protection system reserve a place for corporate bodies, i.e. abstract entities? Are these artificial bodies, whose existence is independent of the human beings who created them, entitled to bring cases before the Court, knowing perfectly well that in making mention of "individuals on application for relief for violation of their human rights", the relevant text intended to refer, without doubt, to natural persons (human beings).

This is one of the most crucial questions facing the Court, for its jurisprudence is criss-crossed today with contradictions regarding this issue, and must be resolved in all urgency. We first need to convince ourselves of this fact.

In the judgment of 17 December 2009 on *National Coordination of Departmental Delegates of the Cocoa and Coffee Sector (CNDD)* **v.** *Republic of Côte d'Ivoire,* the Defendant State simply contested the Applicant's capacity for claiming "human rights". In an expository presentation on Article 10(d) of the 2005 Supplementary Protocol, the Court holds that:

> "... the said text talks of "toute personne victime" without stating whether it is a question of natural person or legal person, or still, whether it is the two at the same time; but the Court would like to emphasise, moreover, that the word "victime", and more precisely the concept of "victim" enables one to understand that it is a question of adjudicating on complaints from any person who may claim that he/it has been harmed or that he/it has suffered from violation of his/its recognised rights to freedom. (…) Whereas, it is trite that rights and freedoms guaranteed by international instruments relating to human rights are so made for individuals, it is nonetheless the case that legal persons equally have rights they can claim. "[57]

---

[57] Judgment No. ECW/CCJ/JUD/05/09 §§23 and 24 of Judgment. The Court then makes abundant references to the case law of the European Court of Human Rights (§25 and 26). But unlike the latter Court, nothing in the texts of the ECOWAS Court of Justice gives proof to that interpretation

One would have thought therefore that the Court's position had finally been established. But in a judgment of 9 May 2011 on *Center for Democracy and Development and Center for Defence of Human Rights and Democracy* **v.** *Republic of Niger,* the Court finds that: "

> … the Center for Democracy and Development and Center for Defence of Human Rights and Democracy in Africa do not provide any justification that they have received a mandate from the people of Niger… "[58]. Subsequently, in a more emphatic manner, the Court declares that "… even if one should suppose that the said association possesses the legal status in their respective countries, they have not evinced their status as victims nor justified that they are qualified to act on behalf of the victims whose mandate they must have received."[59].

The judgment on *Ocean King Nigeria Ltd* **v.** *Republic of Senegal* dated 8 July 2011 keeps faith with the viewpoint expressed above since the Court states therein that "… corporate entities (…) are therefore excluded"[60]. The operative statement itself for the judgment delivered states, in principle, that corporate bodies are not admissible before the Court for human rights violation, and that only individuals (natural persons) are considered as victims.[61].

Curiously however, the Court accepted to adjudicate on a case in which the applicant was not only a legal person, but could not lay claim to any harm in the circumstances of the case. The matter bore similarities to what has just been called to mind, relating to Niger. It concerned *La Rencontre Africaine pour la Défense des Droits de l'Homme* (African Forum for the Defence of Human Rights) – *RADDHO*, which had brought its case before the Court, seeking suspension of the presidential elections scheduled for February 2012 in Senegal, and an order asking the Republic of Senegal to institute proceedings against the security officers involved in the killing of the demonstrators. In a ruling of 6 July 2012, the Court finds that the alleged violations have a "*direct and real link*" with the promotion of human rights and declared admissible the action brought. This should come as a surprising decision because we cannot then see why the two other bodies similar to RADDHO, which had brought their case before the Court against the Republic of Niger in the tense political climate of 2011, saw their application declared

58 Judgment No. ECW/CCJ/JUD/05/11 §18 of the Judgment

59 §28 of the Judgment

60 Judgment No. ECW/CCJ/JUD/07/11 §28 of the Judgment

61 §74 of the Judgment

inadmissible. The two cases had striking similarities and one can hardly fathom the difference in treatment accorded them. Whatever the case may be, the judgment of 6 July 2012 on *RADDHO* **v.** *Republic of Senegal* translates a slackening in the standard of control of applications coming before the Court. We know that finally, and in view of the developments in the situation in Senegal (peaceful conduct of the elections in 2012 and change in political power), the Court, in its judgment of 23 October 2015, declared that there was no point adjudicating on the case[62].

In truth, the danger which has been lying in wait for the ECOWAS Court of Justice, since its mandate turned almost exclusively towards human rights protection, is what one may call the 'syndrome of Banjul', in talking of the African Commission on Human and Peoples' Rights, whose headquarters is located in Banjul. The lodgement of cases before the said Commission, it is common knowledge now, is done in relatively liberal conditions. One of the aspects of this liberalism is precisely the spirit of goodwill with which the Commission receives its 'victims'. More precisely put, it is possible for one to bring a case before the said African Commission without even having to adduce any evidence whatsoever for a harm one may claim to have suffered. Thus, NGOs and law firms located outside the African continent have made submissions before the Commission on behalf of certain given 'people'.[63]

We could certainly give ourselves a pat on the back for such a development, in view of the difficulties of gaining access to channels of redress for transgression of rights amongst the peoples of Africa. The question to be asked however, is whether a court of justice, an international court of justice for that matter, like the ECOWAS Court of Justice, may have the same preoccupations or perspectives as a quasi-judicial body like the African Commission on Human and Peoples' Rights. We do not think so. It is not indeed within the functions of the Court to 'promote' human rights, but just to sanction the violation of human rights. Since the Court has not been assigned any mandate for playing the role of a 'militant', it must be more rigorous than the African Commission on Human and Peoples' in its policy regarding receipt of applications.

---

62 Judgment No. ECW/CCJ/JUD/20/15

63 In *Case Concerning RADDHO* **v.** *Republic of Senegal*, the submissions made in court equally brought out the fact that the Application filed before the Court was written by another body, not found in Senegal, but all the same an organisation for the defence of human rights

In that light, it is recommended to the Court: not to give consideration to the nature of the persons bringing cases before it – whether they are human beings (natural persons) or corporate bodies (legal entities) – but only concern itself with whether or not the prejudice suffered is personal or not in nature. Where the violations alleged have had consequences on the actual circumstances of a given person (either a human being or a legal entity), that person must see his/its application declared admissible. Conversely, if the person in question has not personally suffered from the matters in cause, his/its application must not have any chance of being examined by the Court.

This position seems to us a balanced one, in as much as it first of all avoids the absurdity of having to refuse to acknowledge that legal entities do have 'human rights'. Indeed, who could seriously maintain that an association subjected to "bullying" is not entitled to freedom of expression, or that a company whose assets are unlawfully expropriated cannot claim its right to property before a court of law? Again, the solution being advocated for here equally stands immune from the criticisms of *actio popularis* since the doors of the ECOWAS Court of Justice will not be opened to just anyone interested in human rights, but only those who prove that their own personal rights have been trampled upon. The case law of the Court seems to move in that direction in its recent development, we hope the trend becomes a permanent feature.

C.- States

Can a Member State of ECOWAS sue another Member State before the Court for human rights violation?

In a theoretical sense, the answer is in the negative. In the terms of Article 10 (d) of the 2005 Protocol on the Court, access to the Court is open to: "individuals on application for relief for violation of their human rights".

A glance at other legal instruments of the Community reveals however that the possibility of an inter-State dispute on human rights emerging one day before the Court may well be a tenable hypothesis. Two things must be borne in mind in this respect.

The first is that Article 10 of the 2005 Protocol does not exhaust the grounds for competence of the Court. The Court may indeed be seised on other grounds, in other texts. First of all, the ECOWAS Treaty itself, in its Article 76, provides:

> "1. Any dispute regarding the interpretation or the application of the provisions of this Treaty shall be amicably settled through direct agreement without prejudice to the provisions of this Treaty and relevant Protocols. 2. Failing this, either party or any other Member States or the Authority may refer the matter to the Court of the Community whose decision shall be final and shall not be subject to appeal."

On the other hand, in the terms of Article 9 of the 2005 Protocol:

> "The Court has competence to adjudicate on any dispute relating to… (a) the interpretation and application of the Treaty, Conventions and Protocols of the Community…."

The second point to remember is that a number of these "Conventions and Protocols" contain provisions on human rights. One may cite for that purpose, the 10 December 1999 Protocol of Lome, Protocol relating to the Mechanism for Conflict Prevention, Management, Resolution, Peace-Keeping and Security. But the most relevant instrument in that sense is the Protocol on Democracy and Good Governance, supplementary to the Protocol of Lome. Issues dealt with therein include: participation in public decisions (Article 1(c)); freedom of worship (Article 1(f)); right to equality (Article 1(g)); the right of political parties to be formed and financed by public powers (Article 1(i)); freedom of association and the right to meet and organise peaceful demonstrations (Article 1(j)); freedom of press (Article 1(k)); etc.

On the basis of these two considerations – the competence of the Court in matters of interpretation and application of a certain number of legal instruments of ECOWAS, coupled with the self-generation of human rights provisions in those ECOWAS legal instruments – it becomes perfectly conceivable for a State to bring an action in court against another State which may not have respected the human rights provisions stipulated in the said Conventions and Protocols.

To the arguments above, as derived from the interpretation of the ECOWAS texts, must be added a more general consideration which remains a principle of international law: every State party to a convention acquires the right to insist on the observance of the convention signed by all the other States parties, and can therefore sue another State on account of that right. In other words, even if it is not expressly provided for, any State party to the Conventions and Protocols of ECOWAS is entitled to sue another State party if it considers that the other State has defaulted on its obligations regarding a particular Convention or Protocol of ECOWAS.

One will have to admit however that in that case, one would of course not be finding oneself within the context of human rights violation anymore, as intended by the Supplementary Protocol of 2005. The case would become, more simply and more classically, that of a State in violation of its legally binding obligations. In the hypothetical case of a treaty signed within the framework of ECOWAS, as is at stake, one would even be dealing purely and simply with failure by the State to honour obligations. It is true that till today, the ECOWAS Court of Justice has not recorded a single inter-State case. That reality also demonstrates the extent to which the confinement of judicial settlements within the ECOWAS regional space remains low, even if, we must not deceive ourselves, the States, all States in the world, naturally frown upon dragging their sister States to court, for the good and simple reason that in matters of human rights, none is absolutely blameless.

March 2015

NATIONAL LAW AND THE CASE LAW OF THE ECOWAS COURT OF JUSTICE

The ECOWAS Court of Justice increasingly applies, we are aware, a collection of norms which can be considered as International Human Rights Law. This fact is naturally tied to its jurisdiction, acquired through the adoption of the Supplementary Protocol of 19 January 2005, to try cases of "violation of human rights."

In itself, such extension of powers portended a potential conflict with the norms of national law in general, and with constitutional law in particular. We indeed know that in most of the Member States of the Community, there exist in the preambles or in the actual body of the Constitution, reference to a number of "human rights": either that the Constitution or its preamble contains such prerogatives, fixing the principle and scope, or that the body of laws in question – particularly the preamble of the Constitution – refers to major instruments of human rights protection, like the Universal Declaration of Human Rights of 10 December 1948, the UN Conventions of 1966 (the International Covenant on Civil and Political Rights, and the International Covenant on Economic, Social and Cultural Rights), the Convention for the Elimination of All Forms of Discrimination Against Women (1979), the Convention against Torture, Cruel, Inhuman and Degrading Treatment (1984), or still the 1989 Convention on the Rights of the Child, which all remain legal instruments adopted within the framework of the United Nations. One must obviously make special mention of the African Charter on Human and Peoples' Rights (1981), adopted within the framework of the former Organisation of African Unity (OAU). The latter in particular is indeed almost systematically cited every time the constitutional texts of the Member States refer to instruments of human rights protection.

By acquiring competence in the field of human rights, the ECOWAS Court of Justice thus appeared to become, virtually, a "rival" of the national courts empowered to make pronouncements on violations of human rights within their respective jurisdictions, and in particular, we have already said so, a rival of the constitutional courts. This new prospect, apart from opening a new projection for reflecting on relationships between the ECOWAS Court of Justice and the National Courts of the Member States – in addition to this other angle created by the mechanism of referrals from the domestic courts of the Member States for preliminary determination by the Community Court, as provided by Article 10(f) of the 2005 Supplementary Protocol – constitutes an opportunity for reflecting, in more general terms, on the relationship between the national law of the Member States and the legal order of ECOWAS, as regulated by the ECOWAS Court of Justice.

In general terms, the principles governing these relations may appear simple, at least as regards disputes on human rights violation. As an International Court before which, in matters concerning human rights relations, only States may be sued, since only they are indeed bound by the international texts which stipulate those rights, the Court shall not, in principle, make any room whatsoever for the national law.

Trials before the Community Court are conducted at the level of the international order, and on that plane, only questions of international law may be raised, questions whose sources of reference are found in treaties and conventions concluded by the States concerned, and also, in unilateral acts of supra-national bodies to which States are parties. **(I)**This initially given fact, corroborated by the case law of other International Courts, is satisfactorily affirmed by the Court, and as manifested in its judgments, are numerous and of various forms.

Upon a closer look however, things prove to be more complex. It turns out that the principle of setting aside the national law on the international plane is far from being absolute, and it does occur in more than one instance, that the Court takes the national law into account. The rather simplified theory that the Court is impermeable to the national law must quickly be viewed in relative terms. The fact is that the national law – and even the national jurisprudence – are sometimes taken into account by the Community Judges, and it is the national law which even directly guides, at times, the decisions that the ECOWAS Court may be urged to take. **(II)**We shall therefore attempt to go over the range of instances where the national law creeps into the trial proceedings held at Abuja.

I.- The principle: setting aside the national law

Viewed very closely, the departure from all considerations regarding the domestic law of Member States in the jurisprudence of the Court comes in twin fashion: procedural and substantial. (A). In the first instance, the judges at Abuja take the stand that the Court is not a body mandated to amend or quash the decisions made by the national courts: the Community judge is neither an appeal judge nor a judge with powers to overturn court decisions made by the national judges of the Member States. (B) From the substantive point of view, that is to say, in line with the Rules applied by the Court to the cases submitted to it, the Court shall solely rely on international texts, and not on national texts, which may possibly have enacted the same rights found in the treaties and conventions.

A.- The dimension concerning procedure: the Court is neither an appellate body nor a body set up to quash decisions made by the national courts

Currently, after a decade of practice of contentious jurisdiction in matters of human rights violation, this rule has virtually assumed the status of a legal phrase, and applicants are at times not at fault in citing it, either against their defendants, as a strategy of anticipation, or to prevent an objection the Court may address against them. That is to say, this principle seems 'internalised' today.

That internalisation was far from being automatic in 2005, when that area of the jurisdiction of the Court had just been introduced. The temptation for the Applicants to have recourse to the Constitution of their country could thus be explained, not only by the availability of the constitutional instrument – the instrument they could readily lay hands on and which undoubtedly they best knew – but also by another means, arising from a form of judicial psychology, or psychology, simply put – which was, the absence of the rule of exhaustion of local remedies as a precondition for gaining access to the Court. One may think that the sanctioning of the rule on exhaustion of local remedies in the ECOWAS judicial system may have accorded the proceedings before the Court a more 'solemn' and 'more remote' outlook, and may probably have given weight to the idea that at Abuja, another trial is held, another case is heard, and 'other' rules are applied; in a word, that before the Court, it is international law which is at stake, whereas, until then, that is to say before the judges of the domestic courts, it was the rules of the domestic law that held sway.

Such symbolic separation between the trial at the national level and the trial on the international plane got weakened by the absence of exhaustion local remedies. Not only can one bring cases before the Court while all the domestic courts have not yet been seised with same case, but it has occurred – a position which can be debated – that the Community Court held that once an Applicant had lodged a case before a domestic court, it was obligatory upon the Community Court to stay proceedings till determination of the case which had already begun before the national court. In the judgment on *Aziagbede Kokou and 33 Others* **v.** *Republic of Togo*, delivered on 3 July 2013, one reads:

> Consequently, the Court adjudges that the application (…) is premature; and that it is ripe and appropriate therefore to declare that the allegations and requests made thereto are inadmissible as things stand, since the procedures are still pending before the domestic courts.[64]

Availability of the constitutional instrument, absence of a symbolic hierarchy between the national trial, on one hand, and the international trial, on the other hand (a horizontal relationship expressed therein by the absence of the rule of exhaustion of local remedies), could feature among the reasons for which the national law has had to be cited before the Court in the past.

For some years however, the case law of the Court is settled. We are not going to cite here the entire list of cases in which the Court was faced with the question of taking into account the national law, and where, subsequently, it reiterated its position of the principle.

Thus, in the judgment on *Jerry Ugokwe* **v.** *Nigeria* of 7 October 2005, the Court declared that:

> "Appealing against the decisions of the national courts of Member States does not form part of the powers of the Court (…). The ECOWAS Court of Justice is not a court of appeal or a court of cassation."[65]

In the judgment on *Moussa Léo Keïta* **v.** *Republic of Mali*, delivered on 22 March 2007, the Court:

> "Declares that it is incompetent to adjudicate upon the decision made by the Supreme Court of Mali, as to violation of human rights"[66].

In the judgment on *Al Hadji Hammani Tidjani* **v.** *Federal Republic of Nigeria and Others*, dated 28 June 2007, the Court holds that receiving the application would amount to unjustifiably interfering with the criminal jurisdiction of the domestic courts of Nigeria.[67].

---

64 Judgment No. ECW/CCJ/JUD/07/13, §42.

65 Judgment No. ECW/CCJ/JUD/03/05, § 32

66 Judgment No. ECW/CCJ/JUD/03/07, §39

67 Judgment No. ECW/CCJ/JUD/04/07, §45

Finally, in the judgment on *Alimu Akeem* **v.** *Federal Republic of Nigeria*, dated 28 January 2014, the Court recalls that:

> "It is trite that in those cases where the subject-matter of the dispute essentially had to do with a re-examining of judgments already delivered by the domestic courts, the Honourable Court held that they be dismissed."[68]

It occurs, all the same, that conscious that the Court is reluctant to make assessments on the national law, certain Applicants, proving to be subtle, present their arguments in such manner as to give the impression that they are urging the Court to make a declaration, by taking account of the national law. The strategy will then consist of enticing the Court to concur with or implicitly dismiss the decision from the national court. Rather fortunately, the Court remains faithful to its stance by setting aside, again in that instance, every move whose effect would be to drag it onto that terrain.

The doctrine of setting aside national law shall therefore not be recalled when the Court is expressly requested to invalidate or render ineffective decisions already made by the national courts. It becomes imperative to set aside the national law every time, without having to say so expressly, a request ultimately seeks, by its consequences, that is to say implicitly or indirectly, to reform or neutralise a decision made by a judge at the domestic court. Before the ECOWAS Court, Applicants must therefore be sufficiently advised, at least as to the precautions to be taken in the drafting of one's submissions. It is permissible for Applicants, indeed, not to raise issues in terms of seeking to thwart the ends of a court decision or judgment made by the national judge, but to position themselves exclusively on the terrain of human rights violation as provided for by the international legal instruments.

Again, with regard to this point, a recall of three judgments delivered by the Court will be appropriate.

In the case concerning *Bakary Sarré and 28 Others* **v.** *Republic of Mali,* the Court held that :

> "The Court concludes that it can be deduced from the Application filed by Mr. Bakary Sarré and 28 Others against the Republic of Mali, that the said Application substantially seeks to obtain from the Court of Justice of ECOWAS, a reversal of Judgments No. 188 and No. 116 as delivered by

---

[68] Judgment No. ECW/CCJ/JUD/01/14, §42

the Supreme Court of Mali and it seeks to project the Court of Justice of ECOWAS as a court of cassation over the Supreme Court of Mali. Viewed from that angle, the Honourable Court declares that it has no jurisdiction to adjudicate on the matter."[69]

Then, in the case law of *Isabelle Manavi Ameganvi* **v.** *Republic of Togo*, the Court was of the view that: "

> ... the application to retrieve the lost seats is akin to an application brought against Decision No. E018/10 of 22 November 2010 of the Constitutional Court of the Republic of Togo, which is a domestic court of a Member State; and in following its established jurisprudence, the Court has no jurisdiction to sit as an appellate court or a cassation court, and so it cannot reverse the said Decision.[70].

Finally, in the Court's decision of 23 April 2015, in *CDS Rahama* **v.** *Republic of Niger*, the Court finds that:

> "On the basis of the principle behind this standpoint, it can be deduced that the requests of CDS Rahama concerning the decisions of the local courts of Niger cannot be granted, the reason being that the Court has no remit for examining such decisions; and more generally, after decisions are made by the domestic courts of Niger, the Court has no jurisdiction to examine whether those local courts of Niger adhered or not to their jurisprudence or generally, to the national law of Niger."[71].

The Court does not only recall that it is not a court for reforming or quashing court decisions made at the national level. In the merits of the judgments it delivers, in the choice of its norms of reference, the Court specifically avoids consideration of the national law. Departing from the national law does not only obtain at the procedural or processing stage, *stricto sensu,* it also obtains when the substance of the case is being considered.

B.- The dimension concerning substance: the Court sets aside the national law in its norms of reference

The Court has ceaselessly recalled that it only considers the rules of international law, and not the rules of the national law, notably the rules of the national Constitution. This reminder has a decisive consequence,

---

69 Judgment No. ECW/CCJ/JUD/03/11, Judgment of 17 March 2011, §31.

70 Judgment No. ECW/CCJ/JUD/06/12, Judgment of 13 March 2012, § 17.

71 Judgment No. ECW/CCJ/JUD/03/15, § 51.

in regard to the status of the defendant before the Court, as far as disputes on human rights violation are concerned. If indeed, in that regard, the Community Court relies exclusively on international law, it is for the reason that international law is binding on States only, States which have so agreed to be bound, within the scope of the terms of expression of consent such as enumerated under Article 11 of the 1969 Vienna Convention, which covers:

> "… signature, exchange of instruments constituting a treaty, ratification, acceptance, approval or accession, or by any other means if so agreed."

In other words, it is impossible, in matters of human rights violation, to drag before the Court, any entity or person other than the State. That is a consequence – or may be a cause – of why only the rules of international law are applicable before the Court.

In the case concerning *Center for Democracy and Development and Center for Defence of Human Rights and Democracy* **v.** *Republic of Niger*, which produced the judgment of 9 May 2011, it was declared that:

> "(…) the powers conferred on the Court … shall not be interpreted as implying the exercise of control over the constitutionality or legality of the instruments adopted by the national authorities of the Member States, in application of their domestic law. (…) Consequently, the Court is of the view that it has no jurisdiction to make a declaration on the legality or constitutionality of the acts complained of or to forbid acts of that nature from being taken. Hence, the Court is incompetent to make a declaration as to whether the decisions taken by Mr. Mamadou Tandja are illegal, arbitrary, and null and of no effect.
>
> The Court is equally incompetent to forbid Mr. Mamadou Tandja or the agents of the Republic of Niger from organising the said referendum, for the purposes of holding on to power, or from dispersing the protest marches against the organisation of the referendum."[72]

In the judgment of 19 July 2013, on *Karim Meissa Wade* **v.** *Republic of Senegal*, it is equally written that:

> "… the Court (…) has no jurisdiction to examine the legality of Law No. 81-53 and Law No. 81-54 of 10 July 1981 on the Combat of Illegal-Wealth and the creation of the Anti Illegal-Wealth Court, and any decision made by the Commission of Inquiry of the Anti Illegal-Wealth Court, which is

[72] Judgment No. ECW/CCJ/JUD/05/11, § 24

a domestic court of the Republic of Senegal.".[73]. The Court further states that: "In general terms, (...) the Honourable Court must declare that it lacks the jurisdiction to sit on all the requests altogether, as brought by the Applicant, since examining the case will eventually mean that the Court has overstepped the bounds of its jurisdiction, by interfering in the legislative and judicial matters of the Republic of Senegal."[74].

The judgment on *Abdoulaye Baldé and Others* **v.** *Senegal*, delivered on 22 February 2013, reaffirms that position:

"... the Court holds that the dispute between the Parties in regard to violation of the right to fair trial cannot compel the Court to examine the domestic laws of the Republic of Senegal as to illegal wealth." The Court: "... the Court recalls its consistently held case law that it has no mandate to examine the national laws of Member States or to review decisions made by the domestic courts of Member States."[75].

Much clearer still, in the judgment of 13 July 2015, on *CDP and Others* **v.** *Burkina Faso*, a manner of profession of faith is expressed:

"The first of these principles, which assumes a particular significance in the case submitted before the Court, is the Court's refusal to assume the role of a judge over the domestic law of the Member States. The Court has indeed always recalled that it is not a body set up with a mandate for settling cases whose subject matter is the interpretation of the law or the Constitution of the Member States of ECOWAS. Two effects arise therefrom. The first is that the present judicial argumentation must be devoid of every form of reliance on the domestic law, be it on the Constitution of Burkina Faso, or on any norms whatsoever related to the Constitution of Burkina Faso. In their written pleadings, the Applicants indeed made reference to both the Constitution of Burkina Faso (Article 1) and the Charter of Transition (Article 1).

Such references shall be deemed as inappropriate before the judges of the ECOWAS Court of Justice. As an International Court, its mandate is restricted to sanctioning States' disregard for the obligations arising from the international texts binding on them. The second effect is that there can be no question, in the instant case, of seeking to examine the meaning

---

73 Judgment No. ECW/CCJ/JUD/09/13, § 60

74 § 61.

75 Judgment No. ECW/CCJ/JUD/04/13, §§ 70 and 72

which must be ascribed to the new Article 135 of the Burkina Faso Electoral Code."[76]

It is imperative, in other terms, that the State sued before the Court be an actual party to the conventions relied upon by the applicant, an obvious fact which has at times been circumvented[77].

The ousting of the national law cannot be absolute, however, in the consideration of matters regarding human rights violation. By necessity, and in certain given states of affairs, the international judge, symbolised here by the ECOWAS Court of Justice, will be required to take a look at the national law, and to take it into account, for the purposes of evaluating the requests submitted before him. Thus, it does not turn out as a case of renouncing a position of principle, but reckoning with the specific nature of the case submitted or the "the circumstances of the cause". It is therefore not a matter of criticising the case law – the jurisprudential position taken is perfectly defensible – but only pointing out the limits of the theory of setting aside the national law.

II.- The exception: giving the national law inevitable consideration

The first consideration accorded the national law by the ECOWAS Judge is in reality the consideration of the national juridical procedures through which the case was processed. Indeed, it has occurred, as astonishing as that may appear, that the Court be seised not only with cases which have come to their finale at the national level, but where the Applicant has already obtained the required relief.

---

76 Judgment No. ECW/CCJ/JUD/16/15, §§ 24 to 26.

77 It has unfortunately occurred, inadvertently, without doubt, that the Court, in such regard, had recourse to non-relevant legal instruments, like, as it is actually known, the European Convention for the Protection of Human Rights and Fundamental Freedoms, binding only on the members of the Council of Europe. Such errors occurred in two cases, notably in *El Hadji Mame Abdou Gaye* **v.** *Republic of Senegal* (26 January 2012) and *Kpatcha Gnassingbe and Others* **v.** Republic of Togo (3 July 2013). In the first case, the Court cites, in its *ratio decidendi* Article 5(1) of the European Convention (§39), and in the second, the Court makes reference to the same text in its reasoning (§94). Similarly, by virtue of the theory of setting aside the national law, the Court should not have relied on the Constitution of the States. The Court unfortunately did so, for example, in *Aliyu Tasheku* **v.** *Republic of Nigeria* (Judgment of 12 June 2012), where Articles 34, 35, 36, 41 and 42 of the Constitution of Nigéria were cited (§17). In the judgment on the *Kpatcha Gnassingbe* case cited above, it was the 14 October 1992 Constitution of Togo which was cited, specifically its Article 19 (§ 94).

In other words, the Application brought before the Community judge thus sought to gain on two fronts, a duality which translates into nothing more than a form of unfaithfulness, which the Court has instantly set aside: (A).

On the other hand, there are cases where a return to the national law becomes imperative because it is the national law which constitutes the yardstick for the law whose violation is alleged. Where it is the national legal regime which structures the principle and conditions for the exercise of a right, it is normal that, for assessing any alleged infringement on that law, the judge refers to the standards thus enacted by the State. If the standards are respected, the Community judge will conclude that there is no violation; on the contrary, he sanctions the State. For instance, and in quite a staggering context, it is the international judge who sees to the application of the national law: (B).

On the whole, the consideration of the national law by the ECOWAS judge thus assumes, like in the case of his rejection of the national law as reviewed earlier in our work, a dimension on procedure (taking account of the internal judicial procedures) and a dimension on substance (taking account, inevitably, of the nationally defined standards or criteria).

A.- The dimension concerning procedure: res judicata at the national level

The theory, which we do not spontaneously think of all the time, is that of filing a case before the ECOWAS Court whereas the national judge, before whom the *same* case is filed, has already determined the matter brought before him. In other words, the same case is lodged before the national judge and before the ECOWAS Court. In such instance, we will be dealing with an "objection on grounds of res judicata", which may be defined as "a foreclosure (estoppel), by which means an applicant pleads, as a ground for inadmissibility, the force of a previously decided case, which, where confirmed to be so, compels the judge to declare inadmissible the request of the opposing party".[78]

Such situation, which may once again appear to be strange, has occurred at least twice before the Court in Abuja. Naturally, the Court invoked a sort of objection on grounds of res judicata, in refusing to adjudicate on the case. In such conditions, the Application was declared

---

[78] J SALMON (dir.), *Dictionnaire de droit international public,* Bruxelles, Bruylant, 2001, p 170.

inadmissible. The principle thus applied does not feature anywhere in the texts governing the Court, but no one will fathom contesting its application, if for nothing at all, by virtue of the rule which demands that a case shall not be tried twice (*non bis in idem*).

Every other solution would obviously culminate in the absurd outcome that an applicant may be compensated twice in reparation for the harm done him. It is in vain – we shall see that later – for us to object that the absence of the rule of exhaustion of local remedies, in force before the Court, "disconnects", somewhat, the suit at the national level from trial proceedings at the international level, and explains or even gives weight to that overlap in the procedures. For reasons of simple logic, reproducing before the international judge a trial which has been concluded at the national level cannot be justified. The Court expressed that reasoning in its judgment on *Aliyu Tasheku* **v.** *Republic of Nigeria*, delivered on 12 June 2012. The Court reacted thus:

> "The Court notes that from the exhibits filed in the case-file by Counsel to the Federal Republic of Nigeria, notably with reference to the Judgment of 19 May 2011 cited above, it can be observed that the reliefs sought by the Applicant were granted when the High Court judge (…) ordered that the Nigeria Police authorities must send Mr. Aliyu Tasheku before the High Court on 23 May 2011 at 2 p.m. and granted him a compensation of Five Million Naira (N5,000,000) for unlawful detention (…) The Court cannot retry a case on which a judgment of the domestic court of a Member State has already been delivered and against which no consideration has been raised. Consequently, the Court declares that the Application brought by Mr. Aliyu Tasheku is inadmissible." [79]

Again, it the case law of *Sa'Adatu Umar* **v.** *Federal Republic of Nigeria*, dated 14 December 2012, which declares that the facts brought before the ECOWAS Court "*are essentially the same*" as those tried by the Federal High Court of Abuja. The Court:

> "On these grounds, declares that the instant case is essentially the same as the one that was earlier adjudicated upon in the Nigerian Court; Consequently, the Court declares that there is no need to consider the case brought before it by Sa'Adatu Umar on its merit…"[80].

Finally, in a minor form – thus described because in the context at stake, the Court does not exclude the possibility of returning to consider

---

[79] §§ 11 and 19 of the Judgment

[80] Judgment No. ECW/CCJ/JUD/17/12, §§19 and 22 of the Judgment

the same matter in the future – the ECOWAS judge may consider that a case having been initially lodged with a national judge may render it "premature" for the ECOWAS Court to entertain that same case. Thus, in *Aziagbede Kokou and 33 Others* **v.** *Republic of Togo* (Judgment of 3 July 2013), the Court, upon reckoning with the stage the procedure had reached at the national level, decided that:

> "(...) the application (...) is premature; and that it is ripe and appropriate therefore to declare that the allegations and requests made thereto are inadmissible as things stand, since the procedures are still pending before the domestic courts."[81]

What is interesting in the three case laws is that the remedies given by the judge do not repose, per se, on any particular precise text. They result from an imperative which is grounded on common sense, they are solutions founded on logic only, but remain, for us, irrefutable. The force of common sense may even at times seem to go contrary to the text. In the last case cited, it is certain that a dogmatic understanding of the rule of exhaustion of local remedies could lead the judge to adjudicate immediately on the case, but the Court preferred to "measure the time", and wait for the outcome of the trial pending before the national courts. It is not excluded that in certain cases, the ECOWAS judge takes hold of cases whose procedural developments are not completed, but in that instance, the patience exercised by the Court is justified by a major fact, which should be the Ariadne's Thread of the attitude of the Court: to avoid a situation where the trial of the two cases would result in the same court orders or the same reliefs granted, since they are based on the same requests or seek the same ends. It is therefore a pragmatic, teleological criterion, of a utilitarian bent, founded on the avoidance of superfluous or superimposed reparations, which must guide the judge confronted with a trial still pending at the national courts. If the risk is averted, one cannot rule out the possibility of the ECOWAS Court accepting, without waiting, to adjudicate on the case, and thus set forth a strict concept of the rule of non-exhaustion of local remedies[82]. Everything therefore

---

[81] Judgment cited above, §42

[82] For illustration, one can cite the well-known judgment on *Hadijatou M. Koraou* **v.** *Republic of Niger* (27 October 2008), in which, in a contrary sense, the Court held, in adjudicating on the case, that the fact that the domestic courts had been seised with the case shall have no influence on the jurisdiction of the Court, by virtue of the non-relevance of the rule of exhaustion of local remedies (§§48 and 49). Indeed, what was at stake in the two proceedings was not the same: whereas it was a matter of the applicant seeking civil and criminal sanctions at the domestic level, what was at stake before the ECOWAS Court was

depends on points of fact, the facts of the situation, on logic, in the final analysis.

Objection on grounds of res judicata at the national level is therefore an initial mode of the consideration of the domestic law, of the procedure at the national level. That takes place therefore at the processing stage of the case. From the point of view of substance, the domestic law of the country is given consideration on another platform, which it shall now be appropriate to take a look at.

B.- The dimension on substance: the national law, the barometer for measuring the alleged violations

When the national law confers a right and the right in question is a subject of controversy before the ECOWAS Court, it is inevitable that the Community judge takes a close look at the legal apparatus of such right, which is a domestic apparatus.

This becomes all the more perceptible in cases where the national criminal procedure is in question. It is naturally the case, without exception, that to properly assess the realities of the situation of a person who may have been placed under custody or arrest, or who may have been subjected to a search, to properly assess how an investigating judge employed his powers, the first reflex of the Court, often oriented towards the right direction by the litigant, is that of referring to the relevant provisions of the domestic law.

In *Baldini Salfo* **v.** *Burkina Faso* for example (Judgment of 31 October 2012), the ECOWAS Court expressly cites Article 75 of the Code of Criminal Procedure, just as it makes reference to Law No. 017-2009 of 5 May 2009 on Elimination of Bandits. After indicating indeed, that it appreciates the circumstances in regard to the criminal law of Burkina Faso[83], the Court arrives at the conclusion that the period within which the Applicant was kept in custody exceeded the time-limit of ten days, and even fifteen days, in case of extension, **in violation of Article 5 of the law cited above.** [84].

---

of a more solemn nature, the Court was not only questioning the Republic of Niger and certain cultural practices, but also touching on international norms of an imperatively higher order (like the prohibition of the practice of "slavery" and "servitude"). Hence, one could understand that the ECOWAS judge "sets apart" the two trial proceedings.

83 Judgment No. ECW/CCJ/JUD/13/12, §24

84 §25. Emphasis ours, here in the notes which follow

It is also by reference to the Nigerian criminal procedure that the Court settled the case concerning *Djot Bayi Talbia and 14 Others* **v.** *Federal Republic of Nigeria* (Judgment of 28 January 2009). As the issue of the legality of the duration of detention arose, and in an abundantly clear manner, the ECOWAS Court relied on the national law as applied by the various Nigerian judges:

> "(…) the Court is of the opinion that on the 1st of March 2004, when the Applicants were presented before the trial judge who ordered the release of five (5) among them, it was not unlawful ; but (…) the Court is of the opinion that the prosecution of the ten (10) others and their continued detention till 30th November 2005, is not justified. However, such was the case as seen by **the Federal High Court of Nigeria in her decision of 30th November 2005, which declared that the Nigerian Court does not have jurisdiction** …".

Hence, maintaining the ten Applicants in detention constituted arbitrary detention "*from March 2004 to 30 November 2005.*"[85]

In the judgment of 8 February 2011 on *Sidi Amar Ibrahim and Others* **v.** *Republic of Niger*, the Court equally refers to the provisions of the Niger Criminal Law (more precisely to Articles 80, 32(2) and 41(2) of the Martial Code), in arriving at the conclusion that it is that particular martial code which should have been applied, given the nature of the facts of events in the course of which the successors died (military personnel in active service). Moreover, Articles 46 and 47 of the same Code provide that it is the responsibility of the Minister of Defence and the military authorities to lodge the matter with the competent military courts, and that regardless of that rule, they did not react to the requests for lodgment of the case as addressed to them by the Applicants who were before the ECOWAS Court. The judge concludes thereby that such negligence on the part of the authorities of the Republic of Niger amounts to violation of the Applicant's right to effective remedy **before the competent national courts of the Republic of Niger**.[86].

Finally, in the case concerning *Pascal Bodjona* **v.** *Republic of Togo*, determined on 24 April 2015, the Court held that among the "*rights infringed upon*"[87], the Applicant justifiably pleaded that he was kept in custody for eleven (11) days. That period of time is weighed directly on

---

85 Judgment No. ECW/CCJ/JUD/01/09, §35 and §36.

86 Judgment No. ECW/CCJ/JUD/02/11, §45.

87 §39.

the scales of the provisions of Togo's Code of Criminal Procedure, since, for the Court:

> "This fact (...) could only have been possible upon authorisation to that effect by the State judicial authorities. **Indeed, in the terms of the provisions of the Code of Criminal Procedure of Togo**, the time-limit for keeping a suspect in police custody, which is forty eight (48) hours, shall not be extended unless upon authorisation by the Procureur de la République (Public Prosecutor) – Article 52 of the said Code. One cannot however find any trace of such authorisation in the pleadings of the case filed before the Court."[88]

Many more of such examples could be cited.[89]. They attest to the fact that the facts of the domestic judicial processes of a dispute cannot be systematically set aside by the Community judge. It indeed frequently occurs that the violation of a right finds its source in the very disregard of a provision of the domestic law, which then becomes the actual barometer for measuring the incriminating act. In an attitude which, in the final analysis, has something to do with a form of homage to the national law or national judge, the Court therefore asks the State to look at itself in the mirror of its own law, which the Court then positions in front of the State, so to speak. Violation of the national law thus entails violation the international law: in disregarding the domestic provisions on custody, inquiry and detention, the State – which is now held blameable for the offences of its judicial bodies – transgresses the relevant rules of the international conventions which prohibit arbitrariness; the national law becomes, we need to state it once again, the yardstick and standard for the international law. This can be expressed in another way: the rule at the domestic level is automatically affected in its status by a presumption that it has to conform to the international standard, which implies that taking liberties with the rule of the domestic law constitutes a departure from the international standard.

---

[88] Judgment No. ECW/CCJ/JUD/06/15, §40.

[89] See, among others, Judgment of 31 January 2014 on *Georges Amoussou Constant* **v.** *Republic of Benin*; Judgment of 17 May 2016 on *Farimata Mahamadou and Others* **v.** *Republic of Mali*; Judgment of 10 October 2016 on *Godswill Tommy Udoh* **v.** *Federal Republic of Nigeria*. Similarly, at least on three occasions, the Court made a pronouncement in relying on a declaration of no offence by the domestic courts, and thereby concluded that a detention had been arbitrary See *Mamadou Baba Diawara* **v.** *Etat du Mali* (Judgment of 23 October 2015); *Col. Mouhammed Sambo Dasuki* **v.** *Nigeria* (Judgment of 4 October 2016) and *Maître Djelou Kodjovi and Others* **v.** *Republic of Togo* (Judgment of 6 October 2015).

Certainly, the presumption we have just made is not always necessarily confirmed, but in the absence of an applicable international rule in the given circumstances, in the absence of a comprehensive outline of the international criteria for the "appropriate" rule, one will consider, as a form of optimistic postulate, that State legislations must be in keeping with international requirements. Incidentally, this general attitude also has the advantage of realism and courtesy[90] : in showing the State that it is first of all its own domestic rule that it has disregarded, it then becomes easier to get the State to understand and to accept that it has equally departed from an international norm. Such departure will therefore not appear to have broken out like a thunderstorm in a serene sky, suddenly destabilising a calm and unruffled domestic order. Furthermore, we need not forget that the inverse logic, still more gratifying for the Defendant State, which the ECOWAS Court of Justice has also had occasion to apply: if, contrary to the scenario just painted, the rules of the domestic law have simply been applied, the Applicant's case shall not only be dismissed, and a declaration made thereby, that no offence has been committed, but more essentially, it shall be held that the domestic law was consistent with international requirements – even if, there again, we will only be making a presumption far from being established, that is to say, incontrovertible.

Without going to the extent of describing it as "hydra" or claiming that it haunts the proceedings before the Court, we see that the national law intrudes, through diverse pathways, not only unto a trial proceeding which remains international, but also before a court, one of whose most established dogmas is all the same the principle of setting aside the domestic law. In using the word "dogma", as we have, we immediately get the impression, after reading the foregoing lines, that the term may be undue. Indeed, by necessity and by logic, the Community Court is virtually destined to return, through particular instances, to the law of the Member States: either that the law at stake may already been have stated by the State organs – in the same requests coming before the Court – or else, it is the domestic law which sets out the right or freedom insisted upon and obtained; the national law thus becomes the inevitable standard for the international judge.

March 2016

---

90 Concerning courtesy among judges, See Article *infra, The ECOWAS Court of Justice and the other legal orders or the dialogue of judges as seen from Abuja: some general reflections*

THE ROLE OF THE JUDGE IN DISPUTES ON HUMAN RIGHTS VIOLATION : THE ECOWAS COURT OF JUSTICE BETWEEN ACTIVISM AND SELF-RESTRAINT

The subject-matter of activism[91] and self-restraint of the judge, as to *audacity* for the interpretation of the law, or as to *self-restraint*, are classical issues in judicial literature. Some years after the setting up of the ECOWAS Court, and after the delivery of close to 86 decisions made[92] since it began functioning – judgments essentially delivered on disputes regarding human rights violation – it would be interesting to examine the jurisprudence of West Africa closely along the lines of the role played by the Community judge. Revolutionary in many respects – direct access to the Court for individuals, non-observation of the rule of exhaustion of local remedies, an extremely wide spectrum of legal instruments capable of being invoked – the mechanism for the judicial protection of human rights at ECOWAS must however operate alongside constraints of various kinds, and if the points of originality which we have just mentioned are unquestionably of such nature as to urge the judge to consider his function under a dynamic and ambitious light, other factors exist, which are equally significant to consider – the relatively young nature of the system of protection put in place, a virtually non-existent ideal mechanism for enforcing the decisions made, and, it must be admitted, a wobbling culture of the rule of law – which could hinder the efficacy of the judicial safeguard of human rights.

It is these conflicting trends that we intend to focus on here, on the swing between activism and self-restraint, between audacity and timidity. More precisely, we shall be concerned with certain manifestations of such tension at the heart of the work of the ECOWAS Court of Justice. The approach adopted will thus be simple: we are going

---

[91] The word "activism" may be overlaid with a negative connotation in French, which matter has of course no place in our discussion here. The English expression "*judicial activism*", less marked by value judgments, would certainly be more appropriate.

[92] Statistical figure obtained in July 2017.

to consider in turns **(I)** the activist dimension and **(II)** the motives and workings of self-restraint.

I.- The activist dimension

Two choice areas of the Court's audacity of interpretation of the law, very distinct when one considers the jurisprudence of the Court, are instantly identified. They concern (A) the conditions under which the Court establishes its jurisdiction and (B) the ease with which the Court sets aside arguments raised on the judicial incompetence of the Court purportedly arising from the "nature" or probable peculiarities of certain cases submitted before it. In both instances, the attitude of the Court leads directly to establishing its capacity to adjudicate on the case brought.

A.- In upholding the jurisdiction of the Court

The jurisdiction of the ECOWAS Court of Justice for adjudicating on human rights violation is facilitated by two factors. The first is the extreme abundance of legal instruments that may be invoked against States sued before the Court, and the second is to be found in the judicial reasoning itself, which virtually consists of the presumption of that jurisdiction, by alleging, under conditions sometimes debatable, the burden of proof – proof of competence, which lies with the Applicant.

Regarding the first point, it is appropriate indeed to recall that the Court is right away recognised as competent to examine all violations invoked on the basis of any legal instrument which the Defendant State is party to. We have already made mention of the problems posed in taking such a stand. Not equipped with its own legal instrument of reference, unlike other human rights protection systems, the Community Court thus gets into processes in which it was not originally mandated to enter into. The Court therefore applies texts conceived outside its parent organisation, and for which, above all, special supervisory organs have already been instituted. The Court may thus sanction violation of the 1966 International Covenant on Civil and Political Rights, whereas there exists for the said text an ad-hoc body, the United Nations Committee on Human Rights. Similarly, the Court may make decisions against a disregard for the African Charter on Human and Political Rights, whereas there is the Commission, and the African Court on Human and Peoples' Rights, organs officially put in place to see to the respect of that international treaty.

The resultant effect is that the texts the Court could refer to in cases brought against the States are extremely numerous, the latter having signed and ratified a highly significant number of legal instruments. Indeed, this issue has not posed, as at now, any particular problems. We will however point out two points which the Community judge will need to pay special attention to.

One first of all needs to verify the instrument by which the Defendant State expresses its consent to be bound. Very often, the applicants before the Court omit to mention such unilateral commitment, simply contenting themselves with citing the international instrument of reference, especially when the instrument of reference has been concluded within the UN system and therefore is of universal applicability. This trend can equally be observed when the applicant bases his request on the African Charter on Human and Peoples' Rights. The applicant does not take the trouble to indicate the instrument by which the State is bound, and one is made to assume that the universal recognition accorded an international convention virtually implies that it could be invoked universally against any State. Whereas, it is always necessary that the applicant who pleads an international text produces the evidence that the text in question actually binds the State he is suing. The text could be an instrument of ratification, or a mere signature by the State, if the State intends by its signature, a simplified form of agreement, even a provisional commitment. In the current practice of the applicants, that minimal step of guarantee is not always taken, and it is undoubtedly appropriate that the Community judge reminds the parties of this, we mean the applicant, especially.

The second point, which calls for sustained vigilance, may appear to be a matter of truism, but we need to make mention of it all the same. Indeed, no matter how well known a text may be, and no matter how developed the *référencements croisés*[93] and the comparative case-law may be – striking features of dialogue among judges[94] – the Court must always be cautious not to fall prey to the charm and seduction of following the trend, for the good and simple reason that the texts of

---

[93] The expression is borrowed from HENNEBEL L., meaning "Cross-references among international human rights courts", in *Dialogue Among Judges,* proceedings of symposium organised on 28 April 2006 at l'Université libre de Bruxelles, Bruxelles, Bruylant 2007, pp. 31 and others.

[94] On dialogue among judges, see. *infra* our article entitled: "The ECOWAS Court of Justice and the other judicial orders or the dialogue of judges seen from Abuja : some general reflections"

reference of the other international courts may well not be relevant before the ECOWAS Court, because the State sued before the ECOWAS Court may not be bound by a particular text. It goes without saying that the European Convention for the Protection of Human Rights and Fundamental Freedoms, or the Inter-American Convention are not binding on the Member States of ECOWAS. That means that if there must be "dialogue", if the West African judge may be guided by solutions proffered under other jurisdictions, such dialogue shall not but remain within the context where the disputed law is stipulated concomitantly by a legal instrument which binds the State sued before court.

On the other hand, the very reasoning adopted by the Court when it came to the issue to establishing another aspect of its jurisdiction, demonstrates another extensive conception of its powers, and certainly constitutes an activist approach. Indeed, almost ritually, the Court holds that a mere "allegation" of human rights violation committed by a Member State suffices to establish the jurisdiction of the Court.

Thus, the Court declares in the judgment on *Mamadou Tandja* **v.** *Republic of Niger*, dated 8 November 2010 that:

> "(…) The mere invocation of the violations over which the Court has jurisdiction only suffices for the Court to establish its jurisdiction (…)"[95]. Then in the case law on El Hadji Tidjani Aboubacar **v.** Republic of Niger, 8 February 2011: "The Court finds that for an application to be admissible, in matters of human rights, the mere citing of the facts connected with such description suffices to confer competence on it. That this view is consistent with its case law; that Mr. Tidjani Aboubacar, in accusing the Republic of Niger of having violated his rights, in violation of Articles 17 and 14 respectively of the Universal Declaration of Human Rights and the African Charter of Human and Peoples' Rights, enshrined as right to property and economic and social rights, comes under the jurisdiction of the Court." The Court further holds that the issues in dispute came about on the territory of the Republic of Niger, "… an ECOWAS Member State."[96].

Furthermore, it is the judgment on *Ameganvi M. Isabelle and Others* **v.** *Republic of Togo* of 7 October 2011 which re-echoes that activist approach. As to the admissibility of the application, it is adjudged that the Applicants citing violation of their rights by the Republic of Togo, a

---

95 Judgment No. ECW/CCJ/JUD/03/10, §18 1 (b).

96 Judgment No. ECW/CCJ/JUD/01/11, § 25.

Member State of ECOWAS, on the basis of Articles 9(4) and 10 Supplementary Protocol A/SP.1/01/05 on the Court, largely suffices to declare the application admissible.[97] Finally, in the case concerning *Cheikh Abdoulaye Mbengue* **v.** *Republic of Mali* (judgment equally delivered on 7 October 2011):

> "In his Application, Mr. Cheick Abdoulaye Mbengue makes mention of human rights violations allegedly committed against him on the territory of a Member State of ECOWAS, namely the Republic of Mali. Based on that observation, the Court states that since Article 9(4) of the Supplementary Protocol confers jurisdiction on the Court in matters of concerning human rights and in instances of human rights violation in every Member State of ECOWAS, that power must be applied. The Court deduces thereby that the Application filed by Mr. Cheick Abdoulaye Mbengue (...) is admissible."[98]

One could indeed cite several examples of that nature.[99]. What results from that, is the "ease" with which the Court establishes its jurisdiction. The terms used amply give proof to that: the Court talks of "allegations" or "citing" of human rights violations by the applicant, from which the Court follows up almost automatically, with the declaration of its competence to adjudicate on the case.

This judicial reasoning, which proceeds from an activist standpoint, inspired by an extensive conception of the powers of the judge, calls for three remarks at least, in the form of reservations.

First of all, one can note a form of wavering in the use of terminology, the Court referring now and then to "jurisdiction", and then to "admissibility", concepts which are obviously different from each other. Whereas, it is rather, in our opinion, a question of jurisdiction, since issues relating to admissibility in matters of human rights violation, according to Article 9 of the Supplementary Protocol itself, are limited to only two points: the non-anonymity of the application and the absence of *lis pendens* before another International Court. The Court should therefore, within the context we are interested in, talk of jurisdiction and not admissibility.

---

[97] Judgment No. ECW/CCJ/JUD/09/11, §49.

[98] Judgment No. ECW/CCJ/JUD/08/11, §§26 and 27.

[99] See again Judgment No. ECW/CCJ/JUD/02/11 of 8 February 2011, *Sidi Amar Ibrahim and Others* **v.** *Republic of Niger* § 30 or Judgment No. ECW/CCJ/JUD/03/11 of 17 March 2011, *Bakary Sarré and 28 Others* **v.** *Republic of Mali* (§§34 and 35).

The second reservation arising from the terms employed by the Court concern the appellation *ratione loci* jurisdiction, the judge carefully indicating that the alleged violation occurred on the territory of a Member State of ECOWAS. Truly, such linguistic precaution is prescribed by the very text of Article 9§4 of the Supplementary Protocol, since the text itself clearly provides that the Court has jurisdiction "to determine cases of violation of human rights that occur in any Member State". But one must then agree that the last portion of the phrase – "*in any Member State*"– if understood literally, could lead to an absurd and shocking situation where the Court would decline jurisdiction to adjudicate on a human rights violation committed by a State against a Community citizen for the reason that the transgression did not take place on the territory of a Member State. Now, such a scenario shall be in regard to the actor – the Member State – and of course, the binding nature of the text invoked against the State. The place the violation was committed is not a determining factor. The text seems to establish a sort of equation between the Defendant State and the fact that the violation took place on its own territory. But, not only could the place of commission of such violation be the territory of a Member State, but may as well be outside the West African space.

One can imagine for instance that a violation can be committed by the military personnel of a Member State against a citizen of another Member State – or even of the same State whose military personnel are citizens of that State – but on the soil of Europe or Asia. In that case, it would appeal to reason for the victim to lodge his case before the Court without difficulty, but the literal interpretation of the phrase cited above may result in the judge declining competence to adjudicate on the case. We realise therefore that the addition of the spatial or territorial criterion can lead to absurd results. Let us add, in ending, that not only is the said criterion not relevant, but that of the nationality *per se* of the victim is not: we know, in that sense, and without doubt, that the Court admits that victims who are non-citizens of a Member State are entitled to lodge their case before the Court[100]. In a word, in disputes on human rights violations, the only determining factor is the inclusion of the State sued among the Member States of ECOWAS – it is that inclusion which grants it the status of a litigant before the Court. Every other consideration

[100] See our article on "Access to the ECOWAS Court of Justice in matters of human rights violation: some reflections on the status of the applicant", *supra*, in which the issue of nationality of the applicants is discussed.

would certainly be superfluous and prejudicial to the efficacy of the judicial safeguard of the rights.

The last reservation which gives room for the elliptical justification of the jurisdiction of the Court concerns the actual principle of an approach so expeditious. Indeed, there is a serious problem when the judge declares that the mere allegation of a violation confers jurisdiction on the Court. We stated above[101], that amounts to according the applicant a bewildering amount of powers on two fronts. On one hand, his mere declarations would have the force to commit the Court, so to speak; the Applicant would become a sort of demiurge whose statements would seal the Court's capacity to adjudicate on the case, and he would eventually become more powerful than the judge. That of course would mean conferring unjustified powers on the Applicant; in other words, such powers do not exist, and it must be said that it was by inadvertence that the ECOWAS judge thus founded his powers. On the other hand, in line with the general principles of judicial procedure, it is admitted that a court is always the judge of its jurisdiction; whereas, the assertion repeated above, as made by the Court, simply amounts to jettisoning that fundamental principle.

What remains to be done is that the Court must be confronted with its own contradictions. It has indeed occurred that the judge affirms, at the outset of the adjudication on a case, that the allegation of violation seals its jurisdiction to sit on the case, but further on, admits, at least partially, that he is incompetent to do so. In the case on *El Hadji Tidjani Aboubacar* **v.** *Republic of Niger*, which gave rise to Judgment of 8 February 2011, the Court ended up admitting that it "declines its rationae materiae jurisdiction" (§35), but not long before, it had declared that it was "competent" (§29) to adjudicate upon the case. In the same way, in the case law of *Bakary Sarré and 28 Others* **v.** *Republic of Mali* (Judgment of 17 March 2011), the Court initially reaffirms that it has jurisdiction (§34) but finds itself actually compelled, at the stage of writing its operative statement, to concede, that it has no jurisdiction to adjudicate on aspects of the Application seeking a reversal of the judgments delivered by the Supreme Court of Mali (§41). The result is that the standard formula by which, for a long time, the Court established its jurisdiction, was somewhat an unfortunate one. The ECOWAS judge meant to say less than that. He simply intended to indicate that once

---

[101] See first part of our work, devoted to the central planks of the case law, particularly as it pertains to how the Court establishes its jurisdiction.

human rights violation is alleged, it is his duty to examine the complaint, and that to bring such grievance before him, an applicant shall not be subjected to any further evidentiary requirements at that stage. But it must indeed be admitted: that kind of assertion, which the Court had the habit of making, does not truly serve the purpose intended, and it was absolutely possible to avoid using it entirely. In all instances, it causes more problems – we have borne witness to that – than it may resolve. One must therefore be glad that in its recent case law, the ECOWAS judge has abandoned that course, since we virtually find it nowhere anymore in the decisions made by the Court. That particular manifestation of judicial activism shall henceforth be set aside. The Court therefore quickly needs to take a foothold on another ground, in upholding its jurisdiction, which we shall now turn our attention to.

B.- In rejecting the theory of rationae materiae incompetence

The Court does not succumb, either, to any possibly peculiar features which may characterise a case submitted. The point is clear and simple. It does occur that a State sued before the Court contests the jurisdiction of the Court on the ground that the matter presents a certain peculiarity; that the case is of a specific nature, by virtue of which the Court will have to declare that it lacks jurisdiction to adjudicate on the matter brought. With remarkable consistency, the Court dismisses every claim that it lacks jurisdiction on the basis of the extraordinary nature – in the proper sense of the word – of the matter to be settled. In more precise terms, the Court's firm stand against any form of objecting criteria manifests itself in two ways: by refusing to exclude certain "subject matters" from coming before the Court, and by the will to include certain rights, notably, economic and social rights. In both instances, it is of course the power of the judge which emerges as reinforced.

The most noticeable attempts at putting curbs on the powers of the Court have occurred in instances where disputes are submitted as portraying predominantly "political" features. On several occasions, the claim that such disputes are not triable before the Court has more or less been canvassed, but always dismissed.

In the case concerning *Mamadou Tandja* **v.** *Republic of Niger* (Judgment of 8 November 2010), the judge refuses to put a restriction on his powers, for the reason that the relevant text does not in any way differentiate between various types of disputes on human rights. The Community judge therefore had no business, he thought, to consider the argument of the Defendant State, according to which the detention of Mamadou Tandja was justified by the political nature of the case[102]. In *Barthélémy Dias* **v.** *Republic of Senegal* (Judgment of 12 March 2012)[103] and *Mamadou Baba Diawara* **v.** *Republic of Mali* (Judgment of 23 October 2015)[104], the Court systematically refused to take account of declarations made by politicians regarding the two proceedings. Similarly, the argument regarding *exceptional circumstances*, as justification for rights violation, was set aside (Judgment of 22 February 2013, *Simone Ehivet and Michel Gbagbo* **v.** *Republic of Côte d'Ivoire*)[105]. But it is in the case laws on *Convention Démocratique et Sociale Rahama* **v.** *Republic of Niger* (Judgment of 23 April 2015)[106], *Pascal A. Bodjona* **v.** *Republic of Togo* (Judgment of 24 April 2015)[107] and *Hama Amadou* **v.** *Republic of Niger* (Judgment of 1 July 2016)[108] that the Court undoubtedly dwelt much further on the doctrine regarding that issue.

In the first case, the Court held thus:

> "It can equally be found in the application for expedited procedure, and in the request for stay of execution of judgment, as filed by CDS Rahama, references to allegations of a predominantly political trial of the case. One thus reads in application for expedited procedure, that: "...in order to reward these anti-party activities against CDS Rahama, some were appointed Ministers and Advisers in the Government for a job well

[102] Judgment No. ECW/CCJ/JUD/05/10, §17.1(b).

[103] Judgment No. ECW/CCJ/JUD/05/12.

[104] Judgment No. ECW/CCJ/JUD/22/15.

[105] Judgment No. ECW/CCJ/JUD/03/13.

[106] Judgment No. ECW/CCJ/JUD/03/15.

[107] Judgment No. ECW/CCJ/JUD/06/15.

[108] Judgment No. ECW/CCJ/JUD/21/16.

done." (Page 1 of French version), and in the request for stay of execution, that: "...there is urgency, danger and very serious risk of malfunction of the Party" (Page 2 of the French version).

In its written pleadings, CDS Rahama equally invokes, in support of its claim of unfair trial and impartiality of the State judiciary, that the Chairman of the Superior Council of Judicature postponed the promotion of two (2) judges of the Court on grounds of "... questionable moral character...". It finally avers that the judge rapporteur of the first decision of the appeal proceedings was "... relieved of his duties and transferred to the Ministry of Justice to carry out administrative duties."

The Court is well aware that once it is seised with a matter from a political body, the case will necessarily depict a political landscape. The Court shall however recall, as it has done in other decisions, that the political intents or declarations of one party or the other have no relevance to its legal mandate. More precisely, its mandate, in regard to disputes on human rights violation, is limited to examining, in reality and in concrete terms, whether there is violation of a well-defined right, and the Court does not unnecessarily entangle itself with political motives and statements.

In other words, the mandate and actions of the Court shall not in any way whatsoever be questioned by the fact that a political party, CDS Rahama, has filed a case before it, or by the fact that the judgment of the Court may have objective consequences on the political scene of the Republic of Niger. The Court shall not seek to derive any consequences whatsoever from the very fact that the exercise of its mandate in connection with the instant case could have repercussions on the political or electoral scene.

As a result, the Court shall not entertain the considerations made by CDS Rahama in this instance; and as well, those considerations cannot be entertained by the Court for the purposes of finding out whether human rights violations have been committed or not." (§34, 35, 37, 38, 39).

Then in the case concerning Pascal A. Bodjona **v.** Republic of Togo: "... the Court must first of all recall its own framework of analysis, so as to set aside, first and foremost, a number of considerations either alluded to or raised by the Parties.

In that regard, one may first of all refer to certain political considerations, like the reasons why Mr. Bodjona was removed from the Government of Togo following the reshuffle carried out on 31 July 2012. The Applicant wrote that the dismissal was decided upon "... with the sole aim of circumventing Article 422 of the Code of Criminal Procedure of Togo and the enforcement Judgment No. 48/12 of the Supreme Court...." (Page 4 of the Application in French). Further on, one reads that "... in truth, the Hounourable Minister Bodjona Akoussoulélou Pascal is simply being persecuted for unexpressed political reasons ..." (Page 38 of the Application in French). Finally, the Applicant makes mention of "... loss of opportunity", in terms of harms suffered by him, by virtue of the fact that "... he was destined for a long and brilliant political career, seriously compromised today... " (Page 25 of the Application in French).

There shall be no ground for the Court to be drawn into conducting its analysis upon such a political terrain. The Court shall reaffirm its view, as corroborated by its well established case law, that it shall not examine in any manner whatsoever, the political considerations or allusions contained in the pleadings brought before the Court, and that its mandate is simply to find, upon factual grounds, whether there have been occurrences of violation of the rights of the applicants coming before the Court. Consequently, the Court shall not countenance in the instant proceedings any of the purely political points raised by Mr. Bodjona in his Application." (§34-36).

Finally in *Case Concerning Hama Amadou* **v.** *Republic of Niger*, it is first of all claimed that the rationale behind proceedings instituted against Mr. Hama Amadou can be found in the internal politics of Niger.

The Court has however always put aside the political factor. As a judicial institution mandated to handle only the legal aspects of the cases it examines, even if it ignores neither the context nor the possible political after-effects of such cases, the Court has always refused to see in such political aspects a decisive factor in the exercise of its jurisdiction (...). It is certainly always regrettable that statements made by political authorities may give the impression that politicians are interfering in the judicial procedure. But the Court must recall that any time such arguments have been brandished before it, it has always responded that political considerations do not obstruct the principle of its jurisdiction, nor its traditional methodological approach (pp. 6 and 7 of French version).

Just as the Court does not allow itself to be influenced by theory of the "political" nature of a dispute, it equally does not admit submissions made before it on grounds of the "military" or "top security" nature of the case. The Court dismissed that stand in *Alimu Akeem* **v.** *Federal*

Republic of Nigeria (Judgment of 28 January 2014)[109] and especially in *Djibril Yipéné Bassolé* **v.** *Burkina Faso* (Judgment of 1 July 2016)[110]. In the latter decision, the Court recalls that:

> "It is (…) erroneous for Burkina Faso to invoke the exceptional nature of the political context which prevailed at that material time, as a ground for justifying the acts it engaged in." (p. 12 of the English version).

In refusing to bow to a claim that it has no *rationae materiae* jurisdiction, the ECOWAS Court of Justice affirms its competence and asserts its powers. The Court equally does so when it considers that it could validly adjudicate on economic and social rights, whose justiciable nature is indeed more difficult. Indeed, those rights equally known as "second generation rights" can be distinguished from "rights as freedoms", those of "the first generation" – in the sense that their fulfilment does not imply the State abstaining from an act, but on the contrary, taking an action. Now, a judge will be much more inclined to consider that a matter before the Court has been settled in an instance where he has ordered public authorities to refrain from impeding the exercise of a freedom, than in the situation where it has to impose such freedoms to be enjoyed on the State, the accomplishment of an act to be posed, for the purposes of satisfying the enjoyment of that right. Restoring "rights as freedoms" is easier than rendering justice on "rights as entitlements"; asking the public authority to abstain from an act is less laborious than to ask it to engage in an action. Given that it is so, certain litigants may fall into the temptation to portray such difficulty as an impossibility, and argue, before the bench, as to the virtually non-justiciable nature of economic and social rights. The judge himself, without explicitly being called upon by the parties to rule on such matters, may, by reflex, be tempted to throw in the towel, given the uphill task confronting him.

Such however is not the case of the ECOWAS Court of Justice. On all the occasions that violation of the second generation rights has been alleged, the Court has faced the situation squarely and attempted, as far as practicable, to confer a content on such rights.

One of the first disputes touching upon such rights was the case concerning *Etim Moses Essien* **v.** *Republic of Gambia* (Judgment of 29

[109] Judgment No. ECW/CCJ/JUD/01/14.

[110] Judgment No. ECW/CCJ/JUD/22/16.

October 2007)[111]. The issue at stake was the right to fair remuneration. The Court first of all affirms in that case the necessity of remuneration for work done, followed by the necessity of equal pay for equal work. The right to fair wages and salaries was equally invoked in *The National Co-ordinating Group of Departmental Representatives of the Cocoa-Coffee Sector (CNDD)* **v.** *Republic of Côte d'Ivoire* (Judgment of 17 December 2009)[112]. The Applicant relied on Article 23(3) of the Universal Declaration of Human Rights, in the terms of which:

> "Everyone who works has the right to just and favourable remuneration ensuring for himself and his family an existence worthy of human dignity, and supplemented, if necessary, by other means of social protection".

The Court is certainly going to dismiss the claim by the Applicant, for the reason that it is a private producer and conducts its activities entirely autonomously and receives neither salary nor honorarium from any State organ[113], and that there is no employment relationship between the Applicant and the Defendant State such as to establish a salary obligation on the Defendant towards the Applicant; but as to the principle at stake, the Court never doubted its powers to examine human rights violation of that nature, of the nature of rights as settlements.

As regards Judgment of 30 November 2010 on *SERAP* **v.** *Federal Republic of Nigeria*[114], it raised the issue of the observance of the right of access to education by the Defendant State. What was worth noting here was that, on one hand, the ECOWAS judge affirms the legitimacy of claiming such a right before the Court (Ruling of du 27 October 2009) and on the other hand, that on the merits of the case, the Federal Republic of Nigeria had fulfilled its obligation, in as much as it: "has established institutions (…) to take care of the basic education needs of the people of Nigeria (…)"[115]. Finally, in the case law on *Amédéo Adotevi* **v.** *Republic of Benin* of 28 November 2013, the Court, confronted with observance of the right to protection of the aged and handicapped, makes a sketch of the definition of that right. The Court holds that such protection translates into an obligation upon the State to take more favourable measures to

---

[111] Judgment No. ECW/CCJ/JUD/05/07, §24.
[112] Judgment No. ECW/CCJ/JUD/05/09.
[113] Judgment cited above, §49.
[114] Judgment No. ECW/CCJ/JUD/07/10.
[115] Judgment No. ECW/CCJ/JUD/07/10, §19.

facilitate their conditions of work, their absorption into the labour force, access to health care and a more suitable social security scheme[116].

That the Court did not shrink from venturing into the domain of economic and social rights does not of course mean that it found itself as easy-going as when it was handling rights which are freedoms. In classical terms, we would consider that tracing the contours around the violations alleged is more difficult, more problematic. In the decision cited above, of 28 November 2013, the judge finds all the same that the said obligation upon the States shall be determined partly in line with the economic and material resourcefulness of the States, and partly from the actual political will of the States towards the adoption of effective measures to assist those categories of persons.[117] Such judgment, made with a sprinkling of relativism, perfectly illustrates the judicial unease when the dispute concerns economic and social rights.

Beyond that, judicial restraint simply and purely becomes the order of the day. There is indeed a string of instances within which the Court of Justice simply draws away from examining certain aspects of the disputes submitted before it, voluntarily fixing limits for itself, not to be overstepped. After engaging in activism, the Community judge becomes an adept of self-restraint.

II.– Manifestations of self-restraint

Such judicial restraint, which is also a form of goodwill, may manifest towards both (A) the national judge and (B) other international judicial or political authorities.

A.- Respecting the order of jurisdiction at the national level

The consideration of the national law by the Court, both in procedure and in substance, is a point we have at any rate sufficiently deliberated upon.[118] We thus saw that the Community judge refrained from adjudicating once more on case which had already been adjudicated upon at proceedings at the national level, and wherein the Applicants had expressed the same requests as those they had canvassed previously. Similarly, it is at times on the basis of the transgression of the national law itself that the Court concludes that a human right has been violated,

---

[116] Judgment No. ECW/CCJ/JUD/11/13, §45.

[117] Ibid. §46.

[118] See *infra* our article: "National law and the case law of the ECOWAS Court of Justice"

the national law thus becoming, in direct terms, the barometer for determining the violation in question. Besides, in a more general and systematic manner, the Court has unceasingly recalled that it is not a body set up to modify or quash decisions made by the domestic courts of the Member States, nor, at any rate, a judge over the purely legal or illegal aspects of the State's acts. Those were, already, some marks of regard for the judicial and legal systems of the Member States.

Here, we will need to consider another angle of the incidence of the national procedures on the judicial activity of the Court. Truly, the aspect we intend to look at is incarnated in two forms. Now and then, the self-restraint of the Court takes the form of a presumption of truth attached to the decisions of the domestic courts, whereby the ECOWAS Court directly infers consequences by immediately awarding reparation to the victim; or in other instances, in an approach much more in keeping with the idea of self-restraint, the Community judge refuses to extend the scope of his mandate to an area which now appears as an exclusive reserve of the local judge.

The first prototype is brilliantly illustrated by two cases in which the national courts had already concluded that the applicant was innocent, and the second, by trial decisions, notably taken within the framework of criminal proceedings. In numerous cases, the Court has immediately deduced from the declaration of innocence pronounced by the national judge, violation of the right of the victim, which is thus, one can imagine, the right not to be denied one's freedom and not to be detained arbitrarily. It must be admitted: here, the ECOWAS Court goes beyond self-restraint, it ascribes to the domestic judicial acts a presumption of truth, which, it would not be adventurous to describe as incontrovertible, precisely on account of the Court's principled refusal to make any attempt at modifying such judicial acts.

Therefore, in the judgment of 6 October 2015 on *Djelou Kodjovi, Maître Akumani Koffi and Alipui Ablavi* **v.** *Republic of Togo*, the Court notes that the Applicants, arrested and brought before the law courts for forgery and use of forged documents, were acquitted in the first instance proceedings, appealed and discharged upon appeal. The Court concludes without let or hindrance that the detention of the Applicants was arbitrary in nature, and orders that a monetary compensation be awarded them. It is interesting to lay emphasis on the following passage from the judgment:

"(…) the Court recalls that if by principle, the Court has no powers to review the reasoning for a decision made at the level of a Member State of ECOWAS, whereas the Court neither assumes the role of a national judge in a broader sense, nor that of an Appeal Court or a Cassation Court, it nevertheless remains important that it is the responsibility of the Court to derive all the consequences arising from human rights cases brought before it."[119].

In *Mamadou Baba Diawara* **v.** *Republic of Mali* (Judgment of 23 October 2015), the Court, which had been seised with the case since 2013, immediately changed the course of its analysis, once in January 2015, a judgment of the Supreme Court of Mali had exonerated the Applicant. The Court will content itself, in its decision made almost nine months later, with ordering the reparation of the harm done[120]. The Court upheld the same principle in its judgment of 4 October 2016, on *Col. Mohammed Sambo Dasuki (Rtd)* **v.** *Federal Republic of Nigeria*, a case in which the Applicant was arrested for "corruption". However, failing a legal notification of the charges weighing on him, the national courts had ordered his release. The Court, moving in the same direction, concluded that his detention had been arbitrary, and ordered his release. It held, at least implicitly, that it was reverting to the judgment made by the domestic court:

"We are therefore not deciding on the guilty or otherwise of the Applicant on the charges before the National Court and has only assumed jurisdiction based on the facts before it to establish whether the human rights of the Applicant as alleged has been violated"[121].

The second manifestation of the respect for the order of jurisdiction at the national level is closer to the idea of self-restraint. It relates to the contestation of acts of procedure which have been engaged in at the national level, often by an investigating judge. As an opportune principle which takes high precedence over the issuing of measures, the ECOWAS Court thus demonstrates humility and refuses to institute any form of checks whatsoever in such instances. There are therefore portions of the internal procedures which fall outside the scope of powers of the ECOWAS judge.

---

[119] Judgment No. ECW/CCJ/JUD/17/15, § 22.

[120] Judgment No. ECW/CCJ/JUD/22/15, §§28-29.

[121] Judgment No. ECW/CCJ/JUD/23/16, p.23.

It thus occurs that the Community judge generally holds that opinion on such subject matter. The judgment on *Baldini Salfo* **v.** *Burkina Faso*, delivered on 31 October 2012, puts forth the issue almost in terms of principles: the legitimacy of the measures taken and their chances of materialisation are the principles which guide the Court. When examining a case relating to an ongoing judicial procedure in a Member State, the decisions of the Court are not meant to interfere with the decisions the national courts would be required to take. The Court cannot order measures whose implementation would end up weakening or wiping out the authority and independence of the national judge in the prosecution of the cases brought before him[122]. Then in the judgment on *Aziagbede Kokou and 33 Others* **v.** *Republic of Togo* (Judgment of 3 July 2013), the judge declares:

> "As things stand, the Court may not make any finding concerning the criminal nature of the charges brought, or ascribe any blame whatsoever against the Republic of Togo, without unduly interfering in the conduct of the proceedings pending at the national level, and without violating the freedom of the judge at the domestic court. Furthermore, even though the Court is entrusted with the duty to establish the facts, the Court is nevertheless of the view that for it to set that mandate in motion, consideration must be given to the pragmatic approach whereby appropriate importance is accorded to the proximity between the charges made and the judge at the domestic court, just as the same importance must be given to the prerogatives of the judge at the domestic court.
>
> The Court finds that it is not within its human rights protection mandate to substitute its own viewpoint on the facts of a case for that of the domestic courts seised with the same case, in terms of determining the authenticity of certain exhibits pleaded in relation to charges of a criminal nature. The issue would have been completely different if the question before the Court were to be limited to determining the fairness of the entire procedure which may have been employed at the national level"[123].

These declarations needed to be quoted at length, in as much as they establish a certain doctrine of judicial self-restraint in a way that cannot be contested. Aside highlighting the idea that the mandate for engaging

---

[122] Judgment No. ECW/CCJ/JUD/13/12, § 59.

[123] Judgment No. ECW/CCJ/JUD/07/13, §§38 to 40

in the judicial process devolves rather upon the national judge, these assertions could undoubtedly be reiterated in an instance which can be theoretically daunting for the Court, as made perfectly plausible by the texts: a situation where the national judge could be seised simultaneously as the Community judge, well aware that the rule of exhaustion of local remedies does not apply in proceedings before the Court.

If it turns out therefore that the Court is to handle a case that is absolutely the same as that before the national judge, with the same parties and the same requests, one can without doubt thus expect the ECOWAS Court to abstain from adjudicating on the case, at least on a provisional basis.

We need to recall that the Court has had occasion to label an application as *premature*[124]. Again, let us remember, on a more general note, that an act of jurisdiction always remains within a particular context and that by virtue of the powers vested in him, and by the very propriety of his *juris-dictio*, a judge may consider that the particular forum where he is mandated to make court decisions may not, for a given time, be the desirable or urgent forum for doing so, and in considering, for example, the risks he may be running concerning the authority or credibility of any pronouncements he may make at that given time.

A much more careful look at the case law of the Court shows that the choice area for the doctrine of the *self-restraint* of the Community judge is where measures are to be taken in connection with a court trial at the national level. In the judgment of 7 October 2011 on *Cheikh Abdoulaye Mbengue* **v.** *Republic of Mali*, the Court:

> "... observes that the requests to re-open the judicial inquiry and annul the arrest warrant derive from the sphere of the domestic judicial competence of the Republic of Mali, and that in that respect, the Court recalls its consistently held case law and declines jurisdiction on any application brought seeking to overturn decisions of the domestic courts of ECOWAS Member States ; this Honourable Court is neither an appeal court nor a court of cassation of the of the domestic courts of the ECOWAS Member States (...). Consequently, the Court dismisses all those requests as inappropriate and unjustified"[125].

In the same vein, the judgment on *El Hadji Mame Abdou Gaye* **v.** *Republic du Senegal* of 26 January 2012 enables the Court to remark that it is not within its power to examine, for and on behalf of the national judge, the nature and scope of the guarantees to be provided for a detainee. The Court reiterates that it is the duty of the judge handling the case to assess the relevant factors and to admit or not the guarantee of representation, and, eventually, grant or refuse the provisional release[126]. Finally, in the case concerning *Barthélémy Dias* **v.** *Republic of Senegal*

[124] *Ibid.*

[125] Judgment No. ECW/CCJ/JUD/ 08/11, §38.

[126] Judgment No. ECW/CCJ/JUD/03/12, §44.

(Judgment of 23 March 2012), regarding refusal by the national judge to take account of the guarantees for representation of the Applicant, the Court recalls that all the concepts being dealt with referred to the facts of the case as they related to natural persons accused of an offence, and as a result, came exclusively under the jurisdiction of the domestic courts, and not within the powers of a Community Court seised with a case on human rights violation brought against a Member State of the Community.[127].

If the Court is reluctant to examine the acts endorsed within the framework of the trial of a criminal case, after all is said and done, it refuses to go any further beyond that, and to interfere in more current acts of judicial administration, like the adjournment of a case or the issue of the medical treatment of a person on preventive detention. The first scenario was at stake in the judgment of 23 April 2015 on *CDS Rahama* **v.** *Republic of Niger.* In that judgment:

> "The Court is of the view that it is a normal occurrence, in the course of a proceedings instituted before a court, for the court to adjourn once or several times, either on its own motion (suo motu) or upon a request by a party to the proceedings. As such, adjournments may indeed appear to be buttressed in rights held by the parties pleading their case before the court, but they are not so exclusively limited. Adjournments actually constitute, as well, judicial-administration measures which form an integral part of the mechanism for directing the procedure, or for preparing the causes in subsequent hearings. In that light, whether or not an adjournment or a suspension of deliberation shall be granted remains a matter to be determined within the sovereign powers of the judge in charge of the case. Thereby, it is not within the ambit of an international court like the ECOWAS Court to determine the relevance of the adjournment of a case, or else to assume the role of the domestic judge in adjudging the appropriateness or otherwise of a measure of judicial administration at the domestic level. The experience of the domestic courts shows, at any rate, that the adjournment of court proceedings or suspension of judges' deliberations are not matters over which litigants hold any acquired rights. One may only talk of violation of human rights or violation of the right to fair trial where series of measures of a certain degree of gravity have been adopted, whose cumulative effect result in a concrete prejudice or a significant breach in equality of arms at trial, against the litigant. Nothing shows that such is the case here.
>
> Furthermore, if the ECOWAS Court of Justice were to commit itself to examining such measures as complained of by the Applicant, the Court would very soon find itself in an awkward position vis-à-vis the stand it

[127] Judgment No. ECW/CCJ/JUD/05/12, §25.

has taken above not to act as a court of appeal or as a cour de cassation over the domestic courts of Member States; for the simple reason that, the measures sought for by the Applicant, if granted by the Court, may take the form of a court decision, notably the form of "an order of court"."[128] And in the judgment of 8 November 2010, Mamadou Tandja **v.** Republic of Niger, the ECOWAS judge refuses to make any pronouncement on the propriety of the medical evacuation requested by Counsel for the former Head of State[129].

The mark of difference the Community Court accords the judge in the domestic courts, as manifested by a form of withholding of its jurisdiction, and a form of restriction upon its power to sit on a part or the whole of a case, is thus seen both by a presumption of truth which the Court attaches to decisions made by the local courts, and by the Court's reluctance to enter into certain areas which appear to it as the prerogative of the domestic courts. But such cautious approach, as adopted by the Court, does not only apply to its relations with the judicial order of the Member States, it equally becomes apparent in its relationship with other international bodies.

B.- Respecting the order of jurisdiction at the international level

The Court also demonstrates a measure of regard towards other international bodies, be they courts of justice like itself, or political organs.

Thus, when other international judges are in a position to adjudicate or are actually engaged in adjudicating on a case equally submitted before the ECOWAS Court, the latter manifests a tendency of avoiding conflict by refraining from trying the case. The case cited here has of course nothing to do with *lis pendens*, which presumes identical stakes before two rival courts. At any rate, we have seen that *lis pendens* is a ground which calls for inadmissibility of an application before the Court. Here, the matter brought before the respective courts is not the same, but a head-on collision in decision-making between the judges of the two distinct courts could occur; in determining the case, the Court's decision may "clash head-on" with the one which may be made by the other court seised with the case.

---

[128] Judgment No. ECW/CCJ/JUD/03/15, §§ 27 and 28.

[129] Judgment No. ECW/CCJ/JUD/05/10, §19-4.

That was thus so in an instance where a case was lodged before the Court whereas an organ of the African Union was equally competent to sit on the case. The Applicant, who had been recruited as Deputy Director of the Franco-Arab Cultural Institute, was subsequently dismissed. He argued before the Court that the dismissal was done in violation of the Rules of Procedure of the African Union, the supervisory body of the Franco-Arab Cultural Institute. The ECOWAS judge declined jurisdiction on the ground that disputes on the public service of the African Union cannot be handled by the ECOWAS Court, that the jurisdiction of the ECOWAS Court in Community civil service matters regards ECOWAS institutions, to the exclusion of other international institutions, as held by the judgment of 4 March 2010 on *Mahamat Zeid Abazene* **v.** *Republic of Mali, African Union and Afro-Arab Cultural Institute*[130].

Confronted with a case which had equally been instituted before the International Criminal Court (ICC), the ECOWAS Court adopted the same attitude. The cases concerning *Laurent Gbagbo* **v.** *Republic of Côte d'Ivoire* (23 March 2012) and *Simone Ehivet and Michel Gbagbo* **v.** *Republic of Côte d'Ivoire* (Judgment of 22 February 2013) provide an illustration. In the first case, the Application was lodged on 25 July 2011, but on 30 November of the same year, the Republic of Côte d'Ivoire, in execution of an arrest warrant issued against Laurent Gbagbo by the Preliminary Chamber III of ICC, he was transferred to the ICC. The Applicant asked the Court for an order for his release and according to him, the conditions of admissibility laid down by Article 10 (d) (ii) of the 2005 Supplementary Protocol had been fulfilled, since ICC was not in conflict of jurisdiction with the ECOWAS Court over the matter. The ECOWAS Court however refused to adjudicate on the matter, for the reason that if the ECOWAS Court went further to examine the case and concluded that Laurent Gbagbo's right to freedom had been violated, it would be futile for it to order his release since he was as that time detained at The Hague by the International Criminal Court[131].

The Court further held that it cannot embark on an exercise in futility, and that as a result, it was in the interest of justice to suspend the procedure till the determination of the proceedings before the ICC[132].

130 Judgment No. ECW/CCJ/JUD/02/10, §28.
131 Judgment No. ECW/CCJ/JUD/03/13, §31.
132 *Ibid.* §32.

Almost one year later, when a case was now filed before the ECOWAS Court by Simone Ehivet and Michel Gbagbo, the Court expressly reaffirms its position. In its decision of 22 February 2013, the Court notes that the case concerning Simone Gbagbo had equally been filed before the International Criminal Court, and that by virtue of the issuing of an arrest warrant against her, her situation was akin to that of Laurent Gbagbo, wherein, incidentally, the ECOWAS Court had decided that the change of circumstances implied by the transfer of Laurent Gbagbo before the ICC called for a suspension of the procedure, in the interest of justice[133]. The Court thus adjudged that in the case at hand, it did not find any reason to depart from its former position. Consequently, the ECOWAS Court ruled that there was sufficient ground to suspend the procedure against Simone Ehivet Gbagbo till the case before the ICC was concluded[134].

There are numerous and rich lessons to be derived from these two decisions. It is first of all possible to observe that these decisions were not solely inspired by "goodwill" and judicial "courtesy". Among the reasons which led the Court to refrain from adjudicating on the cases, there are unquestionably objective factors, practical constraints.

Indeed, as noted by the ECOWAS judge himself, especially in the first case cited above, as at the time the ECOWAS Court was seised with an order from the Applicant seeking release from detention, the Applicant was already in the hands of ICC, and under detention. It would be "futile", "in vain", adjudged the Court, to examine the merits of the Application since, whatever the case may be, the Applicant could not be released. There are therefore objective reasons for the self-restraint exercised by the Court. In the final analysis, it shall be permissible for one to ask whether the Court could not simply have held that as at the time it was asked to try the case and make an order, the matter brought was "not triable", another way of acknowledging that it is practically impossible to try such a case or that there would be no point for a judge to sit on such a case[135].

That being so, one would be wrong to see in this policy of self-restraint nothing more than the manifestation of an objective restraint. There are also, in the explanatory factors of such self-restraint, points deriving from

---

[133] *Ibid.*, §25

[134] *Ibid*, §26.

[135] See infra, in relation to this point, the article entitled: "The no-case phenomenon before the ECOWAS Court of Justice"

ordinary judicial courtesy, of a renunciation freely granted. It must be noted in that regard that the ECOWAS Court, in the two cases cited above, had not completely given up its powers, and renounced in ultimate terms its power to determine the cases in question. The Court only *suspended* the proceedings brought before it. The Court thus admits a sort of circumstantial priority, of a provisional pre-eminence of ICC. We are not operating under a pyramidal model, in a hierarchical order which would imply that the Sub-Regional Court irrevocably gives up a case to a superior court. The temporary concession made by the ECOWAS judge does not arise, far from that, from a formal obligation; it must therefore be understood as a manner of goodwill linked to a set of circumstances which are typically transient in nature.

The second factor which illustrates the policy of self-restraint resides in the peculiar nature of the second case. In the latter case – and contrary to the first –the Applicants were not, at the time the Court had to adjudicate, transferred before the ICC nor deprived of their liberty. The actual constraint which stood in the way of the Court in the first case did not exist in the second. The ECOWAS judge was at liberty to determine the case. But by the mere fact that the case had been "*filed before*" the ICC, and an arrest warrant issued, the Court refrained from sitting on the case and "*suspended*" the consideration of the dispute. In that lies the proof that there is more than the objective constraint or the actual impossibility as grounds for the self-restraint of the judicial functioning of the legal organ of ECOWAS. One can thus justifiably estimate that in its relations with the ICC, the West African Court practices a respectable self-restraint.

The legal organ of ECOWAS adopts the same goodwill towards the organs of UEMOA. It is undoubtedly with UEMOA the sister organisation, which occupies the same geographical space, that the Community judge engages the most in relations of that nature. And indeed, it is towards UEMOA that the policy of self-restraint has manifested itself the most. At least two major decisions may be cited here in that regard. The first is the case concerning *El Hadji Tidjani Aboubacar* **v.** *Republic of Niger* (Judgment of 8 February 2011). The Defendant State, Niger, sued before the Court for human rights violation, contested the competence of the ECOWAS Court to determine the case, pursuant to a provision in the Rules of Procedure of the UEMOA Court – for it was an issue of application of a decision made by the UEMOA Council of Ministers, adopted in 2003 and in relation to the circulation of certain monetary currencies. For Niger, it is the UEMOA Court which has the exclusive jurisdiction to adjudicate on the matter, and Niger cited in that regard Article 15 of the Rules of Procedure of that court, unequivocally establishing the principle of its jurisdiction on issues concerning extra-contractual liability. Without entering into a technical debate on the issue at stake – human rights violation and extra-contractual liability within the meaning of the cited provision – the Court followed the argument of the Defendant State. After finding that it was indeed an issue regarding application of a decision by the UEMOA Council of Ministers, and that UEMOA

> "... has, among other institutions, a Court of Justice for applying its Community law (...)", the ECOWAS judge held that: "... this provision attributes exclusive competence to the Court of Justice of UEMOA when its institutions or officers are in issue as regards the exercise of their functions ; that since the facts in the case are essentially constituted by Decisions and Acts made by the monetary authorities of UEMOA, in the exercise of their functions, Article 15 paragraph 4 of the Rules of the Court of Justice of UEMOA are binding; (...) that if the Honourable Court does not decline its avowed rationae materiae jurisdiction, it will inevitably be led to assume a right it is depositary of and whose implementation is conferred expressly and unequivocally on another Regional Court. (...) The Court is also of the opinion that although its rationae materiae jurisdiction is relevant, it is incumbent upon it to decline that jurisdiction (...)"[136].

What is particularly relevant to note here is that twice, the ECOWAS Court admits that it is within its powers to sit on the matter at stake, but prefers not to examine the case.

The judgment of 1 July 2016 delivered in the case concerning *Djibril Yipéné Bassolé* **v.** *Burkina Faso* provides another occasion for the Court to decline its jurisdiction and give way to its sister court of UEMOA. The Applicant here was claiming a right from Regulation No. 05/CM/UEMOA of 1 January 2015 and argued that certain provisions of that instrument be applied to him, in that those provisions granted lawyers registered with the bar of a Member State the right to plead in courts of any other Member State. According to the ECOWAS judge:

> "The Court must first of all recall that it has no mandate whatsoever to act as a watchdog over the legality of a sister organisation such as UEMOA. In every instance it has been requested to interfere in the

---

[136] Judgment No. ECW/CCJ/JUD/01/11, §§31 and 32.

relations among organs of UEMOA, or to assume the role of any such organ of UEMOA, notably the Court of Justice of UEMOA, the ECOWAS Court of Justice has declined jurisdiction in the matter, in due regard for those alternate legal or judicial orders. (…) The Court must reaffirm that position of principle in the case at hand. The ECOWAS Court of Justice has no mandate to keep watch over a legal system obtaining in the same sub-region but for which specific mechanisms of sanction are provided. The ECOWAS Court of Justice cannot therefore arrogate to itself the duty regarding the observance of the Rules of Procedure of UEMOA"[137].

It cannot therefore be contested that the ECOWAS Court demonstrates self-restraint where it could be led, in the exercise of its judicial functions, into conflict with other judges. One may even ask if this policy of restraining oneself from deciding on a case is not at times beyond acceptable limits, and whether the Court is not showing more than restraint before these other judges, but a sort of subservience not necessarily justified. It has occurred, in the relations between the Court and *la Cour Commune de Justice et d'Arbitrage* (CCJA), an offshoot of *l'Organisation pour l'Harmonisation du Droit des Affaires en Afrique*, (OHADA), that the Court declined its jurisdiction whereas the conditions for *lis pendens*, which seemed to be the alibi of the Court, were not met: not only had CCJA already adjudicated on the case at the time the matter came before the Court (there was no situation of the two cases pending before the two courts at the same time), but the two courts were not seised on the same grounds (before CCJA, the orders sought concerned enforcement of a court decision whereas before the ECOWAS judge, the matter was on human rights violation)[138].

Besides, the policy of self-restraint goes beyond the judicial domain, *stricto sensu.* The Community Court does not only engage in self-restraint towards other courts of justice like itself, but applies that policy in its dealings with political bodies, in regard to a specific aspect of certain requests addressed to the Court: that of getting the States to carry out their Community obligations in general, and more particularly, getting the States to enforce court decisions.

The Court refuses to grant requests aimed at leading it towards both the delivery of a judgment and the execution of that same judgment. The reason behind such restraint is simple: execution of the obligations upon

---

[137] Judgment of ECW/CCJ/JUD/22/16, pp.8-9

[138] We will not return to the details of this argument, already discussed above. See Part I of this work

States in general arise from another procedure, which has to do with default proceedings, and must be dissociated from matters brought for human rights violation. It must clearly be stated here that proceedings for default on such State obligations can only be enforced by another Member State, or by the Commission through its President (Article 10 of the Protocol on the Court as amended by the 2005 Supplementary Protocol).

Without doubt, it is in the judgment on *Mamadou Tandja* **v.** *Republic of Niger* dated 8 November 2010 that the Court expressed itself in the clearest terms in that regard. To the request by the Applicant to order the Defendant State to execute the judgment delivered, the Court responded as follows in its reasoning: that considering that the Member States of ECOWAS are under obligation to execute decisions of the Court in accordance with Article 22 of the Revised Treaty and Article 24 of the Supplementary Protocol on the Court, that on that ground, the States shall take all the necessary steps to comply with those provisions; that therefore, there will be no point for the Court to order the immediate implementation of its own decisions, which are binding on the States once they are notified[139]. In the Decision of 17 May 2016, on *Bodjona Pascal* **v.** *Republic of Togo*, the Court reaffirms its stand vis-à-vis the request made before it to consider the enforcement of an earlier decision made in favour of Mr. Bodjona by holding that it is not the duty of the Court to interfere in the execution of a court decision delivered by itself, and that it is the responsibility of each party to follow the laid down processes provided to that end by the legislative texts of ECOWAS, notably those found in the Supplementary Protocol A/SP.1/01/05 of 19 January 2005 and Supplementary Act A/SA.13/02/12 of 17 February 2012. The Court held that in the instant case, it had already settled the case by delivering a judgment on the merits of the case for both parties, in accordance with the provisions of Article 19(3) of the 6 July 1991 Protocol on the Court which states that: "The Court shall give only one decision in respect of each dispute"[140].

Judicial restraint is demonstrated here by a degree of terseness, through a clear and firm refusal, even if in the judgment on *Karim Meissa Wade* **v.** *Republic of Senegal* of 19 July 2013 paints the picture of a somewhat pedagogical court devoting a little more attention to the

[139] Judgment No. ECW/CCJ/JUD/05/10, §20.

[140] Judgment No. ECW/CCJ/JUD/06/15, §§21-22.

channels through which it may be seised on questions relating to the enforcement of its own judgments[141].

The jurisprudential approach adopted here reposes therefore on the idea that the issue of enforcement of judicial decisions is not judicial. Truly, that viewpoint stems from a number of considerations internal and external to ECOWAS.

From the internal point of view, it shall be appropriate to recall the existence of Supplementary Act A/SP.13/02/12 of 17 February 2012 on the Legal Regime of Sanctions against Member States which do not honour their obligations towards ECOWAS. Article 1 of that legal instrument cites among the obligations upon the Member States: application and respect for the Acts of the Authority of Heads of State, and of the Council of Ministers, as constituted by the Treaty of ECOWAS, the Conventions, Protocols and Supplementary Acts, Regulations, and Directives of the Community, as well as the Decisions of the Community Court of Justice. Then, it is Articles 15 and 16 of the said Supplementary Act which describe the implementation of the sanctions. The procedure is as follows: upon established complaint,

---

[141] Judgment No. ECW/CCJ/JUD/09/13. *The Court thus rules in the following terms: in §§ 80 and 81 : "From all the provisions cited above, it is apparent that the dispute which may arise out of the non-implementation of a decision made by the Court, falls within the domain of having to examine the failure of Member States to fulfil their obligations, because such a dispute essentially has to do with determining whether the State dragged before court acted in line with its primary obligations regarding the Community law (The Revised Treaty of ECOWAS and The Protocol on the Community Court of Justice), by respecting the binding force of the judgments of the Court and by "... taking immediately all necessary measures to ensure execution of the decision of the Court."*

In terms of the request for suspension of the Republic of Senegal from participating in all ECOWAS activities, the Court makes it clear that a mechanism is provided under Supplementary Act A/SP.13/02/12 of 17 February 2012 on the Legal Regime of Sanctions, which sets out the obligations of Member States and prescribes sanctions for non-compliance. In its Article 2(3), the said instrument enshrines respect for the decisions of the ECOWAS Court of Justice as one of the categories of obligations binding on the Member States, and whose non-implementation may call for sanctions. The instrument clearly and undoubtedly portrays the frame of mind of the Community law, as to the content of the obligations that may call for the application of Articles 9(1)-d and 10(a) of the Protocol on the Court. In the existing Community legal order, the cited Supplementary Act constitutes an auxiliary means through which the Court may interpret and apply the said Articles."

Then the Court refers to Supplementary Act No. A/SP.13/02/12 of 17 February 2012 on the legal regime of sanctions thus: "... *the Court makes it clear that a mechanism is provided under Supplementary Act A/SP.13/02/12 of 17 February 2012 on the Legal Regime of Sanctions, which sets out the obligations of Member States and prescribes sanctions for non-compliance*". (§82).

notably before the President of the Commission, of default on obligations – such complaint capable of being brought by any other natural or legal person from a Member State, a Community Institution or Member State – the President of the Commission shall notify the State in question of the complaint and grant it a time-limit of thirty (30) days to comply with the law and file its defence. If upon expiry of that period, the President of the Commission notices that the non-observance persists, he reports accordingly to the Council of Ministers through a memorandum, the Council grants the defaulting State another time-limit to honour its obligations, and upon expiry of the time, he makes recommendations to the Authority of Heads of State concerning sanctions and the scale of sanctions is stipulated in Article 6 of the text. The text itself describes the sanctions as "political", and they are adopted by an organ indeed very "political", the Authority of Heads of States and Government. One understands, under such conditions, that the Court of Justice avoids any inconsiderate entry into discussions on the issue of refusal by States to enforce its decisions, because the refusal to implement the Court's decisions automatically poses so much of a political problem, of the sanctions to be taken.

Some considerations of comparative law equally compel us to think that the refusal to obey judicial decisions poses a predominantly political problem whose resolution therefore rests with non-judicial bodies of the organisation. In its judgment on *Soering* **v.** *United Kingdom* delivered on 7 July 1989, the European Court of Human Rights responds to the request made before it – asking it, at the reparation stage, to assist the parties in the execution of the judgment – by indicating the consequences derivable thereof, that the

> *"The Court is not empowered under the Convention to make accessory directions of the kind requested by the applicant (...) responsibility for supervising execution of the Court's judgment rests with the Committee of Ministers of the Council of Europe"* [142].

---

[142] §127 of the judgment. Article 54, as applicable to that judgment, is today Article 46 of the European Convention on Human Rights. Entitled "*Binding force and execution of judgments*", it provides :

"*1. The High Contracting Parties undertake to abide by the final judgment of the Court in any case to which they are parties.*

2. The final judgment of the Court shall be transmitted to the Committee of Ministers, which shall supervise its execution.

3. If the Committee of Ministers considers that the supervision of the execution of a final judgment is hindered by a problem of interpretation of the judgment, it may refer the matter

In a system like that of the Inter-American Court of Human Rights, reputed however for granting a considerable margin of liberty to their judges in their power of determination of how judgments are to be enforced, the necessity has recently arisen to further associate political organs like the General Assembly or the Permanent Council of the Organisation of American States (OAS) in the procedure of execution the judgments of the Court of San José[143]. Within the very framework of the 1981 African Charter on Human and Peoples' Rights, the power of sanction of the violating State rests, in principle and in the final analysis, in the hands of the Assembly of Heads of State and Government of the African Union. Article 59 of the Charter, irrespective of the mode of sanction applied against the defaulting State by the Commission – complaint brought by another State or by individuals – it always rests with the Assembly of Heads of State and Government to decide whether to publish the report made by the African Commission of Human Peoples' Rights, a publication perceived as the ultimate sanction against the offending State. The mere production of the annual report of the Commission – which may make mention of cases of refusals to implement decisions made – does not seem to escape the attention of the *imprimatur* of the 'supreme decision making body' of the African Union, bearing the most eloquent testimony of the thesis of the political nature of the execution of delivered judgments[144]. This tide does not seem to

---

to the Court for a ruling on the question of interpretation. A referral decision shall require a majority vote of two thirds of the representatives entitled to sit on the committee.

4. If the Committee of Ministers considers that a High Contracting Party refuses to abide by a final judgment in a case to which it is a party, it may, after serving formal notice on that Party and by decision adopted by a majority vote of two thirds of the representatives entitled to sit on the committee, refer to the Court the question whether that Party has failed to fulfil its obligation under paragraph 1.

5. If the Court finds a violation of paragraph 1, it shall refer the case to the Committee of Ministers for consideration of the measures to be taken. If the Court finds no violation of paragraph 1, it shall refer the case to the Committee of Ministers, which shall close its examination of the case".

It is true that much more recent tendencies have revealed that the Court examines much more closely the execution of its judgments. But one will note that it is especially on the basis of a text, which is Resolution 2004 of 12 May 2004, that this developing trend is carried out. In that resolution, the Committee of Ministers ask the Court to detect 'underlying structural problems' which may be raised by certain human rights violations. It is on the basis of that text that the Court delivers its well-known 'pilot judgments'.

[143] See report entitled : *Bases para un Proyecto de Protocolo a la Convencion americana sobre los derechos Humanos...* , cited by par HENNEBEL L. and TIGOUDJA H., *Traité international des droits de l'homme*, Paris, Pédone 2016, p.1435 note 10.

[144] Article 59 of the African Charter:

have been stemmed by the adoption of the 1998 Protocol establishing the African Court on Human and Peoples' Court, since it is granted that if the Court may make determinations on violations ascribable to States, it shall always be the duty of the political organ of the African Union to carry out the actual sanctions whose scale of gravity is featured in Article 23 of the instrument establishing the African Union.

February 2017

"*1. All measures taken within the provisions of the present Charter shall remain confidential until such a time as the Assembly of Heads of State and Government shall otherwise decide.*

2. However, the report shall be published by the Chairman of the Commission upon the decision of the Assembly of Heads of State and Government.

3. The report on the activities of the Commission shall be published by its Chairman after it has been considered by the Assembly of Heads of State and Government."

THE ECOWAS COURT OF JUSTICE AND THE OTHER LEGAL ORDERS OR THE DIALOGUE OF JUDGES AS SEEN FROM ABUJA : SOME GENERAL REFLECTIONS

The subject-matter of inter-court dialogue is without doubt one of the most discussed topics these last years. The reason is simple. It stems from the quick-paced increase – proliferation, as some would say – of international courts and tribunals and the attendant risk of conflict and contradictions in case laws, or even, more seriously still, the danger of fragmentation of international law, deriving from a plurality of the sources for interpreting the rules[145].

Whereas, not in the too distant past, the international field was quite sparsely populated, with notably the International Court of Justice (ICJ) sitting enthroned amongst them and symbolising, by the rules governing access before the Court and its jurisdiction, a domination of the model of inter-State justice as well as the fundamental willingness which governed the Court, the world is opened in the last decade of the century, to other forms of justice, a transformation which has systematically given place to the establishment of new judicial bodies. On a universal scale, justice has become specialised, thus giving rise to a considerable flourishing of a subject like International Law, with the establishment of the International Criminal Court (ICC) (1998 Treaty of Rome), but equally ad-hoc courts, like the International Criminal Tribunal for the Former Yugoslavia (ICTFY) (Resolution 827 of 25 May 1993 adopted by the Security Council), the International Criminal Tribunal for Rwanda (ICTR) (Resolution 955 of 8 November 1994 adopted by the same Security Council), without mentioning, of course, the numerous internationalised criminal tribunals (in Cambodia, Kosovo, Sierra Leone, Timor etc.) which have come into existence. Equally established by way of specialisation, was the International Tribunal of the Law of the Sea

---

145 Among the highly numerous works, we will only cite t
he symposium of la Société Française de Droit International on *Judicialisation of international law,* symposium of Lille, Pédone 2003; and that of Montréal, *International Courts : Complementarity or Rivalry?*, Bruylant 2005, directed by DELAS O., CÔTE R., CREPEAU F., and LEUPRECHT P.

(ITLOS, which was provided for under the United Nations Convention on the Law of the Sea 1982) but was only set up so many years later.

One must add this other aspect constituted by the *regional factor*[146]. Our era is indeed characterised by the phenomenon of regional integrations, solidarities based on proximity. Now, the creation of such groupings of States is almost systematically accompanied by the institution of judicial organs, specifically entrusted with the duty of seeing to the correct application of the system of rules put in place by the said organisations. It is a global phenomenon, but it attains its full potential on the African continent, where in the 1990s, one witnessed a metamorphosis of international organisations. At the continental level of Africa, the creation of the African Union (1999-2000) – which took over the Organisation of African Unity, created in 1963 – also saw the creation of a judicial organ, the Court of Justice of the African Union (Article 18 of the Treaty). And with specific regard to human rights protection, a system was put in place under the African Charter on Human and Peoples' Rights (concluded in 1981), which, originally, makes provision solely for one supervisory body of the judicial apparatus: the African Commission of Human and Peoples' Rights.

At the sub-regional level, new organisations equip themselves with their respective courts of justice: West African Economic and Monetary Union (UEMOA), is established in 1994, the Economic and Monetary Community in Central Africa (CEMAC) in 1994, the Southern African Development Community (SADC) in 1992, Common Market for Eastern and Southern Africa (COMESA) in 1992 also, and the East African Community (EAC) in 1999.

Against the background of such profusion of courts and tribunals, one needs to highlight the new competent judicial organs put in place to cater for human rights. At the continental level, the system of protection has progressed much further, we have had the African Court on Human and Peoples' Rights (established under the 1998 Ouagadougou Protocol), and it is a question, in the terms of another Protocol adopted on 1 July 2008, of merging with the Court of Justice of the AU, as provided for in the instrument establishing the African Union (a court which was actually created by the 2003 Maputo Protocol). We need to add that in 2014, a Protocol amending that of 2008 came into being, conferring on the

[146] According to the expression of Laurence BOURGORGUE-LARSEN in his presentation at the symposium of Lille cited earlier: *The regional factor in the judicialisation of international law*, p.203.

already established *African Court on Justice and Human Rights* jurisdiction over criminal matters (Article 28A). At the same time, the Sub-Regional Courts were equally granted powers in the area of human rights: the ECOWAS Court, of course (the 2005 Supplementary Protocol on the Court), and also the East African Court of Justice (the said jurisdiction having been provided for in Article 27 of the treaty establishing the organisation and implying the adoption of a specific protocol for that purpose) and the SADC Court (the adoption of a particular protocol being equally necessary here, the Heads of State of the Member States taking the trouble to recall, on the heels of the 32nd Summit and before the inclinations towards judicial activism, that the jurisdiction of the Court remained for the time being within the confines of the interpretation of the Treaty only).

The result is a fairly complex landscape, an intermingling of judicial orders made all the more complex by the fact that certain courts, as we just stated, have not hesitated to add to the jurisdiction stated in their texts, powers derived from a somewhat extensive reading of the rules governing them. In this general context – an upsurge in the creation of courts both at the world level and on the African continent – a reflexion on the dialogue among judges certainly assumes a particular significance, and the very experience of the ECOWAS Court is a proof of the relevance of the subject-matter.

The concept of dialogue of judges, in truth, makes reference to ambivalent considerations, to a two-faced coin. The face of disagreement first of all, which is the most obvious, is that which automatically emerges in a situation of proliferation of the interpreters of the law – the judges. Let us not forget: in a pluralism, the risk of dissenting views is all the more great since no one is subject to anyone else, in that the judges are independent of each other. But there is the other face, that which actually warrants a discussion on "dialogue": the face of agreement, of convergence, of congruence. The plurality of courts and tribunals does not merely bring forth the danger of dissent and splits, it equally generates interest in the other, and attention to the other, for the judge is not alone: he is sensitive to his environment, and open to his neighbourhood. Cohabitation or coexistence creates as much risk of discord as promise of convergence, the test of inter-subjectivity sways between the temptation of alterity and solidarity.

We must further add that such dialogue is not limited towards international judges, at least as far as our perspective is concerned. It is not a doctrinal bias or a personal understanding of things, it is a requirement which arises from the texts themselves, for, in the case of the ECOWAS Court of Justice, the texts make provision for mechanisms of collaboration or dialogue between the national judge and the Community judge, notably through a procedure modelled after the Treaty of Rome establishing the Rome Treaty, which instituted the European Economic Community (1957), referral for preliminary determination before the Community Court of Justice (former Article 177 of the said Treaty). But there is more than referral for preliminary determination. The fact that the ECOWAS Court of Justice is inclined, in line with the facts, to remain a human rights court, creates an opportunity for dialogue with other human rights judges constituted by the national constitutional judges.

In relation to the legal organ of ECOWAS, dialogue amongst judges must therefore be envisaged both towards **(I)** the national judges and **(II)** the international judges.

I.- Dialogue with the national judge

The components of this dialogue exist. The ECOWAS Court demonstrates sufficient respect towards the jurisdiction of the national judge, and is cautious, in the exercise of its mandate, not to go too much against the domestic courts. (A) The manifestation of that goodwill comes in numerous ways. (B) That being the case, we are still far from having attained the conditions of an optimum dialogue. So much still needs to be perfected in that regard, and it will suffice to recall some lost opportunities, some instances lost as at today.

A.- The reality of the dialogue

It will suffice here to refer to the previous study on national law and the case law of ECOWAS[147]. We saw there that the forms of goodwill expressed towards the national judge are many. The first among them is the refusal to retry a case which has already been adjudicated upon by the national judge, *in a context where the two actions before court seek the same orders, notably of monetary compensation.* We have seen the purely logical reasons of such reticence. A way of respecting the assigned mandate of the domestic court and of averting the dishonesty of litigants tempted to gamble before the two fora with the objective of obtaining

[147] Cf. supra

double compensation, the refusal to retry a case amounts to conferring on the national court a dignity and a status similar those of the Court itself. There is a sort of alliance of justices, the national and the international, which is opposed to disregarding each other or giving the other a cold shoulder. Along the exact lines of this dogma, largely shared by courts, according to which the international judge is not an appeal court judge over the cases at the domestic courts, nor does he have the power to quash judgments made at the national level, the position held by the ECOWAS Court must indeed be applauded. Let us recall that the Court's position was notably expressed in the judgments on *Aliyu Tasheku* **v.** *Federal Republic of Nigeria*, delivered on 12 June 2012, and *Sa'Adatu Umar* **v.** *Federal Republic of Nigeria* dated 14 December 2012[148]. With the case law of *Aziagbede Kokou and 33 Other* **v.** *Republic of Togo* (Judgment of 3 July 2013), reverence towards the domestic courts is expressed in more principled terms, and justified more systematically: the ECOWAS Court held that bringing the case before it was "*premature*" in so far as the matter was pending before the domestic courts[149]. This last point is significant because the issue has been raised as to whether the Court may decline to sit on a case which is pending at the same time before the national courts and the Community Court of Justice, given that the rule of exhaustion of local remedies does not apply before the Community Court. In the formal sense of it, nothing, in such an instance, prevents the Court from adjudicating on the case; no rule forbids the Community Court from sitting on the case. It is however desirable, in our opinion, that the ECOWAS judge abstains, albeit provisionally, from doing so, for at least an easily predictable reason. Indeed, if the Court were to endeavour to state the law, it could create itself, the very situation it seeks to avoid when it refuses to try a case which has been settled by the national judge, for a second time. It suffices to imagine that just as may have been ordered by the local judge, the Community Court orders a reparation for violation of a right. Equipped with two writs of execution (the two judicial decisions), the applicant could then seek to be compensated twice.

The jurisprudence regarding "premature lodgment", in our understanding, must be maintained, *on condition, the point must be firmly made, that the two actions before court seek the same orders*. This position derives from pure logic, and is devoid of any narrow

---

[148] Judgment No. ECW/CCJ/JUD/17/12.

[149] Judgment No. ECW/CCJ/JUD/07/13, §42 of the Judgment.

understanding of the texts, likely to conclude upon absurd results. The rule of exhaustion of local remedies must not lead to shocking or unreasonable situations. As such, where two actions before court do not seek the same reliefs, and do not have the same issues at stake, nor call into play the same system of rules, the ECOWAS Court may absolutely adjudicate upon the case, at the same time that the matter is pending before the national judge. This was what occurred in *Case Concerning Hadijatou Mani Koraou* **v.** *Republic of Niger* (Judgment of 27 October 2008), the ECOWAS judge having determined the case before it, for reasons absolutely defensible in the given instance[150].

Whatever the case may be, the doctrine of "premature lodgment", understood within the perimeter we have just indicated, has the merit of according the national judiciary due respect; in so doing, it does contribute to dialogue amongst judges. Equally demonstrating such respect, such "judicial diplomacy"[151], are all the instances where the ECOWAS judge refrains from entering into what he considers to be the "reserved ground" of the national judge, like measures of instruction in criminal proceedings, generally, or processes which postulate a "proximity" – a term used in the judgment of 3 July 2013 on *Aziagbede Kokou and 33 Others* **v.** *Republic of Togo* – with the case, a clear-sighted discernment of the circumstances of the case[152]. The Court again educates us in the judgment on *Baldini Salfo* **v.** *Burkina Faso* (31 October 2012), and scrupulously sees to it that it does not weaken the authority and independence of the national judge in the trial of the cases lodged before him.[153].

The Court must be given credit for keeping faith with that line of action. It is imperative to acknowledge however that all the potentials for dialogue with the national judge have not been explored, far from that. Besides glaring proofs of what President Costa of the European Court of Human Rights called "*judicial diplomacy*"[154], there are yawning gaps, shortcomings and lost opportunities for dialogue. It is that room for perfection, as things stand now, that the Court must be interested in.

---

150 Judgment No. ECW/CCJ/JUD/06/08, §§49 to 53 of the Judgement.

151 The expression is borrowed from J-P COSTA, former President of the European Court of Human Rights in *Judges for Freedom,* Dalloz, 2013, p.224.

152 See supra, article entitled: "The role of the judge in disputes on human rights violation: the ECOWAS Court of Justice between activism and self-restraint".

153 Judgment No. ECW/CCJ/JUD/13/12, §59.

154 COSTA J-P., *La Cour européenne des droits de l'homme. Des juges pour la liberté,* Paris, Dalloz, 2013, p.224.

B.- The limits of the dialogue

In the looking at dialogue with the national judge, two unfortunate points could be put forward. They relate to two broad categories of functions assigned to the Court. As a judge of the norms for economic integration, the Court is equipped with an instrument of collaboration which is underutilised: the referral of issues from the domestic courts to the Community Court, for preliminary determination. As a human rights judge, the ECOWAS judge has incurred an undoubted deficit in the intellectual partnership it could have engaged with the constitutional courts of the Member States, who are the partners of the Community judge in determining cases on human rights.

With regard to the first point, it will be appropriate to express the bitterest regret regarding the current situation. More than fifteen years after it was established, the ECOWAS Court has never had a case referred before it from the domestic courts for preliminary determination. The procedure is to be triggered by the judge at the domestic court, so much the reason why the judges at the Community Court cannot be blamed for inaction. Indeed, in the terms of Article 10 of the 2005 Protocol:

> "Access to the Court is open to the following: … (f) Where in any action before a court of a Member State, an issue arises as to the interpretation of a provision of the Treaty, or the other Protocols or Regulations, the national court may on its own or at the request of any of the parties to the action refer the issue to the Court for interpretation."

This mechanism, patterned after the European system, (former Article 177 of the Rome Treaty of 1957 establishing the European Economic Community, EEC), certainly constitutes an effective measuring instrument of the rate of penetration of the ECOWAS law into the legal orders and judicial attitudes of the Member States.

It is unfortunately the case, that since inception, no case has been so referred before the ECOWAS Court of Justice, whereas under other community jurisdictions, national courts have already referred domestic matters before supranational courts similar to the ECOWAS Court of Justice, such as the courts of justice of UEMOA, CEMAC and the East African Community. It is true that at the regional level itself, the overall figures remain rather insignificant: only the Court of Justice of UEMOA has had a referral for preliminary determination at least three times, the other two having done so only once, with the Court of Justice of

ECOWAS recording the same figure as the courts of justice of the Common Market of Eastern and Southern Africa (COMESA), and of the Southern African Development Community (SADC), barring any error on our part. Nonetheless, the low figures recorded in the collaborative effort with the judges of the Member States remains a concern. It must be interpreted as it ought to be: the Community law is not yet optimally employed or invoked in the Member States. This state of affairs, in the final analysis, has a connection with access to and knowledge of the Community law itself. In fact, the Community law is largely unknown, since it is not widely taught, either as a university course or as a subject in career judicial programmes (training of lawyers and judges).

More than fifteen years after it was put in place, the virtual abandonment of the referral procedure thus remains a regrettable case, in as muchsafeguarded, as already stated, it constitutes the most privileged avenue for the penetration of the Community law. Now, one must not lose sight of the fact that behind the challenge concerning the law, which also does provide a justification for the establishment of the ECOWAS Court and all the procedures for gaining access to the Court, what is at stake is of an overriding practical concern: the law and its mechanisms are a means for defending concrete interests, rules made to serve the purpose of integration, a unified economic space, free competition, freedom of movement of peoples, capital, goods, etc. It is the process constituting the event by which these concrete pursuits shall materialise. When the materialisation of that pursuit delays, or when the resources it makes available are not sufficiently harnessed, it provides a ground for one to believe that the formal rules, the rules of integration, are, at least partially, detached from the reality.

Another lost opportunity for dialogue is that which could have been engaged with the Constitutional judges of the Member States. That is where the ECOWAS judge, as a human rights judge, is concerned. One is aware, incidentally, that since 2005, the year such judicial power was given birth to, the Court has essentially been seised with cases on the grounds of the human rights jurisdiction of the Court. Whereas, there exists in the Member States, at least in the virtual sense, another judge, a human rights judge. We are referring here to the Constitutional judge, the interpreter and custodian of the Constitution, the fundamental law which often embodies the declarations of rights. What is more? An opportunity for dialogue is provided here by an attractive legal instrument constituted by the African Charter on Human and Peoples' Rights. This treaty is very frequently invoked by the applicants before the ECOWAS Court, and it is at any rate "constitutionalised" by almost all the Member States[155]. Indeed, a court like the Constitutional Court of Benin has produced a very rich case law on the African Charter. There is no reflection however on dialogue among judges centred on that instrument.

One of the reasons of the difficulty for undertaking such an exercise of reflection could however be traced to the fact that the ECOWAS Court relies on a somewhat overwhelmingly large number of legal instruments. Indeed, disputes on human rights violation before the West African judge is peculiar in the sense that any legal instrument binding on a Defendant State may be invoked before the Court in a case brought against that State. When it is known that there are, in the international order, a huge number of treaties on human rights binding on the States, one becomes apprehensive as to the scope of the rules that may have to be taken into account. Such "wide scope" of the Community judge obviously makes it difficult for one to have a dialogue at the centre of which one could find only one reference, organised around a single text. Therein lies another reason for the difficulty involved in conducting here a dialogue with the national constitutional judge.

II.- Dialogue with the international judge

With the international judge, the ECOWAS Court equally engages in a form of long-distance conversation. Things are however more complex here. Indeed, dialogue is not but made of consensus; dialogue does not solely consist of agreeing all the time, it also consists of, as surprising as that may appear, disagreements, the independent posture adopted now and then by one party or the other, as we shall see, equally forming part of the dialogue. It is worthy to note that besides (the A) proclaimed areas of convergence, there are (B) divergent stands assumed by the ECOWAS Court

A.- Proclaimed areas of convergence

Three forms of convergence may thus be identified.

The first takes the shape of goodwill, courtesy, leading the ECOWAS Court of Justice to carefully shut itself out, to act discreetly, and avoid entering into competition with other international judges. Such attention, accorded to the other, is a component of dialogue with the judges, the

155 Thus, the Charter is cited in the preamble to the Constitutions of the following States: Benin, Burkina Faso, Côte d'Ivoire, Guinea, Niger, Senegal and Togo.

avoidance of contradiction, which implies abstinence from making a pronouncement on a pending case, is surely a way of lending a listening ear to the other courts. This first mode of dialogue has been examined under the policy of self-restraint on the part of the Court[156]. This was seen in the light of the risk of competition with the UEMOA Court of Justice[157], the *Cour Commune de Justice et d'Arbitrage* (CCJA) of OHADA[158], the semi-judicial organs of the AU[159] and even with the International Criminal Court (ICC)[160]. It indeed seems that the context of the English term *comity* as applied to a comity of courts of justice may be appropriate for expressing the attitude of the judge here. As written by Julie Allard and Antoine Garapon,

> "... half-way between thought and action, between information and constraint (...), the comity designates a form of friendly civility among equals (...). Judicial comity is contrary to judicial competitiveness: it refers to a positive frame of mind towards the other systems of justice, and the feeling that one has something to learn from the others."[161]

In another context, the ECOWAS Court goes further. It no more contents itself with renouncing a place of pride, it expressly taps the ingredients of its solution from other sources, from other courts of justice. In an explicit, open manner, it borrows from other judges, the essentials of which constitute the grounds for its own pronouncements. The dialogue is thus taken a notch higher, one no more limits oneself to "tolerating" the other, by ceding to the other person the room for decision-making, the other person becomes an ally, a supporting base for the judgment to be delivered.

Indeed, such collaboration may first of all take a discreet and subtle form, with the jurisprudence of the ECOWAS Court going in the same

---

[156] See: *The role of the judge in disputes on human rights violation: the ECOWAS Court of Justice between activism and self-restraint*, our article cited above, *supra*.

[157] Judgment of 8 February 2011, *El Hadji Tidjani Aboubacar* **v.** *Banque Centrale des Etats de l'Afrique de l'Ouest and Republic of Niger*; Judgment of 1 July 2016, *Djibril Y Bassolé* **v.** *Etat du Burkina Faso*.

[158] Judgment No. ECW/CCJ/JUD/04/12 of 31 January 2012, *Aziablévi Yovo and 31 Others* **v.** *Société Togo Télécom and Republic of Togo*.

[159] Judgment No. ECW/CCJ/JUD/02/10 of 4 March 2010, *Dr. Mahamat Seid Abazene* **v.** *Republic of Mali*.

[160] Judgment of 23 March 2012, *Laurent Gbagbo* **v.** *Republic of Côte d'Ivoire and Alassane Ouattara;* Judgment No. ECW/CCJ/JUD/03/13, of 22 February 2013, *Simone Ehivet and Michel Gbagbo* **v.** *Republic of Côte d'Ivoire*.

[161] ALLARD J. and GARAPON A., *Les juges dans la mondialisation. La nouvelle révolution du droit,* Paris, Seuil, 2005, pp.59-60.

direction as that of other court, but which the Court does not necessarily cite. On certain issues, judges of human rights are indeed faced with the same problems, and they may be urged to proffer solutions already advocated for by some of their colleagues.

It is clear for example that the case law of the Court on amnesty laws was inspired by judgments delivered by other courts confronted with the same problem. There is a similarity in inspiration between the judgment on *Cantoral Huamani* of 26 May 2010 delivered by the Inter-American Court of Human Rights and the judgment on *Heirs of Ibrahim Baré Mainassara* **v.** *Republic of Niger* of 23 October 2015 delivered by the ECOWAS Court of Justice. In the first, the American judge rules that the rules on amnesty, on time bar and on grounds for exoneration from liability, which aim at preventing inquiry and sanction of the authorities, from serious human rights violations such as torture, extra-judicial, summary or arbitrary executions and forced disappearances, those prohibited by virtue of the fact that they violate the inalienable rights recognised in international law, are inadmissible[162]. The ECOWAS judge expresses similar reservations on the efficacy of amnesty laws. The ECOWAS Court sets forth a doctrine which is typically its, in terms which deserve to be reproduced at length:

> "The issue before the Court to determine is therefore quite simple and may be formulated as follows – Does a legally instituted amnesty shut the door to every form of judicial investigation? – Does it foreclose or constitute an estoppel to every form of attempt to seek information on a matter, purely speaking, – in terms of seeking the truth or enquiring about the facts thereon?
>
> The Court cannot share such a tyrannical concept of effects of an amnesty measure. The Court recalls that it has had occasion in the past to consider, regarding the same State – Niger –, the scope of such a law. Indeed, in Case Concerning Sidi Amar Ibrahim and Others **v.** Republic of Niger (Judgment of 8 February 2011), the Court was called upon to examine the effects of Order No. 2009-19 of 23 October 2009 on amnesty, concerning events which had occurred between 2005 and 2009. Even if the Court had recognised the existence of the order, and accepted the decision taken by the authorities of Niger to set aside every form of judicial proceedings on the matters at stake, the Court nevertheless made a pronouncement as to

162 See also the judgments on the *Barrios Altos,* 14 March 2001, §§43-44; and *Massacre of la Rochela* **v.** *Colombia,* 11 May 2007, Series C n°163, §294.

the inefficacy of the amnesty law in situations of serious and widespread violation of fundamental human rights (§51).

The Court considers, today, that it shall be appropriate to raise the requirements of the law on amnesty, and prop up the level of acceptability of amnesty laws (...) Amnesty laws cannot constitute an unreasonable cover-up for the past, an estoppel which may automatically be invoked against every legitimately inquiring mind attempting to know the truth (...).

The Court is of the view that if the necessity to forget or to forgive, on a massive scale, may be imperative and applicable to a society at a given time in its history, such necessity cannot imply that one must treat with scorn, the right to know, the right of access to the truth, which victims in a cause are entitled to. The Court is not ignorant in any way whatsoever of the sovereign right of a State to adopt, in a given situation, measures of amnesty. Equally, the Court is not seeking to cripple the effects deriving from amnesty provisions, but it holds that the scope of an amnesty measure is limited within the confines of the criminal issues at stake, and should not in any way affect the civil reparation for the victims of the incidents involved. In other words, the Court finds that amnesty laws do not wipe off criminal accusations, but they leave unimpaired victims' right to reparation, no matter the form such reparation may take. Before this Court therefore, amnesty laws must be properly situated within their exact confines, i.e. within the limits of incriminating charges and criminal proceedings, to the exclusion of individuals' civil rights (...) amnesty does not justify inertia, and respect for victims' rights is not incompatible with the necessity of social reconciliation."[163]

Similarly, when the ECOWAS Court of Justice is to explain why the absence of simultaneous filing of a case before an international court is a condition of admissibility of the action instituted before it, it largely delves into the rules obtaining before courts inclined towards the safeguard of human rights, to provide the points of justification for its ruling. In the judgment on *Hadijatou Mani Koraou* **v.** *Republic of Niger*, of 27 October 2008, the Court cites, in that regard, as much from the European doctrine[164] as from provisions from the European Convention

---

163 Judgment No. ECW/CCJ/JUD/ 23/15, §§ 51 to 54, 57 and 58.

164 COHEN-JONATHAN G., *La Convention européenne de sauvegarde des droits de l'homme et des libertés fondamentales"*, Paris, Economica, 1989, p.143 (§50); TRECHSEL S., *Die europäische Menschenrechts-konvention, ihr Schutz der persönlichen Feiheit und die schweizerischen Strafprozessrechte*, Stämpfli Bern, 1974, p.125, cited in Judgment No. ECW/CCJ/JUD/06/08, §52.

on Human Rights[165] or from the American Convention on Human Rights[166], or yet still from conventions concluded within the framework of the United Stations.[167].

Called upon to make a pronouncement on the "arbitrary" nature of the detention of a former Head of State, in *Case Concerning Mamadou Tandja* **v.** *General Salou Djibo and Republic of Niger* (Judgment of 8 November 2010), the Court equally refers to the proceedings of the United Nations Human Rights Commission, more precisely, to the Working Group on Arbitrary Detention, which had outlined the relevant criteria[168]. The points drawn from the conclusions of the UN body were equally recalled in the case law on *Agba Sow Bertin* **v.** *Republic of Togo* (Judgment of 11 June 2013)[169].

Finally, the judgment of 13 July 2015, on *Congrès pour la Démocratie et le Progrès (CDP) and Others* **v.** *Burkina Faso* provided an opportunity for the Court to confront its position with that of other international courts, as to restrictions on the right to present oneself for elections. To set aside the claim of the new authorities to exclude dignitaries of the ousted regime from the electoral race, the Court criticises the disputed measure before buttressing its position on other decisions made at the international level. In that connection, the Court cites United Nations Human Rights Committee and the European Court of Human Rights[170]. Somewhat surprisingly, a certain doctrine has come out with criticisms of the approach adopted by the Court in that judgment[171].

---

165 Article 35.2.b. of the Convention (§51).

166 Article 46.c of the Convention (§51).

167 Article 5.2.a) of the First Optional Protocol relating to the International Covenant on Civil and Political Rights (§51).

168 Judgment No. ECW/CCJ/JUD/ 05/10, §19.1 of the Judgment.

169 Judgment No. ECW/CCJ/JUD/05/13, §33 of the Judgment.

170 Judgment No. ECW/CCJ/JUD/ 16/15, §§35 and 36 of the Judgment.

171 An initial critique consisted of a negative remark against the Court for citing the European Court of Human Rights, the judgment on *Paksas* **v.** *Lithuania* (6 January 2011), whereas it appeared that one should have cited another judgment, *Zdanoka* **v.** *Leetonia* (16 March 2006). The critique was made by J. Andriantsimbazovina (in *Human Rights Protection by Supranational Courts*, Paris, Pédone, pp.24-25) and by J-F Akandji-Kombe (*The ECOWAS judge and the Burkinabe democratic revolution. Brief remarks on a worrying decision.* http:// jfakiblog.com/ 2015/07/21/ le-juge-de-la-cedeao-et-la-révolution-démocratique-burkinabé/). The criticism would be that the decision cited is rather characterised by the recognition of a freedom for the State authorities to shrink the right to participate in elections, whereas the ECOWAS Court rather shrunk that very right in its decision. To such criticism, one only needs to respond that the Court neither committed an error nor

"inconsistency", the Court did not merely refer "in general terms" to the judgment of the European Court, but indeed did cite an extract of the said judgment which falls perfectly in line with the thinking of the Court, whose terms we may well remind ourselves of : "The European Court of Human Rights recalls in its Judgment of 6 January 2011 in Case Concerning *Paksas* **v.** *Lithuania*, that - *In the Court's view, it is understandable that a State should consider a gross violation of the Constitution or a breach of the constitutional oath to be a particularly serious matter requiring firm action when committed by a person holding that office. (...) However, that is not sufficient to persuade the Court that the applicant's permanent and irreversible disqualification from standing for election as a result of a general provision constitutes a proportionate response to the requirements of preserving the democratic order.*" The Court thus reaffirmed that the free expression of the opinion of the people in choosing their legislative body must at all times be preserved. (§104 and 105, also see ECHR Judgments, 22 September 2004, *Case Concerning Aziz* **v.** *Cyprus*)." The extract corresponds exactly to the reasoning of the ECOWAS Court. It was therefore not cited "*without discernment*" (J. Andriantsimbazovina); one does not see why one should interpret another person's thoughts in his place. Similarly, blaming the Court for its balance between the duty to try "actual" or "concrete violations", and that of adjudicating on "imminent violations" (M. Hébié, *What about if the ECOWAS Court of Justice had it all wrong or almost all wrong*?, Burkina 24, 31 July 2015) amounts to disregarding the necessities of a jurisdiction founded upon urgency and necessity, so much logical and so systematically provided for, to anticipate untoward events.

On the merits, the discussion becomes obviously difficult when, in a purely hypothetical political case, after considering that "*the insurrection of 30 and 31 October was celebrated for its legitimacy...*", one considers that the ECOWAS Court of Justice was at any rate incompetent to adjudicate on the case (M. Hébié). Similarly, the argument consisted of justifying the prohibition to participate in elections by the necessity for the State to *"defend itself"* or to avoid a *"destruction of democracy"* (J-F Akandji-Kombe) appears to us as dangerous, in that it opens the door to the worst abuses on the part of the political rulers. J-F Akandji-Kombe regrets that "*jurists have so much difficulty thinking along the lines of revolutions"* (p.2), but the human rights judge is not under obligation to subject himself to the negating logic of the rights of minorities, the judicial power is indeed a fixed point in the torment of revolutions whose essence, meaning or twists it is always adventurous to claim to have understood. As for the theory of "*margin of appreciation of national institutions"* which J-F Akandji-Kombe makes mention of, it appears to us questionable on two grounds: on one hand, applying it would end up negating the very judicial examination of the acts of the State, and on the other hand, particularly, the court that applies it the most – the European Court of Human Rights – is far from envisaging it in a mechanical or systematic manner, since this theory is brandished only in cases where not only the conventional legislation lacks firmness or precision, but where the legislations and national practices differ quite considerably, when therefore there is lack of consensus on the issue at stake. We certainly did not find ourselves in that situation in the case tried by the ECOWAS Court.

The same author also criticised the judges of the Court for "*constituting themselves into authorities of democracy"* (p.6). The criticism seems to us somewhat misplaced for, all international judges sanctioning rights violation in a State necessarily act as proponents of democratic norms. Has the European Court of Human Rights not produced abundant case law on what must be *"a democratic society"* (status of political parties, freedom of expression, requirements of fair trial) ? And when the Inter-American Court makes pronouncements on the framework and implementation of political rights, like that of

The ECOWAS Court of Justice thus practises "judicial diplomacy" either by avoiding entering into competition with other judges – national or international, or in more "directly", by openly adopting solutions already applied to cases similar to the ones brought before the Court. At that stage, we are engaged in full dialogue amongst judges. The Court "*rubs its mind*", to paraphrase Montaigne, with the minds of other judges in similar circumstances. In cultivating interest in the other judge, even wilfully copying him, the judge maximises the quality of the judgment he delivers – what is shared becomes more credible and more acceptable. We need to quote J. Allard and A. Garapon:

> "While engaging in his judicial business, the judge seeks to ascribe to his personal opinion, a more general basis, and thereby give it a more acceptable status. Since he seeks to claim a higher degree of rationality, he thus gives his decision a more universally applicable outlook. In that regard, the authority he recognises in the foreign decisions is not binding, but rather persuasive (persuasive authority)"[172]. Again, one of these writers states that: "Dialogue enables the judges to discuss the efficacy of the various foreseeable solutions, and to permanently evaluate the legal systems. An alternate external view, highlighted for present purposes, enables one to assess one's own rules, legal culture and case law. Thereby, one may find a means of improving upon one's judiciary, and at any rate, contribute to a form of standardisation of the justice system"[173].

The last form through which dialogue is engaged takes the shape of meetings, a practice equally widespread among the galaxy of international courts. Through colloquiums, seminars, "sensitisation missions" and other training sessions, the judges of ECOWAS get

---

participating in elections, does it not define the democratic standards (Judgment on *Yatama* **v.** *Nicaragua,* 23 June 2005, where, precisely, the issue at stake was the restriction of the right to compete in elections)? In the current context, a human rights judge, whether national or international, as in the present case, necessarily acts as an assessor of the democratic rules.

We will end on a general note which all of us need to bear in mind. It is the duty of the judge to recall the requirement to respect the rights of each and every party, beyond the political upheavals, turmoil and alternations. The power to make laws, irrespective of who is in power, cannot be used for the systematic banishment of political opponents. Resigning oneself to the state of affairs, or justifying it, is to turn the State into a theatre for a ceaseless settlement of scores.

172 *Ibid*, p.59 (?)

173 ALLARD J., Le dialogue des juges dans la mondialisation (The dialogue of judges in globalisation), *in Le dialogue des juges,* Actes du colloque organisé le 28 avril 2006 à l'Université libre de Bruxelles, Bruylant, 2007, p. 85.

engaged in meetings with other judges or courts and other actors of the judicial world such as legal and judicial officers, university lecturers, and top functionaries. This is even a significant aspect of the Court's official work programme.[174].

The fact that the Community judge should be so much concerned with what goes on in other courts of justice, naturally comes in to mitigate the risk, real from the outset, of the Community Court being tempted by any form of judicial imperialism. The risk was given birth to within the context of the Court's own willingness, as already mentioned, to enter into human rights protection systems equipped with their own organs and mechanisms for sanction. Indeed, the Court, we know, sanctions violation of such conventions, which the Defendant State is party to, thus presenting the Court with a huge array of rules that may be invoked by litigants coming before the Court. We do not find ourselves in a context, as in the case of the European or American model of human rights protection, where it is the application of a specific convention which poses a problem – the 1950 European Convention on Human Rights and the 1969 American Convention on Human Rights. Here, the scope of the legal instruments that may be invoked is wide and extensive, and applicants virtually find themselves in a dilemma – a convention invoked by an applicant in a case only needs to be relevant, and then the State must be a party to that convention. The West African Court therefore contributes its quota by ensuring that the States effectively discharge their obligations, whereas the very presence of the Court within that configuration resulted from a unilateral decision. In such circumstances, there could indeed be a risk of seeing the Court "going it all alone", or adopting an extraordinarily extensive view on its functions. All that we

---

[174] We may cite "at random", from a long list of possible examples, some concrete cases of meetings in which the Court participated in recent years. Lome Symposium of April 2010 on "Africa and the internationalisation of constitutionalism : actor or spectator?" ; Symposium on "Administration of justice in West Africa and enforcement of judgments delivered by the ECOWAS Court of Justice", April 2008, at Dakar ; Symposium on : "Community institutions at the service of the realisation of Vision 2020", March 2013, at Lagos ; Bamako Seminar, jointly organised with GIABA, on "Combatting money laundering and terrorism financing" for French-speaking and Portuguese-speaking judges of ECOWAS, March 2010; Visit to the Court of Justice of the European Union (Luxembourg), November 2016 ; Abidjan Symposium organised by the Superior Courts of Judicature of French-Speaking countries on "Uniform laws in Africa: myth or challenge to be surmounted ?", November 2013 ; Arusha Colloquium on "African courts of human rights and similar institutions", October 2010, etc. The Court equally engages in relations with universities, takes part in various training sessions, through the individual participation of the members of the Court, and receives other courts to its seat at Abuja, the last example being the visit of the Court of Justice of UEMOA in 2017.

have just seen is however of such nature as to reduce that risk; it has turned out that the Community judge pays so much attention to his peers elsewhere on the international scene, the fear of an expansionist drift in the Court's functions has not occurred. On the contrary, it is dialogue which has become the order of the day.

One must not be deceived however by the existence of these spheres of convergence. The relations between the ECOWAS Court and other international courts do not merely consist of totally agreeing on all issues. It does occur that on specific issues, there be, on the contrary, divergent stands. These areas of divergence must not be overshadowed by the points of convergence, nor be swept under the carpet, for they form part of the dialogue amongst judges.

B.- Divergent stands assumed

Indeed, dialogue does not mean all differences are to be wiped off, and the rationale behind dialogue is not the kind of uniformity that negates specific features and the particular nature of specific contexts.

> "Dialogue among judges does not as such presuppose that they reason in the same way, nor that they always arrive at the same conclusions. Dialogue, with its own constraints, does not necessarily engender uniformity of decisions".**J. Allard further writes**[175]

He adds that:

> "Judicial business among judges cannot be exclusively envisaged from an angle of a cordial conversation amongst enlightened and open minds: it equally takes more competitive and more conflicting forms"[176].

With reference to the ECOWAS Court of Justice, that irrepressible autonomy was made manifest in case concerning *Hadijatou Mani Koraou* **v.** *Republic of Niger* (Judgment of 27 October 2008). One of the arguments of the Defendant State, Niger, was that regardless of a directive in that connection, the Court should have applied the rule of exhaustion of local remedies, considering it as golden rule ordinarily observed by international courts adjudicating on human rights. The Republic of Niger precisely "… considered such absence as a lacuna which should be filled by the Court"[177]. The "jurisprudence" of the

---

[175] ALLARD J., *Le dialogue des juges dans la mondialisation*, previously cited, p.89.

[176] J. ALLARD and A. GARAPON, Op cit, p.35.

[177] Judgment No. ECW/CCJ/JUD/ 06/08, § 36 of the judgment.

African Commission on Human Rights was invoked in support of such viewpoint, as well as the principle according to which charges cannot be made against a State at the international level except where it has defaulted on its obligations at the national level, that is to say when the courts before which the cases were actually lodged, did not sanction the defaults. In response, the Court recalls first of all that the rule of exhaustion of local remedies is far from being absolute, that not only may the States parties to a convention freely renounce it, but that international jurisprudence has relaxed numerous aspects of the rule. Then – and that is what is of interest to us here – the Court states that whatever the case may be, it is not bound by the practice of the African Commission on Human and Peoples' Rights, the supervisory organ for the correct application of the Charter:

> "The adherence of the Community to the principles of the Charter signifies that in the absence of ECOWAS legal instruments relating to human rights, the Court ensures the protection of the rights spelt out in the Charter, without necessarily proceeding to do so in the same manner as the African Commission on Human and Peoples' Rights.
>
> Indeed, from the interpretation of Article 4(g) of the Revised Treaty, one cannot deduce that the modalities for the protection and promotion of human rights by the Court must be those provided for by the Charter"[178].

We may cite a second example of the autonomy in the Court's approach. It concerns the conception of the status of "victim" and of "locus standi". We know indeed that the relevant provisions are crystal clear, with Article 10 of the new Article 10 only providing for "*individuals on application for relief for violation of their human rights*". The West African judge has made a relatively strict construction of the notions of "victim" and "locus standi". To that extent, the Court's position is clearly diametrically opposed to that of the African Commission on Human and Peoples' Rights, before which one may well assert that *actio popularis* is admitted[179]. In other words, claims brought before the Commission may originate from a person or an entity not a direct victim, that person or entity may not have suffered the effects of the default complained of. And in fact, it has occurred that the Court admit cases from non-governmental organisations, and even from

178 *Ibid,* §42 and 43.

179 See, for example, *Bakweri Land Claims Committee* **v.** *Cameroon,* Decision of 24 November -7 December 2004, Petition No. 260/02, §46; *Law Society of Zimbabwe* **v.** *Zimbabwe,* Decision of 19-25 February 2013, Petition No. 321/06 §58.

ordinary law firms at times incorporated outside the African continent, with charges made against States.

Again, forming part of this liberal practice is the option adopted by the ECOWAS Court to institute a "right for making charges", granted to entities that may not have suffered the harm. Such entities are recognised as having the power to defend the interests of the victim by filing complaints on the violations the victim may have suffered. There again, the African Charter sets itself apart by glossing over every requirement related to the status of a "victim", Articles 55 and 56 being silent on that point, opening up the possibility, we have thus deduced, of the applicant before the Commission not being the one that may have been the victim of the violation in question. Along the same lines, Article 44 of the American Convention on Human Rights provides that:

> "Any person or group of persons, or any nongovernmental entity legally recognized in one or more member states of the Organization, may lodge petitions with the Commission containing denunciations or complaints of violation of this Convention by a State Party."

From the opposing angle of that stance, the ECOWAS Court of Justice adopts a relatively strict view of the concepts of "victim" and "locus standi". The Court has first of all laid emphasis on the necessity that the harm suffered, and resulting in the disputed violation, shall be personal to the applicant, and this shall constitute the basis of the locus standi. In its judgment of 9 May 2011 on *Center for Democracy and Developpement and Center for Defence of Human rights and Democracy* **v.** *Mamadou Tandja and Republic of Niger*, and after citing the terms of Article 10 the 2005 Protocol, the Court finds that:

> "... it can be deduced from the points of the case that the Applicants are legal persons incorporated under the laws of the Federal Republic of Nigeria and of the Republic of Benin, as regards respectively, the Center for Democracy and Development and the Center for the Defence of Human Rights and Democracy in Africa. Now, in the circumstances of the case, even if one should suppose that the said association possess the legal status in their respective countries, they have not evinced their status as victims or justified that they are qualified to act on behalf of the victims whose mandate they must have received.(...). The Court (...) finds that the decisions taken by Mr. Mamadou Tandja have effect on only the nationals of Niger and possibly on residents of the said country. But, the Applicants are not Associations formed from the laws of Niger and do not have any justification either as constituting a part of the

Republic of Niger. The said decisions cannot therefore be against them and does not concern them either intimately or remotely; they cannot therefore constitute victims of the consequences of such decisions. Ultimately, they cannot be identified as victims[180].

Similarly, in the case law on *Oumar Mariko* **v.** *Republic of Mali* (Judgment of 12 February 2014), the Court holds that Oumar Mariko cannot claim the status of being a victim of violation of his rights, since he was not a candidate to the presidential elections, within the meaning of the electoral law of Mali; consequently, his case was dismissed[181].

Still, the Court's demanding conception of *locus standi* and the ensuing necessity which "deals with" the victim in the case, compel the Community judge to ask for the production of a power of attorney when the personal or direct victims decide to delegate somehow the locus standi. For the Court, the presence of the victims shall always be recalled, and it shall not be a question of them "disappearing" or "winding up". This is apparent in the judgment of 17 March 2011 on *Bakary Sarré and 28 Others* **v.** *Republic of Mali* where the Court states that:

> "It follows from this provision (i.e. Article 10 of the 2005 Supplementary Protocol on the Court, as cited in the above-stated judgment), that the admissibility of an application is linked, among other criteria, to the status of the victim. This condition necessarily entails that the applicant, acting on personal grounds as a result of a legally protected injured interest, reserves the right to come before a judge to have his claims examined; alternatively, an applicant, authorised to act by virtue of a power of attorney on behalf of another person or for a group of people whose legally protected interests have been harmed, shall exercise the power of representation in the action (...). Bringing an action before a court of law is a vested power, and it is up to the holder of that prerogative either to execute it himself or entrust that power to a third party (...). Thus, the said power of attorney which accords joint powers of representation does not confer on Mr. Bakary Sarré any legal title to act before the Court of Justice of ECOWAS on behalf of the said year-group. As a result, there are grounds for concluding that Mr. Bakary Sarré does not have the locus standi for lodging the instant case in the name of the judges of his year-group"[182].

---

[180] Judgment No. ECW/CCJ/JUD/ 05/11, §§28 and 29.

[181] Judgment No. ECW/CCJ/JUD/03/14, §29.

[182] Judgment No. ECW/CCJ/JUD/03/11, §§ 37 and 38.

This viewpoint of the Court is reaffirmed in several other decisions[183], one of the latest being that of 30 June 2015 on *167 Former Workers of SONIDEP Represented by Eli Haggar and B. Kanfideni* **v.** *Republic of Niger and SONIDEP*, where the judge observes that those claiming to be representing the Applicants had not given proof of their power of attorney. Indeed the Court ruled that they had not registered any such power of representation for and on behalf of the purported principals of the applicants; that they did not file any pleading authorising them to represent the Applicants before the Court of Justice. The Court therefore concluded that they did not qualify to act on behalf of the Applicants[184].

This jurisprudence, in relation to that of the African Commission on Human and Peoples' Rights, in our view, deserve to be commended. It is appropriate indeed to remind ourselves that the two bodies are not the same and they do not have the same mandate, nor the same powers. The Court remains a judicial body, whose mode of operation is embedded in texts, and is required to keep to a rigorous application of certain standards of procedural law. Unlike the Commission, the Court is not a body devoted to "promoting" human rights, it does not have that "militant" dimension, and essential limitations, necessarily linked to its status of a court of justice, brings about specific consequences as to the applications brought before it.

The Court is necessarily less "generous" than the Commission, which does not mean that in other respects, it cannot manifest the attitude of being "flexible" or accommodating, vis-à-vis the feeling of abandonment in the peculiar picture of an individual who has decided to sue a State, a non-egalitarian configuration, which often characterises proceedings on human rights. And in actual fact, it has occurred that the Court interpret some of its rules in a way manifestly favourable to the applicant[185].

---

183 Judgment No. ECW/CCJ/JUD/04/12 of 31 January 2012, *Aziablévi Yovo and 31 Others* **v.** *Société Togo Telecom and Republic of Togo* (§§10 and 11); Judgment No. ECW/CCJ/JUD/04/14 of 12 February 2014, *Boureima Sidi Cissé* **v.** *Republic of Mali* (p.10)

184 §IV.13, 15.

185 Such "generosity" is thus manifested by the fact that even if the Court does not admit applicants "*actio popularis*", it all the same makes provision for individuals to be defended by an "agent", who is not necessarily a professional lawyer, but could be an NGO or an "activist" group. That is a case of an independent stand of the notion of "agent" being, without doubt, associated with the presence of the State at the trial (notably like the International Court of Justice at The Hague). Despite the end of the monopoly of States in court actions, and the consequent appearance of private persons on the judicial scene (reform of the 2005 and jurisdiction of the Court in matters of human rights violation), the possibility of being represented by an agent is nevertheless maintained. In fact, it was a question of enabling private persons to be defended before the Court, not only by "lawyers",

As we can see, dialogue amongst judges is a reality in the proceedings at the ECOWAS Court of Justice. Such dialogue, which is sometimes engaged in like Molière's Monsieur Jourdain, who was writing prose without being conscious of doing so – that is to say, spontaneously, and without being aware at times –, assumes several shades. With the domestic judge, the dialogue essentially takes the shape of a restraint, a goodwill which leads the Court to put on an attitude of reluctance towards trying or retrying either part or the entire case. To abstain in that manner is to pay homage, a way of raising the national judiciary to the same level of dignity as that of the international. The judges and the judiciaries are of equal merit, a presumption of equality which also operates like a principle of economy: one may dispense with re-examining what has already been settled by a peer, one may, at most, draw lessons from the initial pronouncement. But we also saw that the same dialogue had room for perfection, riddled as it is with huge gaps, flaws, untapped avenues, like in the area of referrals for preliminary determination, or communication with the other human rights judge, in the shape of the constitutional judge.

With the international judge, dialogue or confrontation of case laws brings to light disagreements, which must not raise any undue cause for alarm. The status of the courts, their rules of reference, the conditions of access, may be some of the factors which explain why they do not agree on all things at all times. In the current circumstances, disagreement is an ingredient of dialogue, and may even constitute the salt of dialogue. The fact still remains, however, that the zones of convergence supersede the bones of contention. As a human rights judge – a description which, more than other descriptions, lends itself to judicial diplomacy, and urges one to look out for what is going on elsewhere – the judge at the ECOWAS Court thus demonstrates that he is a product of the contemporary world, even if he still has more to do, in that regard, to forge ahead.

June 2017

---

but equally by the so-called "agents". That is a demonstration of judicial goodwill and a tacit acknowledgement of a form of peculiarity associated with the trial proceedings on human rights violation, thus bringing in the inequality of arms between a private person and a State, and calling forth a form of assistance for the applicant.

THE FUTURE OF THE ECOWAS COURT OF JUSTICE

More than 25 years after the drafting of its Rules of Procedure, and in particular, more than 15 years after it was actually put in place, the ECOWAS Court of Justice has come up with a practice, and has produced a jurisprudence comprised of elements which give room for initial stock taking. But more than taking stock here, *per se*, we intend to acknowledge what has so far been achieved, as a springboard, for reflecting on the future of the Court; it is a question of peeping into the future, on the basis of the gains made by the Court in the course of its practice. It is still appropriate to indicate that we are much less concerned here with a projection of the future of the Court in terms of a prophesy or a prognosis, than with a totally justified standpoint which is aimed at emphasising the dangers lying in wait for the Community Court and the options which appear to us as plausible, in line with the mandate assigned the Court, and the tasks ahead of it. Making pronouncements on these matters appears so necessary to us that today, when it has become a question of putting the Court in a context of "institutional reform"; the 51st Summit of the ECOWAS Heads of State and Government (Monrovia, 4-5 June 2017) has just emphasised the importance of its implementation, certain aspects of which undoubtedly deserved to have been discussed more globally and with an in-depth approach[186]. There is even the fear that the current reform may throw off balance the institutional stability of the Court and spring up unpleasant surprises.

It is appropriate to state that even before the said institutional reform was embarked upon, the Court took the initiative to propose a preliminary draft of a Protocol, normally expected to be examined by experts from the Member States (representing notably the Ministers of Justice) before being submitted to the ECOWAS Council of Ministers. The initiative taken by the ECOWAS Court, on the basis of the 1991 Protocol[187], was submitted to the ECOWAS Commission, the supervising authority of the

---

[186] Press release of 4 June 2017, Monrovia, N° xxx/2017

[187] Article 33 §1 of Protocol A/P1/7/91 of 6 July 1991: "1. *Any Member State or the President of the Court may after consultation with the other members, submit proposals for amendments of this Protocol.*"

procedure which should lead to the adoption of the text. But nothing indicates, unfortunately, that the process will be carried out to a successful end. Several reforms have been designed in the past for the ECOWAS Court, the texts governing the Court remain dispersed and sometimes incoherent, and it does not appear that one has a clear idea of what has been envisaged for the future of Court, hence the necessity of a prospective view on the said judicial body. A discussion towards the future of the Court must not in any way jettison the current achievements, some of which, in our view, must be maintained and safeguarded. That is the status of such a judiciary, of which an author said – in another context, but the terms which would be appropriate to reproduce here – that, it be actually examined

> "... against the background of two constants which behove the judge to reconcile. On one hand, legal security, like equality before the law, require foreseeable solutions and demand that similar cases be given identical treatment: the unity and continuity of jurisprudence form the basis of the legitimacy of the judge. On the other hand, new questions are raised, concepts evolve, and the law and the citizens do come up with expectations which have to be dealt with by jurisprudence through flexibility, innovation and inventiveness. An immovable jurisprudence would mark the decline of the judge. Marrying stability and creativity appears, in the final analysis, as the key to the quality of the jurisprudential norm"[188].

The present contribution, which serves the purpose of a viaticum, will lean on the current two dimensions of the ECOWAS Court: **(I)** as a court of justice set up to serve the ends of integration, and **(II)** as a human rights court.

I.- The Court, as mandated to fashion out integration

Such was the initial mandate of the Court, in effect; it is appropriate never to lose sight of this. (A): Unfortunately, certain current rules hamper the successful conduct of that mandate, in as much as they weaken the status of the Community Court of ECOWAS. (B): The other matter of concern is the deficit in collaboration between the national judge and the Community judge, a reality which is no more than the

---

[188] STIRN B., La qualité de la norme jurisprudentielle *in Autour de la qualité des normes,* Proceedings of the Colloquium of Aix en Provence, 24 and 25 October 2008, directed by FATIN – ROUGE STEFANINI M., GAY L., PINI J., Brussels, Bruylant 2010, p. 262.

judicial manifestation of the weakness of the Community integration, or the alleged perception, by the judicial actors who should, ideally, be the bearers of the norms of that very integration.

A.- Weakness in statutory provision

In the course of reading through the rules governing the Court, one cannot avoid being confronted with two points which are not only categorically proved in the light of the norms obtaining under similar regional legal frameworks, but are obviously of such nature as compromise the overall efficiency of ECOWAS.

One rule concerns the tenure of the judges. It is, in the terms of the reform carried out by the Supplementary Protocol of 14 June 2006, "*four years non-renewable*". This rule, a revision of the tenure of five years, renewable once – provided for in the 1991 Protocol – constitutes an obvious heresy. One may even wonder how it got adopted and on what bases it was defended. Incidentally, the ECOWAS Court of Justice is, to our knowledge, the only international court which provides for such a short tenure, and fails to guarantee the minimal equanimity for the judges, and a stable jurisprudence. Actually, there is a consolidation of work ethics, and deliberation amongst judges, with regard to jurists of different training backgrounds (Common Law judges or Romano-Germanic system, which often refer to different practices and linguistic expressions, training of juridical actors – judges, lawyers; – or academicians – professors, juris consults; – practice of "civil" law or "private" law or on the contrary, "public" law, even public international law, etc.). In contrast, for example, to a court like the UEMOA Court, the members of the ECOWAS Court necessarily come from different legal backgrounds – if for nothing at all, from the linguistic point of view – and they do not have the same judicial practices, the very rules of their recruitment clearly stating the diversity of their professional origins. It would have been desirable to take account of this, and accord the judges a little time to iron out these potential sources of conflict. Instead, it was preferred to adopt a uniform rule of general application, equally applicable to the members of the ECOWS Commission. The short duration of the tenure is an absurdity, and to streamline the tenure of the officers of a legal organ on the same basis as the administrative or executive organ is equally absurd, as can be deduced from the comparative tables below:

Comparable courts of justice	Tenure
UEMOA Court of Justice	6 years renewable
CEMAC Court of Justice	6 years renewable
SADC Tribunal	5 years renewable
OHADA Court of Justice	7 years renewable once
African Court on Human and Peoples' Rights	6 years renewable once
COMESA Court of Justice	5 years renewable once
International Court of Justice	9 years renewable
International Tribunal for the Law of the Sea	5 years renewable
Court of Justice of the European Union	6 years renewable
European Court of Human Rights	9 years non-renewable
International Criminal Court	9 years renewable
Inter-American Court of Human Rights	6 years renewable once

A close look at the international standards being observed on the issue under consideration does reveal that in all the currently operating international courts, the statutory regimes applicable to the tenure of judges either provide for a long non-renewable term of office or a relatively shorter renewable tenure.

Besides, putting the tenure of the legal arm at par with that of the executive arm of the organisation does not practically exist anywhere in the world.

ORGANISATION	Tenure of executive organ	Tenure of judges
UEMOA	Commission : 4 years renewable	6 years renewable
CEMAC	Commission : 5 years renewable	6 years renewable once
SADC	Secretariat : 4 years renewable once	5 years renewable once
COMESA	Secretariat : 4 years renewable	5 years renewable once
AFRICAN UNION	Commission : 4 years renewable	6 years renewable once
EUROPEAN UNION	Commission : 5 years non-renewable	6 years renewable
ECOWAS (before 2006)	Commission (formerly Executive Secretariat) : 4 years renewable once	5 years renewable once
ECOWAS (currently)	Commission : 4 years non-renewable	4 years non-renewable
UNO	General Secretariat: 5 years renewable	9 years renewable

The question of the tenure of judges is not the only one which poses a problem in terms of statutory guarantees[189]. A word must be said on the absence of a bridge between the Court and other arms of ECOWAS, notably the inter-governmental organs like the Authority of Heads of State and the Council of Ministers. Even though the judges of the Court are appointed by the Authority, or by its current Chairman, there is no means of communication between the Court and the Authority. There is however a simple means, and relatively current, of carrying out such communication: the preparation of an annual report by the Court, which the Court could, on an annual basis for example, address to the other organs of ECOWAS. As at now, that kind of report does not exist. The only modality by which the Court reports on its programmes and activities remains relatively informal, because in fact, it is by way of a "contribution", prepared upon the request of the Commission, that the latter incorporates the information provided in its own annual report. In other words, the activities conducted by the Court and the reporting made thereon are "drowned" in the account related by the ECOWAS body which assumes the role of a secretariat. It follows therefore that such practice cannot bring out the "visibility" of the Court within the context of the institutional debate which should ideally have taken place at ECOWAS.

Beyond the mere formality of producing an annual report, a report prepared by the Court will not only have the merit of providing information on the accomplishment of its mandate, but would confirm the dignity conferred on the Court by the texts. It is worthy to recall that the Court is the only ECOWAS institution whose founding treaty calls for independence (Article 15). We will add that the 14 June 2006 Supplementary Protocol raises very clearly the level required for the recruitment of a judge, in providing notably that a judge at the Court shall – again – be **"independent",** and be:

> "...selected and appointed from nationals of the Member States who are persons of high moral character, and possess the qualification required in their respective countries for appointment to the highest judicial officers, or are juris consults of recognised competence in international law (...) community law or the law of regional integration." (Article 3(1) new).

---

[189] Another worrying prospect could be the reduction in the number of judges (from seven to five, as is being whispered at the time these lines are being written), a reform which is not only diametrically opposed to the surge in number of applications coming before the Court, but hinders the accomplishment of other functions assigned the Court, such as arbitration – a Rules of Arbitration having been drafted already – without considering other areas of competence not yet operational, but which can be activated at any time, as we shall see later. The rationale of "cost reduction" being put forth by the proposed reform project should be absolutely inappropriate here. Apart from the significance of the expected "savings" being doubtful, such reform would simply tilt negatively towards "reducing the value" of the ECOWAS Court, in disregard, at any rate, of the very texts on the Court.

The words used do send our minds to the qualities required of members of the principal judicial organ of the United Nations, the International Court of Justice, at The Hague.

In the draft proposal prepared by the Court itself – unfortunately left in limbo –the two concerns which have just been expressed were however taken into account. Amendment of the judges' tenure and the institution of an annual report were proposed. By coincidence, such a report, a true means of expression for the Court, will only be destined for the inter-governmental organs of ECOWAS. For the fluidity of the ECOWAS inter-institutional conversation, it has been proposed that the document in question be equally transmitted to the ECOWAS Commission and the ECOWAS Parliament, through their respective heads of institution.

Outside these issues of statutory order, the future of the ECOWAS Court cannot be reflected upon minus a worrying phenomenon: the low rate at which the norms of integration are invoked, both before the Court itself and before the domestic judge.

B.- Abandonment of the law of integration

As paradoxical as that may seem, it is indeed the marginality of the law of integration that one needs to discuss. Integration law, it is the least we can say, is largely under-utilised, largely untapped.

It suffices to refer to the two procedures which, *par excellence*, make a demand on the norms of integration: cases on default to fulfil a Community obligation (before the ECOWAS Court) and referrals for preliminary determination (triggered by a domestic court)[190]. In the first, it is a question of a State having defaulted in its obligations as a member of the Community of States; the State has thus failed to observe the norms laid down by the Community, irrespective of the legal instrument which enacted the rule (original or derived law). In principle, an action for default is initiated by a Member State or by the President of the ECOWAS Commission (new Article 10(a) of the Supplementary Protocol on the Court). Now, till today, no action for default has been instituted before the Court. Far from depicting a strict observance of the obligations of the Member States, the absence of actions for default in

[190] These two procedures, like other processes provided for before the Court, were largely inspired by the 1957 Rome Treaty establishing the European Economic Community. Other integration bodies in Africa, equipped with a legal organ, have also adopted those provisions (UEMOA and CEMAC notably).

obligations rather indicates either an ignorance of the rules produced by ECOWAS, or a clearly diplomatic form of reluctance in suing a Member State before the Court, for fear that such a step may result in a deterioration of the quality of relations between the suing State and the State being sued. If the latter point is not to be ignored, if almost all the States are are sensitive to that fact – including organisations like EEC/EU, known for their very "integrated" nature – one must not hide the fact that it is all the same worrying that the Court has never had, in more than fifteen years of functioning, an occasion to tackle a case of violation of the Community law by a State.

This fact particularly shows that the law argued before the Court is not the ECOWAS law. And indeed, essentially, and since the 2005 reform, the Court has virtually become a judicial body mandated to sanction human rights violation, and that – the more important point here – these human rights are provided in instruments not engendered by ECOWAS. Most of the time, indeed, the conventions relied on by the applicants were either made by the United Nations (The 1966 Conventions and others) or the OAU/AU (African Charter on Human and Peoples' Rights).

The other contentious jurisdictions remain marginal before the Court, be it actions for examining the legality of acts by the Community or those concerning Community public service, these two procedures being thus initiated by private individuals whose interests are threatened. Consequently, it must not be deduced from the functioning or case law of the Court that the law of integration is promoted or defended, for, indeed, that law is not in contention. The reality is not pleasing, for the Court is to serve the purpose of integration, the objective for setting up the Court is situated within a broader economic outlook, and there is some disappointment in seeing the Court somewhat distanced from that perspective.

The current picture can even, from a purely psychological point of view, constitute a disservice to the image of the institution. Adjudicating almost entirely on issues of human rights violation, it may acquire the image of an essentially "repressive" arm of ECOWAS, and coming before the Court may be seen as an occasion for snubbing the States, instead of serving the interests of the flourishing of the economies of the States. This is the reason why it is urgent to think of the means by which the law of integration may be revived, the law for whose preservation the Court was given birth to.

In terms of the national judge, it is through the referral for preliminary determination that one could have had an idea of the extent to which the Community law may have been invoked or applied, but the overall result from our expectations, there again, remains desperately poor. Unlike other sister courts, such as the Court of Justice of UEMOA or the Court of Justice of CEMAC, the ECOWAS Court of Justice has indeed never been seised with an application by the domestic courts, for preliminary determination.

We need to remind ourselves that the mechanism of referrals from the domestic courts to the ECOWAS Court, for the purposes of preliminary determination on specific matters of the Community law, is a procedure whereby the national judge, confronted with an issue on Community Law, submits the matter before a judge at the ECOWAS Community Court, for the interpretation of such ECOWAS norm, excluding comments on validity or invalidity.

In principle, it is the frequency of such referrals before the ECOWAS Court which would have given us an idea of the rate of penetration of the ECOWAS law into the Member States, and into their judicial practice. If we should limit ourselves to those statistics and no more than that, one would thus have to conclude that the rate of penetration is low, that the law of integration, in the Member States, is actually disregarded or abandoned. Certainly, the national judge is positioned on the front line of the Community law, for nothing prevents him from proceeding, himself, to interpret and apply the ECOWAS law, once he considers that the conditions are met (notably on the basis of clarity of meaning). There could therefore be instances of application of the Community law which may not necessarily be known to the Court of Abuja. But, in truth, nothing enables us to affirm that there is any statistically significant figure for such spontaneous application of the Community law by the domestic courts. One can safely bet that if one should proceed to take a count of the frequency of use of the Community law by the national courts, the relevant cases obtained would constitute a rare commodity.

Now, the paucity of the final figures is a far cry from the splendour of the mandate assigned to the Court by the texts. The Preamble to the 2005 Supplementary Protocol assigns to the Court the role of carrying out "*elimination of the obstacles to the realisation of Community objectives and accelerating the integration process*", and that of "*effectively ensuring that Member States fulfil their obligations*". The least which can be said is that the current result does not rhyme with the task assigned.

The Court must be absolved from all blame in connection with the situation. Not invested with the power to try cases on its own, the Court can only try cases brought before it and, in principle, within the terms pleaded by the parties in the trial. It is, on the contrary, up to those pleading for the parties, that is to say the lawyers, to argue points having a bearing on the rules of integration. It is up to them to remember, for example, that a State bringing charges against a Community citizen of another Member State for illegal immigration may necessitate reference to laws enacted by ECOWAS on freedom of movement of persons, some of which date back to the 1980s; it is up to them to have recourse to the rules of freedom of establishment or equality of treatment within the ECOWAS space when restrictions are imposed on the exercise of a liberal profession or registration in a university in another Member State; it is up to them to look into the ECOWAS law for rules relating to free competition so as to defend a company or businessman who considers himself unfairly treated within the territory of the Community, etc.. Scenarios of disputes of these nature abound, and there is no lack of rules of the Community law, at least awaiting to be applied. The real question is rather, as we can see, the awareness of the relevant rules or access to those rules. It should be expected that with time, the hindrances to the deficit of application of the rules of the Community law of integration will reduce. From that standpoint, the intensification of intra-Community exchanges could be a huge catalyst. It is out of the trading of goods and amongst the inhabitants of the Community space that judicially fertile contradictions will be born, that is to say, issues will arise, and require to be settled by trial proceedings in court.

II.- The Court, as a human rights court

It is as a human rights court that the Court delivers almost all its judgments today. This function is not negligible, even if it has been stressed that the initial mandate of the Court was – and remains – to serve the ends of the interpretation and application of rules of economic integration. On the role of the Court as a body mandated to make judgments on matters of human rights, several reflections on the future of the Court may be made, intermittently, on (A) the trial conducted before the Court; and on (B) the decisions made by the Court.

A.- The trial conducted by the Court

It would be desirable that, in three areas, options will have to be made.

The first has to do with *the jurisdiction of the Court and the mandate assigned it*. We are concerned with drawing attention to the risks of overloading the Court, and in the end, adulterating its role. It must be recalled that the Court was originally assigned the role of interpreting and applying rules of integration. The Court itself, we have seen, had a "militant" mandate; it was required to promote the Community law through its operation. That was the reason why the mode of organisation of trial proceedings before the Court was exactly the same as that of the first Court of Justice of the European Communities (CJEC), a creation of the 1957 Treaty of Rome. Then came in the 2005 reform granting the Court jurisdiction in the area of human rights violation. We know that, for now, it is virtually on the basis of that jurisdiction alone that cases are brought before the Court. There are two possibilities however, sometimes advocated, for extension of the powers of the Court: as a criminal court and as an arbitration court.

The probability for the Court to exercise criminal jurisdiction – and thus to try private persons guilty of offences – truly remains quite unlikely, no decisive act having been made in that direction. But it shall be appropriate to put forward a word of caution against such temptation, which rears its head from time to time. Conferring on the Court such powers would amount to adulterating it once and for all, and to sow seeds of confusion. As a "jack of all trades", the Court runs the risk of delivering muddled or unreadable judgments. Being the legal organ of an organisation seeking economic integration, it is desirable that it remains so, and resist the distracting calls for the "criminalisation" of its jurisdiction, which has somewhat become fashionable. Indeed, within the context of an African continent that gives a cold shoulder to a universal criminal justice system, which it accuses of not being sufficiently "criminal" in justice, voices have been raised at regular intervals to claim an endogenous justice, that is to say African courts mandated to sanction high profile violations of the law. Under such circumstances, the idea of turning spontaneously to courts which have been set up for protecting human rights, to carry through that mission, could be tempting. The ups and downs experienced by the African Court on Human and Peoples' Rights equally prove our point.

Established under the 2008 Ouagadougou Protocol, the said court was thereafter "fused" with the Court of Justice of the African Union (whose establishment was provided for in the Constitutive Act of AU), within the terms of the 1 July 2008 Protocol on the African Court of Justice and Human Rights. Another Protocol amended the latter protocol, in 2014, by adding to the jurisdiction of the Court that of sanctioning a number of "crimes" (Article 28A)[191]. We thus see that assigning criminal competences to the ECOWAS Court would corrupt, not only the nature and rationale behind the establishment of the Court, but engender conflicts with the African Court of Justice and Human Rights. If tomorrow, the judge on the bench of the West African Court is to make judgments on criminal cases, it must be understood that the very organisation and functioning of the ECOWAS Court would be transformed. The Court will need new institutions and a new apparatus, for example, for conducting inquiries – including, of course, investigations on the crime scenes – a prosecution panel for organising and putting in place, the means for execution of the sentences, etc. These tasks, on their own, suffice to make the hands of the Court very full. If one should add to that the current function of the Court, already daunting enough – because it involves being a judge over enforcement of all the relevant conventions binding on States in matters concerning human rights – one can legitimately wonder if such a project is feasible.

Equally related to the issue of extension of the mandate or jurisdiction of the Court is the possibility that it may be made to play the role of an arbitration body. This angle of the matter is not, like the previous one, a pure conjecture, since it features in the ECOWAS Treaty itself. Indeed, in the terms of Article 16 of the said treaty:

> "There is hereby established an Arbitration Tribunal of the Community. The status, composition, powers, procedure and other issues concerning the Arbitration Tribunal shall be set out in a Protocol relating thereto."

It is provided that pending the establishment of the Tribunal, the Court shall equally act as an Arbitrator[192], and a draft Rules of Arbitration of the Court has already been prepared, as indicated above. Two questions may thus be asked. The first is of the quantitative aspect. It

[191] Article 28A : "Subject to the right of appeal, the International Criminal Law Section of the Court shall have power to try persons for the crimes provided hereunder:

1) Genocide 2) Crimes Against Humanity 3) War Crimes 4) The Crime of Unconstitutional Change of Government; 5) Piracy 6) Terrorism 7) Mercenarism 8) Corruption 9) Money Laundering 10) Trafficking in Persons 11) Trafficking in Drugs 12) Trafficking in Hazardous Wastes 13) Illicit Exploitation of Natural Resources 14) The Crime of Aggression".

[192] New Article 9 §5 (2005 Protocol).

requires that we interrogate ourselves as to the viability of the option made by the text, considering the fact that the number of disputes submitted before the Court is not sufficiently huge to warrant such a generous offer of modes of settlement of the cases coming before the Court. Virtually no State has yet come before the Court as an applicant in a case.

We have already said, that the contentious matters coming before the Court are essentially made up of cases brought for human rights violation, in which it is a State that is sued at court. The current posture of the cases and trials before the Court leave very little space for the conduct of arbitral functions by the Court, at any rate in the short term.

But supposing even that the quantitative issue be resolved, the transformation of the Court into an arbitral tribunal could pose a problem, from a qualitative point of view. Indeed, if the Court were to make arbitral awards, it could create a situation which would result in a dilution of the Community law, since the mastery of the law applicable by the parties – a mastery postulated of the arbitral mode of settlement – is capable of leading those litigating on behalf of the applicants, to choose a body of rules which has nothing to do with the Community law of ECOWAS. The emergence or autonomy of the ECOWAS Community law could therefore suffer as a result. We may be permitted to recall thus that

> "It is doubtful that such 'justice à la carte' is what would be needed by organisations which have fixed for themselves the objective of realising integration among States"[193].

Strangely, at any rate, a provision of the 2005 Protocol seems to be out of sync with the introduction of arbitral justice into the ECOWAS system since it is entitled "*Exclusivity of Competence and Recognition of the Decisions of the Court*", and states in its paragraph 1 that

> "No dispute regarding or application of the provisions of the Treaty may be referred to any other form of settlement except that which is provided for by the Treaty or this Protocol"(Article 22 of the 1991 Protocol).

Incidentally, it must be recalled that even within the framework of its strictly judicial powers, the Court is competent to adjudicate on a range of disputes whose elasticity cannot always be predicted. Indeed, apart

---

[193] SALL A., *La justice de l'intégration. Réflexions sur les institutions judiciaires de la CEDEAO et de l'UEMOA*, Dakar, CREDILA, 2011, p. 43. (The Justice of Integration: Reflections on the Judicial Institutions of ECOWAS and UEMOA)

from the most commonly known kinds of cases capable of coming before the Court, and which are provided for in the new Article 9 of the 2005 Protocol[194], the Court shall have jurisdiction over three other types of cases, according to the same text:

> "... over any matter provided for in an agreement where the parties provide that the Court shall settle disputes arising from the agreement.(new Article 9 §6); over any other matters or issues thus – "This Court shall all the powers conferred on it by the provisions of this Protocol as well as any other powers that may be conferred by subsequent Protocols and Decisions of the Community (§7), or any other dispute the Authority deems fit to bring before the Court: "The Authority of Heads of State and Government shall have the power to grant the Court the power to adjudicate on any specific dispute that it may refer to the Court other than those specified in this Article"(§8).

To all these provisions of the Protocol, one needs to add the provisions of the ECOWAS Treaty itself, where we read that any dispute regarding the interpretation or application of the provisions of the Treaty may come before the Court for determination (Article 76). The Court is thus potentially vested with powers to adjudicate on so many different kinds of disputes, just by virtue of being the legal organ of ECOWAS. Under such conditions, there is cause to be apprehensive about projections towards assigning more powers to the Court, be they under criminal or arbitral jurisdiction.

The second significant area of interrogation concerns *actors in the trial, more precisely, the issue of "amicus curiae"* before the Court. As at now, this particular point has not been provided for in any provision. The only traces found in the texts partly concern recourse to expert opinion, and partly, intervention procedure. Regarding the first, Article 16 of the 1991 Protocol states that:

> "The Court may, in any circumstance, and, in accordance with its Rules of Procedure, order any manner of judicial enquiry summon any person, organisation or institution to carry out an enquiry or give an expert

[194] We are talking of interpretation and application of the original and derived law of ECOWAS, and adjudication on disputes relating to: legality (of rules, regulations, directives, decisions of subsidiary legal instruments adopted by ECOWAS), failure to fulfil Community obligations, disputes on Community public service, action for damages against a Community institution or Community official, and human rights violation occurring in any Member State.

opinion"[195]. Moreover, Article 21 of the same document (entitled Application for Intervention) stipulates that: "Should a Member State consider that it has an interest that may be affected by the subject matter of a dispute before the Court, it may submit by way of a written application a request to be permitted to intervene"[196].

If these provisions are cited, it is because, without making any exact reference to the participation of an *amicus curiae* in the trial proceedings, they more or less match up to the role that an amicus curiae may play before the Court, but in truth, as we shall see, amicus curiae interventions must be substituted with a more precise and more satisfactory rule.

To the very approximate nature of the legal basis for the presence of amicus curiae in the current state of the texts, one must add the fluctuating jurisprudential stands adopted on amicus curiae intervention in the trials proceedings. Indeed, now and then, the Court, without blinking, has had to admit *amici curiae* to the trial (refer *Tokumbo Lijadu-Oyemade* **v.** *Executive Secretary of ECOWAS and Others,* Judgment of 10 October 2005 ; *Linda Gomez and 7 Others* **v.** *Republic of The Gambia,* Judgment of 14 February 2014 ; pending case *Federation of African Journalists and 3 Others* **v.** *Republic of The Gambia*), and sooner or later, the Court has had to reject them, on the basis of Article 21 of the above-cited Protocol, by virtue of a faithful reading of that text: only States shall be admitted to "intervene", within the meaning of the article (cf. *Case Concerning CDP and Others* **v.** *Burkina Faso,* Judgment of 13 July

---

195 The Rules of the Court equally provide in its Article 45:
"*The Court may order that an expert's report be obtained. The order appointing the expert shall define his task and set a time limit within which he is to make his report. 2. The expert shall receive a copy of the order, together with all the documents necessary for carrying out his task. He shall be under the supervision of the Judge - Rapporteur, who may be present during his investigation and who shall be kept informed of his progress in carrying out his task. 3. The Court may request the parties or one of them to lodge security for the costs of the expert's report. 4. At the request of the expert, the Court may order the examination of witnesses. Their examination shall be carried out in accordance with Article 43 of these Rules. 5. The expert may give his opinion only on points, which have been expressly referred to him. 6. After the expert has made his report, the Court may order that he be examined, the parties having been given notice to attend. 7. Subject to the control of the President, questions may be put to the expert by the representatives of the parties. 8. Before carrying out his task, the expert shall take the following oath in written form or before the Court: "I swear or declare that I shall conscientiously and impartially carry out my task".*

196 Article 89 of the Rules of the Court stipulate, besides, in detailed form, the procedure of intervention before the Court.

2015, in terms of a non-State entity applying to take part in the trial as amicus curiae).

There is another thing. It is that the very concept of *amicus curiae*, at the international level, does not have one and the same meaning. Following the courts and judicial cultures, the content of that function may vary considerably. Let us recall first of all that *amicus curiae* is *a friend of the Court*, the concept refers to:

> "The prerogative accorded a personality or a body, non-party to a judicial procedure, to provide a court or tribunal with information of such nature as may throw more light on certain questions of law or fact"[197].

But before a court such as the European Court of Human Rights, things may turn out to be more complex since the notion of *amicus curiae* may indeed be subsumed in the concept of "third party intervention", introduced in the 11th Additional Protocol, which is capable of blending with three instances of intervention, all cited in Article 36 of the European Convention on Human Rights: intervention of States in trials in which their citizens are a party, a mechanism reminiscent of diplomatic protection (Article 36§1), intervention of a State party to a Convention but not party to a trial, or of any person with interest in the matter before court, upon invitation by the President of the Court and in the interest of an efficient administration of justice (Article 36 §2), and finally, intervention of the Commissioner of Human Rights, Council of Europe, in any case handled by a Chamber or the Grand Chamber (Article 36§3).

The abundance of illustration here is obviously not for clarifying the role of an *amicus curiae.* It must be added that the Court of Strasbourg itself does not excel in its own consistency and precision, since it talks as much of "*intervening party*"[198], as of "*amicus curiae*"[199] and of "*intervener*"[200], quite simply. If we should turn our attention to a court like the Inter-American Court of Human Rights, we may be confronted with the same scepticism when the said Court declares, in one of its judgments, that the absence of independence of a friend of the Court is not a justification for a rejection of his declarations or his witness[201]. Such

---

197 SALMON J. *Dictionnaire de droit international public*, cited above, p.62. (Dictionary of Public International Law)

198 Judgment on *Tashin Acar* **v.** *Turkey,* 6 May 2003.

199 Judgment on *Goodwin* **v.** *United Kingdom,* 11 July 2002.

200 Judgment on *Mamatkulov and Abdurasulovic* **v.** *Turkey,* 6 February 2003.

201 Judgment on *Suarez Rosero* **v.** *Ecuador*, 12 November 1997, series C, N°35, §32.

assessment seems to go contrary to the idea that an *amicus curiae* acts for the Court and not for a cause, and that the clarity of his contribution will be much guaranteed if his position were to be at equidistance between the parties.

In truth, the issue concerning the mission of the *amicus curiae* remains fairly undefined, such that the practice of the courts, to that extent, may manifest divergent approaches. That is why it is important that the ECOWAS Court of Justice defines itself the outlines and essential features of the concept, without giving the impression that the definition and content of the notion are shared by all the international judges. Indeed, we have seen that the case law of the Court on the matter is not stable, for lack of codified rules. We need to add that when the Community judge admitted the *amici curiae* before the Court in the above-cited cases, he did not see any need to justify their presence in the trial proceedings, as if an amicus curiae already had an acquired right for appearing in the procedure. For all these reasons, a clarification becomes imperative. There is a last point for which issue there is a justification that the ECOWAS Court pay further attention to: it is the quasi-generalisation of the practice before international courts. The West African judge cannot escape the realities of his time, and there is already a premonition that those pleading the cases in court themselves have taken the initiative to present themselves as *amici curiae* whereas there is no provision in that respect in the texts governing the Court. It is the sign that the practice could become a judicial custom that may be invoked in international courts. Let us add, in ending, that the phenomenon harbours, considering its philosophy, a significant relevance for courts devoted to human rights protection.

The concept should translate a consciousness of the necessity of delivering justice by taking extra account of certain constants the modern world, in defence of general interest, transparency, publicity, and even "democratisation of international law"[202].

With a view to formally admit an *amicus curiae* before the Court, the rules fixed could be based on the following principles[203] :

---

[202] MENETREY S., *L'amicus curiae, vers un principe commun de droit procédural ?*, Paris, Dalloz, 2010, p.211 (wok with rich content). (Amicus Curiae : Towards a Common Principle of Procedural Law)

[203] These principles are largely inspired by the conclusions of the work by MENETREY S., cited above.

- There is no acquired right for participating in the proceedings as *amicus curiae*; it is up to the Court to decide, according to the nature of the case, who the Court invites or admits in such capacity;
- The Court shall examine the capacity of the *amicus curiae* in accordance with the following criteria: independence, impartiality, scope of representation. The *amicus curiae* shall indeed be *a friend of the Court*, and shall help the Court to take its decision, but is not a party "interested in" or defending any of the points argued by the principal parties;
- The Court may *suo motu* request an individual or entity to intervene as *amicus curiae.* In that case, he is not bound to show the interest of his participation;
- An *amicus curiae* shall file a reasoned application to the Court, detailing the interest of his participation in the procedure; he must not suddenly "intrude" upon the hearing in court, for, it must be said once again, there is no automatic right for coming before the Court in the capacity of an amicus curiae; such application by the *amicus curiae* shall be transmitted to the parties;
- The Court shall serve the parties with the memorial lodged by the *amicus curiae* and receive, where necessary, the observations made by the parties, for the parties to have an interest in that regard;
- The participation of an *amicus curiae* shall not have any connection with the actual facts of the dispute, and shall concern the general background of the case, the context of the case. The facts constituting the dispute shall be the exclusive preserve of the parties and of the Court;
- The opinions of an amicus curiae shall not be binding on the Court;
- An *amicus curiae* shall bear his own procedural costs; he shall not under any circumstance whatsoever ask the parties or the Court to pay his costs, except where his intervention in the procedure arose from an express invitation by the Court.

It is appropriate to indicate that the principle of an *amicus curiae* was retained in the draft proposal of the Protocol prepared by the Court in the year 2017, which seems to be of no relevance today. The text makes reference to the Rules of the Court, to set out the modalities for intervention, which are on the points which have just been made above[204].

There are other matters for querying on the future of the Court. They no more concern the trial before the Court, but the judgment delivered by the Court, still as a human rights court.

B.- The decisions made by the Court

From the point of view of the quality itself, there is still room for improvement in two regards today, in the decisions of the Court.

In their formal pattern, the judgments delivered do not *systematically have the same style of presentation.* Now, this practice of varying the manner of writing the decisions is not satisfactory. It is in the interest of a court to have "a trade mark", it is desirable for it to have a traditional form of presentation. That originality does not yet exist at the ECOWAS Court. To achieve that, two avenues could be explored: a systematic reading – and correction – of the draft decisions by all the judges, if possible, at least by the judges constituting the "panel", that is to say the "chamber", or the establishment of a service unit for writing the judgments, the latter option appearing to us however more difficult to realise, given the current state of affairs.

In terms of substance, the quality of the decisions made could be improved upon if a mechanism were to be devised through which, internally, the judges could be assisted. Such "assistance in judgment writing" could quite simply take the form of instituting a function of "Advocate General" or "Law Commissioner" - what name to call it may not matter much – whose job function would be to present in all independence, conclusions on the cases brought before the Court.

The discussion on the draft decision, as presented by such "solution provider", would certainly be of such nature as to raise the level of the demands of the decision, and would of course ensure added value for the judgments.

[204] In case it is impossible or difficult to work on the Protocols – which are in principle, international treaties – or even on the Rules of the Court, it would still be possible to rely on Article 100 of the Rules, which offers the possibility of *Practice Directions*, which could be formally adopted by the Court. The Court may take such steps by relying simultaneously on Article 16 of the 1991 Protocol, which opens an avenue for hearing "experts", or any "institution" or "body" which may further assist the Court in making its decision.

Regarding the verdict itself, it is known that as a human rights court, the ECOWAS Court sanctions transgressions attributable to States. But, experience shows that that judicial sanction is essentially exhaustive in two ways: compensatory reliefs, and more rarely, the order given to the State either to restore a person's freedom, or to institute a trial for someone.

A first question raised thus concerns *the mode of reparation chosen and possibilities of refinement.* Indeed, the case law of the Court excels on that point in its manifest clarity based on the fact that by fixing the amount of the reparation, the Court exercises a discretionary power. This principle is alluded to or recalled in a number of judgments, like in the Judgment of 7 June 2012, *Groupe RACECO* **v.** *ECOWAS Commission,* in which one reads that in making use of its discretionary power, the Court fixed CFA F 1,500,000 as the sum to be awarded him[205], or in Judgment of 8 February 2011, *El Hadji Tidjani Aboubacar* **v.** *Republic of Niger*, where the Court, in employing its discretionary power, fixed the sum of CFA F 10,000,000 to be awarded to him for all the harm done him[206]. In other instances, the West African judge makes reference to equity to justify the impressionist nature which surrounds the determination of the amount for reparation, as in the judgments of 3 July 2013, *Monsieur Kpatcha Gnassingbe and Others* **v.** *Republic of Togo*[207] or that of 6 November 2013, *Chude Mba* **v.** *Republic of Ghana*[208]. It is true that having recourse to equity obtains before several other courts of human rights protection[209]. That being so, an attempt at objection of the amounts awarded would partly have the merit of showing that the evaluation of the harms done against victims is not done capriciously or dogmatically, and also that, those pleading the cases in court as counsel are indeed not treated in an unequitable manner, considering the degree of unpredictability in the mode of calculation of the compensating reliefs. It would be desirable that in future, the determination of such amounts be made as much as possible on objective and consistent bases.

One may even envisage that such reparation may not consist of a compensation. The system currently being practised before the Court, by

---

205 Judgment No. ECW/CCJ/JUD/08/12, §32.

206 Judgment No. ECW/CCJ/JUD/01/11, §38.

207 Judgment No. ECW/CCJ/JUD/06/13, §102.

208 Judgment No ECW/CCJ/JUD/10/13, §105.

209 See for example Article 41 of the European Convention on Human Rights, Article 63§ 1 of the American Convention on Human Rights, or still Article 27 §2 of the 1998 Ouagadougou Protocol establishing the African Court on Human and Peoples' Rights.

its automatic nature and by its invariableness, shows signs of immaturity. Before a prejudicial act of psychological, non-economic type, it is not certain that a compensatory relief will always be appropriate. It is worthy to recall at this juncture the materials of general international law, in relation to monetary compensation. Far from being systematically envisaged, monetary compensation rather seems confined, limited to material and economic harms only. Such, at least, seems to be the philosophy of Article 37§1 of the Draft Articles on Responsibility of States for Internationally Wrongful Acts as prepared by the International Law Commission (ILC). In the terms of that provision:

> "The State responsible for an internationally wrongful act is under an obligation to give satisfaction for the injury caused by that act insofar as it cannot be made good by restitution or compensation".

Viewed from that angle, the award of a sum of money is no more considered as a second-best solution, as compensation for lack of a better mode of relief, but rather as a mode of reparation appropriate for a specific category of prejudice, it is never automatic.

The question is therefore that of finding out if there are no possibilities for transcending the systematically compensatory conception of the reparation arising out of the violation found by the judge. In other words, is it conceivable to grant a victim a form of compensation which may not be, or else may not solely consist of the monetary type?

A development upon the mode of reparation seems to us expected indeed, in as much as we need to guard against the tendency of the responsibility of a State which has committed a human rights violation, deteriorating into a form of civil responsibility that is only remediable by paying a sum of money. Because it is actually a matter concerning human rights, that is to say, a question of values, it may be judicious to *explore other forms of sanction of States, of a more symbolic order, of a more psychological connotation.* One can thus imagine the Court issuing a symbolic order against a defaulting State, typical of a "satisfaction", this other mode of reparation of injury known in international law, and of which the ILC tells us:

> "... may consist in an acknowledgement of the breach, an expression of regret, a formal apology or another appropriate modality." (Article 37§2 of the above-cited ILC document). T

The ECOWAS judge could thus enjoin the State to carry out certain acts such as public acknowledgement of a default – in precise forms which remain to be determined, and without confining it to a snub – or still the publication of the decision of the Court, as pertains both before the European Court of Human Rights and the African Court[210]. With regard to this point, we know that Article 13 § 6 of the Rules of the Court provide that when an action is instituted before the Court:

> "Notice shall be given in the Official Journal of the Community of the date of registration of application initiating proceedings, the names and addresses of the parties, the subject-matter of the proceedings, the form of order sought by the applicant and a summary of the pleas in law and of the main supporting arguments".

But there is no article or clause providing that the judgments of the Court shall be published, even if we know that in principle, they are published by the Registry Department of the Court. It is known however, as illustrated in domestic law, that an order to render a court decision public, can, by "cleansing" the victim in the eyes of all, constitute a suitable mode of compensation. It may also constitute a deterrent to human rights violation.

For the purposes of refining the sanctions pronounced, and because it is a question of norms relating to human rights, it is permissible to think that the ECOWAS Court of Justice will be made to at least *relax its doctrine of non-interference in the legislative matters of the Member States.* The Court, in begging the question somehow, does regularly recall that it does not make pronouncements on the legality or otherwise of the domestic laws of Member States, or that it has no jurisdiction to examine *in abstracto* the national laws of the Member States. That is true, and it must be well understood: we are not contesting how well-founded or not that position is. But we can safely bet, that with time, and with the development of the human rights protection mandate, the Court could be made to evolve its position further and accept to criticise legislations which are pre-disposed to violating human rights. It is certain, for instance, that the Court could validly criticise a law which unduly puts curbs on the practice of a profession, and not limit itself to finding violation of the individual rights of the applicant; the exercise of the Court's judicial functions will go beyond the strict case submitted before it. Similarly, when it is in the provisions of the criminal code of procedure that one can find the disregard of the rights of defence, one can indeed

---

[210] See the important Judgment of 13 July 2014, on *Reverend C. R. Mtikila* **v.** *Republic of Tanzania*, §37.

see the judge criticising the source norms of the violation in question, beyond the intermittent acknowledgement of transgression of the rights of the applicant.

That approach may even be considered as an end in itself, of any human rights protection system. If we should indeed operate on the basis of the principle that the States do not necessarily regard unfavourably the increase in level of rights protection for people, we may think that a critical appraisal of their own legal system, emanating from an international body, enables them to correct imperfections that they had genuinely not taken notice of, or which they could not have foreseen, simply as a result of the extreme multiplicity of disputes handled on individuals, or that the apparent hotchpotch of cases whose feedbacks had to be dealt with, thus preventing them from understanding what their structural weaknesses were. The appropriate criticism of "bad" laws, is, in the final analysis, a bonus for the domestic judicial order.

But for now, the cautious attitude of the Court can be understood. It arises from at least two factors. The first is linked to a general context, which is the novelty of judicial control, as carried out in an environment that is not always conducive, considering the relatively low level of the culture of the rule of law, and even, more simply, of the tradition of observance of human rights. Let us add that the technical conditions for gaining access to the domestic judge may at times negatively affect the sensibilities of the States (exemption of the rule of non-exhaustion of local remedies, in the case of ECOWAS). A second reason for the cautious behaviour of the Court is due to the fact that it is not the supervising ad-hoc organ of execution of the conventions whose application it periodically appraises. Indeed, such international commitments have the peculiar feature of putting in place, almost systematically, mechanisms for assessing the attitude of States (periodic reports to be provided) and especially, they establish supervisory organs specifically commissioned for the assigned task, be they semi-judicial organs (United Nations Committees, or Human Rights Commissions in America and Africa) or judicial organs in the proper sense of the word (Courts of Justice). Now, it is obvious that such ad-hoc bodies will have a more guaranteed competence and a sharper idea of the sanctions that may be imposed on the States parties, than a Court of Justice which is an outsider of a sort to the system, and to the balancing acts and reasoning patterns of such ad-hoc bodies. Indeed, as we have already noted, the ECOWAS Court, in making judgments on the manner in which States execute the relevant conventions, step onto grounds which are unknown to the Court, and "encroaches", one may say, "on the territories" of other entities. This stand is not of such nature as to enable it to go too far in the appraisal of the appropriate modes of compensation, especially if it is the treaty itself which pre-determines the types of sanctions possible. One must therefore understand the quantitatively minimal options adopted by Court – in the monetary sense, one could say – as a form of restraint, a mark of the resolve not to go too far, knowing that it has already gone a little far by electing to sit as a judge of the convention whose provisions it is applying.

Apart from the development trend expected from the mode of reparation the Court employs almost systematically, *the problem of actual implementation of the decisions of the Court exists*. The issue is hardly peculiar to the ECOWAS Court, one could even argue that courts devoted to human rights protection find themselves quite regularly confronted with the problem of actualisation of their own pronouncements[211].

For the ECOWAS Court, there is currently no means or barometer for measuring systematically the rate or level of enforcement of its judgments. That is a regrettable omission, but occasionally, a report is made of one Government or the other being reluctant or refusing to comply with a delivered judgment. An exploratory reflection on the ways and means of guaranteeing the execution of the delivered judgments is of absolute necessity.

In that sense, three considerations appear to us as capable of being taken into account.

The first would involve a "rediscovery" of the new Article 24 of the Protocol on the Court, introduced in 2005. According to paragraph 4 of that provision:

> "All Member States shall determine the competent national authority for the purpose of receipt and processing of execution and notify the Court accordingly".

---

211 See, in that regard, significant contributions at the colloquium on *La protection des droits de l'homme par les cours supranationales*, (Human Rights Protection by Supra-national Courts) cited above : « L'effectivité des arrêts des Cours supranationales de droits de l'homme » (The Significance of Supra-naional Human Rights Courts) (GUTIERREZ RAMIREZ L-M., pp. 177 à 193) et « La remise en cause de l'autorité des cours supranationales » (TOUZE S., pp. 195 à 211). (Critique of the Authority of Supra-national Courts).

This provision constitutes, in our opinion, the first gear one can apply for improving upon the execution of the court decisions. It is appropriate however to recall that till today, only 4 States out of the 15 in the Community, have fulfilled this requirement, without necessarily being at any rate a sign of refusal by the States to comply with their commitments[212]. If the States were to appoint their national authorities – which a sustained effort before the national authorities could yield – they could act as precious spokespersons for the Court. A mere follow-up of the relationship with these "liaison officers" would make them feel that it is important that decisions made by the Court in disputes which concern their States be monitored and implemented. It is the institutionalisation of a dialogue, or the possibility of bringing that dialogue to life at any moment, which will be of such nature that the appointed national authority will always be urged to track the enforcement of the judgments. And if this approach of silent pressure does not work, it would always be permissible for the ECOWAS Court to find things out from its spokesperson, in direct and express terms, in order to be sure of what has become of the pronouncements of the Court. It is therefore important, in our opinion, to see to the effective application of Article 24 of the Protocol, that is to say, that the Member States honour first of all the laid down obligation. The potential benefits which may be derived from this provision, in terms of guarantee for enforcement of the judgments, are numerous. Some of them are, as we have seen, simply "psychological" in nature. Without doubt, the optimal implementation of the said Article would help actualise the decisions of the Court.

Another gear we can apply is the annual report of the Court. It has been said, currently, such report does not exist. Putting in place such a report was however advocated for in the draft proposal made by the Court in 2017. Certainly, instituting an annual report on the Court could help maximise the chances of seeing the judgments executed. What matters is that such document must not be reduced to a purely factual account of the activities engaged in by the Court, but focus on the challenges the Court could be made to face, and the means for surmounting them. In

[212] These four States are, at the time of writing these lines, Nigeria, Togo, Guinea and Mali. However, when the issue is raised, before the Member States, they often show their surprise, which gives them away for "forgetfulness" or "ignorance". The duty in question is relatively simple: not only can a Member State appoint any individual or entity for the intended purpose (a top functionary, a registrar, a judge, etc.), but the accomplishment of the duty is not formally circumscribed in any way (any legal instrument, even a simple letter addressed to the Court may fulfil that purpose). One may reasonably suppose that it is not by malice, but at worst by negligence, that the States have still not carried out that formality.

adopting such an ambitious method, the issue of enforcement of judgments will necessarily form part of the matters for discussion, even if one must be careful, in any case, not to turn the annual report into an instrument for stigmatising the States, or a means for investigating their case. A comparison with the practice of comparable international courts may be instructive. Their annual reports are not only meant for giving accounts of the work they do, they are also a means for reflection on the various problems the judges faced, including execution of the decisions they make. Before the Inter-American Court of Human Rights, it is provided, regarding the Court, that:

> "To each regular session of the General Assembly of the Organization of American States the Court shall submit, for the Assembly's consideration, a report on its work during the previous year. It shall specify, in particular, the cases in which a state has not complied with its judgments, making any pertinent recommendations."[213] Again, in the African system, the 1998 Protocol of Ouagadougou which established the African Court on Human and Peoples' stated the following on the Court: "The Court shall submit to each regular session of the Assembly, a report on its work during the previous year. The report shall specify, in particular, the cases in which a State has not complied with the Court's judgment."[214]

We also know that within the United Nations human rights protection system, and notably before the Human Rights Commission, the annual report submitted to the General Assembly represents an opportunity to draw attention of the plenary session of the General Assembly, to the reluctance of certain States to respond positively to observations addressed to them.

Devising an annual report for the ECOWAS Court would undoubtedly produce several benefits for the Court. Apart from the possibility of giving the Court the greatest visibility, which should be in keeping with the Court's proclaimed independence, the annual report could otherwise constitute, as obtains in sister courts, an avenue for frank surveillance regarding execution of obligations arising from conventions, at least a mild means of stock-taking whose mere outlook of advertisement could deter wrongdoing on the part of the States. It must

---

213 Article 65 of the American Convention on Human Rights.

214 Article 31 of the Protocol.

be said here that the Court of Justice proposed the production of such report in the reform proposals it made in 2017.

The last point of reflection on improvement upon the execution of the decisions of the Court is that of political sanction. Truly, the use of a coercive force by the Authority of Heads of State and Government is not, currently speaking, plausible nor desirable, in so far as it would end up in a failure, the failure of bringing a recalcitrant Member State into a state of repentance. Given such a scenario, the chances are high that things could quickly turn sour, and finally end up in termination of a State's treaty commitments or the exercise of its right of withdrawal from the international organisation[215]. Nevertheless, there are two texts today, on the basis of which a State having disregarded a judgment of the Court, could be sanctioned. On the other hand, Supplementary Act A/SA.13/02/12 on the regime of sanctions against Member States which do not honour their obligations towards ECOWAS provides that among the obligations for the Member States feature also compliance with the decisions of the Community Court of Justice (Article 1), and therefore, the refusal to execute decisions of the Court constitute a default. Besides, in the terms of Article 77 of the ECOWAS Treaty, sanctions may be imposed on a Member State which: "*fails to fulfil its obligations to the Community*". It has however been stated: there is very little chance, as at now, that these extreme provisions may be implemented, like, incidentally, what is happening before similar judicial organs[216].

The future of the ECOWAS Court of Justice is taking shape in a nuanced form – it is neither dark nor bright. As custodian of the system of rules for integration, the Court has struggled to assert itself, for lack of suitable cases to adjudicate upon. As a judge over human rights, it has unquestionably proved to be efficient, in its own context, even if the mode of delivery of that mandate remains to be perfected. It is for the purpose of perfecting the mandate of the Court, in general terms, that the draft reform was conceived, but it is not certain that it will be adopted. There are serious reasons however, for doubting the suitability of the choice the Community authorities seem to have made. It is imperative to

---

215 See, for example, as regards the American Convention of Human Rights, termination (based on Article 78 of the Pact of San José) made by Trinidad and Tobago in 1998, by Peru in 1999 and by Venezuela in 2012.

216 Our mind goes to "actions for failure by a State to fulfil its obligations" provided not too long ago under Article 46 §4 of the European Convention on Human Rights, which enables one to access the Court for non-execution of judgment by a Member State, which has till today not been implemented.

notice that currently, not only are the reforms being made, one after the other, piling up in a disorderly, piecemeal fashion, but they are inspired by a strait-jacketed managerial rationale for international standards, obsessed by a need "to reduce costs", but in substance, ignorant of the peculiar callings of the institutions.

The calling of the Court has a human dimension, including the mission of a "justice enforcer", which cannot be justifiably forgotten. One needs to have seen litigants whose eyes were illuminated upon hearing the verdict of the Court, whereas in their own countries, all the doors to justice had been shut before their very eyes. One needs to have met the widow, Mrs. Mainassara Baré, sobbing her heart out after witnessing before the Court, and relieved thereafter, after having had access to a platform upon which she could make her story heard. One can never forget those two Benin nationals, one rendered virtually incapacitated by a quack doctor who had administered an absolutely unthinkable therapy on her, the other, a young housemaid savagely battered by her boss – both of them having won their respective cases before the domestic courts of their countries of origin, but whose hopes for redress had all but vanished, because their case-files "got lost" when the matter went before the Appeal Court in their country, etc. etc. One needs to have seen all these persons – who, had it not been for the ECOWAS Court of Justice, would have had to live the rest of their days in denial of justice – to convince oneself of the fact that the Court did not exist, or does not exist, for nothing.

June 2017

TABLE OF CONTENTS

PART I

THE CASE LAW OF THE COURT

PART II

REFLECTIONS ON THE COURT FROM THE POINT OF VIEW OF DOCTRINE

Le Sénégal aux éditions L'Harmattan

Dernières parutions

L'ESTHÉTIQUE SOCIALE DES PULAAR
Socioanalyse d'un groupe ethnolinguistique
Sy Harouna
L'esthétique sociale pulaar est une mise en ordre éthique de la vie sociale. Elle est l'inventaire systématique de ce qu'il y a de beau et de laid dans le social relativement à ses valeurs, à ses normes, à ses règles et à ses codes qui commandent des postures, des relations, des rapports et des qualités appropriés. L'analyse des contradictions de la société pulaar du Fuuta Tooro a révélé des logiques et des stratégies fondées sur des rapports de castes et sur les représentations sociales que ces rapports produisent.
(31.00 euros, 304 p.)
ISBN : 978-2-343-11189-6, ISBN EBOOK : 978-2-14-002810-6

LE BAYNUNK GUNAAMOLO, UNE LANGUE DU SUD DU SÉNÉGAL
Analyse phonologique, morphologique et syntaxique
Diop Sokhna Bao - Préface de Denis Creissels
Le Sénégal est un pays multilingue avec des langues majoritaires et des langues minoritaires, de par le nombre de leurs locuteurs, mais également de par la quantité de travaux dont chacune dispose. Les langues majoritaires ont fait l'objet de nombreuses recherches, à la différences des langues minoritaires. Ce constat est à l'origine du choix porté sur la description de la variante gunaamolo du baynunk (parlé au sud du Sénégal, plus précisément à Niamone, dans la région de Ziguinchor) qui est une langue en danger très peu décrite. L'utilité et l'intérêt de ce travail résident dans la sauvegarde et la connaissance de cette langue et sa communauté. Elle peut servir aussi de référence à des recherches futures.
(Coll. Études africaines, 38.50 euros, 392 p.)
ISBN : 978-2-343-09614-8, ISBN EBOOK : 978-2-14-002913-4

DE L'HÉRITAGE ARABO-ISLAMIQUE SAINT-LOUISIEN
Une illustration par les œuvres d'Abbas Sall et d'Abdoulaye Fall Magatte
Fall Cheikh Tidiane - Préface de Samba Dieng et Postface de Mouhamed Habib Kébé
Cet ouvrage porte sur la réhabilitation du legs culturel arabo-islamique ouest-africain en général et saint-louisien en particulier. Revaloriser un pan du patrimoine culturel par l'entremise de l'imagination poétique locale de deux intellectuels demeure l'objectif principal de cette étude. Une partie descriptive constituée de la traduction d'une cinquantaine de poèmes suivie d'un volet analytique constitue la méthodologie de ce travail de recherche. La moisson tirée de ce travail préliminaire apporte quelques éclairages sur l'intérêt de la traduction de manuscrits arabes, notamment ceux produits par d'éminents ulémas du Sénégal, tels les deux poètes faisant l'objet de cette étude.
(Harmattan Sénégal, 35.00 euros, 340 p.)
ISBN : 978-2-343-11306-7, ISBN EBOOK : 978-2-14-003014-7

L'AGRICULTURE DU SÉNÉGAL SOUS LA COLONISATION
Diop Ismaïla
L'introduction de l'arachide au Sénégal au début du XXe siècle révolutionne le paysage agricole. La France décide alors de faire du Sénégal une colonie arachidière. Le Sénégal devient la troisième puissance arachidière du monde après les États-Unis et l'Inde. Cette monoculture extensive aboutit à un déficit vivrier chronique, une dégradation des sols, une dépendance vis-à-vis des importations de riz en provenance d'Asie. Pour y remédier, le rapport de la mission Roland Portères de 1952 recommande des mesures d'aménagement du territoire, de restauration des sols, de promotion de l'agriculture intégrée sérère.
(Harmattan Sénégal, 23.50 euros, 218 p.)
ISBN : 978-2-343-11129-2, ISBN EBOOK : 978-978-2-14-002836-6

CASAMANCE
À quand la paix ?
Bassène René Capain - Préface du père Nazaire Diatta
Malgré leur volonté et leur engagement affichés d'aller vers la fin du conflit armé en Casamance, la position des parties en guerre n'a jamais réellement évolué. L'État du Sénégal se dit prêt à négocier sur tous les points, sauf sur ceux relatifs à l'intégrité territoriale et l'unité nationale, alors que, de son côté, le MFDC soutient une position contraire en déclarant être disposé à ne négocier que sur la question se rapportant à l'indépendance totale de la Casamance. Cette situation montre que le conflit armé est encore loin de finir en Casamance.
(28.50 euros, 276 p.)
ISBN : 978-2-343-10426-3, ISBN EBOOK : 978-2-14-002593-8

PARCOURS D'UN JOURNALISTE AUTODIDACTE
Ndiaye Pape Ngagne - Préface de Mamoudou Ibra Kane
Pape Ngagne Ndiaye, par son style, est devenu un rendez-vous incontournable de l'espace audiovisuel sénégalais. L'émission « Faram Faccce » qu'il anime présentement sur TFM est très courue des hommes et femmes politiques pressés de se soumettre au feu roulant et nourri des questions du redoutable interviewer, unique dans son genre. Ce livre n'est pas seulement une autobiographie, mais aussi une réflexion thématique et une sélection rigoureuse de certains numéros de la célèbre émission qui se veut « un décryptage des questions majeures de l'actualité nationale ».
(37.00 euros, 360 p.) *ISBN : 978-2-343-09916-3, ISBN EBOOK : 978-978-2-14-002822-9*

DES FRANCENABE AUX MODOU-MODOU
L'émigration sénégalaise contemporaine
Fall Papa Demba - Préface du Professeur Abdoulaye Bara Diop
Principalement centré sur la France et ses anciennes colonies d'Afrique, le champ migratoire sénégalais s'est, de manière originale, progressivement étendu à des destinations naguère méconnues ou peu fréquentées (comme les États-Unis, l'Italie, l'Espagne, l'Afrique du Sud ou le Brésil). Peu à peu, les migrants sont devenus des acteurs incontournables du développement. La prise en compte de ces populations, et de leurs mouvements, devient donc nécessaire aux programmes et politiques de développement durable.
(Harmattan Sénégal, 40.00 euros, 559 p., Illustré en noir et blanc)
ISBN : 978-2-343-10796-7, ISBN EBOOK : 978-2-14-002539-6

« DOYEN » AMADY ALY DIENG, LE TRANSMETTEUR INTÉGRAL (1932-2015)
Économie biographique ou sémio-Histoire
Ngaïdé Abdarahmane
Amady Ali Dieng nous a quittés il y a un an. Pour lui rendre hommage et s'en rappeler les enseignements, l'auteur de cet ouvrage a décidé de compiler ses nombreux écrits ou interventions. Les quatorze textes qui composent cette anthologie sont représentatifs et significatifs de la personnalité, du style et des préoccupations d'Amady Ali Dieng. On y retrouve son style, son humour et son esprit critique.
(Harmattan Sénégal, 23.50 euros, 228 p., Illustré en noir et blanc)
ISBN : 978-2-343-10855-1, ISBN EBOOK : 978-2-14-002561-7

41 RULES TO BE HAPPY
Kane Babaly
Seeing that happiness is the goal towards which all men strive for, the author wrote this book to help the reader in treasuring the joyous of life and realizing his desires in entirety, to be fulfilled, to claw his way to the top and to assure him it will turn out well in the end. Moreover, this book intends to give the keys us to get the secret for reaching we want in this life. 41 rules to be happy is a little self help book which has 41 rules that are meant to allow every reader to live life in full potential.
(Harmattan Sénégal, 14.50 euros, 138 p.)
ISBN : 978-2-343-10904-6, ISBN EBOOK : 978-2-14-002583-9

SÉNÉGAL
Les limites du Plan Sénégal Émergent
Mansour Samb El Hadji
Cet ouvrage présente une analyse profonde des politiques publiques en décortiquant le Plan Sénégal Émergent (PSE) qui jusque-là n'a fait l'objet d'aucune analyse critique sérieuse. Le Sénégal est face à un défi, le défi de son émergence, un défi qu'il compte relever avec tous ses fils. Ce défi qui mobilise aujourd'hui tout le monde doit nous pousser à proposer de nouveaux chemins et à animer un débat nécessaire et incontournable dans tout processus d'émergence.
(Harmattan Sénégal, 27.00 euros, 276 p.)
ISBN : 978-2-343-09721-3, ISBN EBOOK : 978-2-14-002372-9

SÉNÉGAL
Dynamiques paysannes et souveraineté alimentaire
Le procès de production, la tenue foncère et la naissance d'un mouvement paysan
Diop Amadou Makhouredia - Préface d'Yves Guillermou ; Postface de Fodé Niang
Le présent ouvrage contribue à la compréhension des stratégies développées par la petite paysannerie et les dynamiques qui animent les exploitations agricoles familiales permettant la production de biens nécessaires à l'alimentation et l'entretien des familles. La capacité des paysans à prendre en main leurs propres préoccupations a été mise en évidence par l'émergence d'organisations, de groupements, d'associations et d'unions dans tout l'espace rural sénégalais.
(Harmattan Sénégal, 26.00 euros, 256 p.)
ISBN : 978-2-343-10852-0, ISBN EBOOK : 978-2-14-002457-3

HISTOIRE ET SOCIOLOGIE DES RELIGIONS AU SÉNÉGAL
Tamba Moustapha
Le Sénégal reste une exception dans le domaine religieux : 90 % de musulmans, 5 % de chrétiens et 5 % d'adeptes de l'animisme. C'est aussi le pays où les musulmans et les catholiques partagent le même cimetière, où les conjoints partagent des religions différentes, où les écoles privées catholiques comptent 60 à 70 % d'élèves de confession musulmane, etc. Ce phénomène n'est pas dû au hasard. L'histoire et la sociologie des religions permettent de l'expliquer amplement. Cet ouvrage souligne cette exception sénégalaise pour montrer qu'au moment où notre monde est en proie au fanatisme, à l'intolérance et au terrorisme religieux, le Sénégal propose un autre « modèle ».
(Coll. Études africaines, série Economie, 41.00 euros, 426 p.)
ISBN : 978-2-343-10424-9, ISBN EBOOK : 978-2-14-002506-8

FIGURES DU POLITIQUE ET DE L'INTELLECTUEL AU SÉNÉGAL
L.S. Senghor - M. Dia - A. Ly - CH. A. Diop A. Diouf & F. Mitterrand - J.R. De Benoist - A. Seck - TH. Fall - A. M. Samb - A.M. Samb JR - TH. Monod - H. Bocoum - G. R. Thilmans
Samb Djibril
Cet ouvrage réunit des personnalités politiques et/ou intellectuelles très diverses : Léopold Sédar Senghor, l'Immortel Noir ; Mamadou Dia, le brillant économiste ; François Mitterrand et Abdou Diouf, deux experts politiques, ou encore Théodore Monod, le savant probe. Ces figures sont autant de coryphées auxquels l'auteur a voulu rendre hommage, afin de rappeler que la terre africaine du Sénégal ne manque pas de princes de l'esprit ni de nourriture intellectuelle.
(26.00 euros, 266 p.)
ISBN : 978-2-343-10731-8, ISBN EBOOK : 978-2-14-002513-6

TÉLÉVISIONS AU SÉNÉGAL
Entre désert de contenu et sécheresse intellectuelle
Djimbira Cheikh Mouhamadou
« Il faut lire ce livre en considérant qu'il a été sciemment écrit dans l'intention de nuire à la société spectaculaire. Il n'a jamais rien d'outrancier. » Cette pensée de Guy Debord nous permet de comprendre à bien des égards, l'ouvrage de Cheikh Mouhamadou Djimbira qui est un plaidoyer pour la création de programmes audiovisuels de qualité.
(11.50 euros, 80 p.)
ISBN : 978-978-2-343-10790-5, ISBN EBOOK : 978-978-2-14-002528-0

UN SCOUT SÉNÉGALAIS
L'aventure citoyenne (deuxième édition)
Ndene Pascal - Préface de Jacques Moreillon
Lorsque nous parlons de l'adolescence, nous évoquons l'autonomie, la responsabilisation, la citoyenneté, le jeu, les relations avec les parents et avec les pairs. Toutes ces questions sont abordées dans ce livre qui montre avec humour le parcours éducatif d'un adolescent dans le scoutisme. Ce livre s'adresse à tous les jeunes, garçons et filles, aux parents et éducateurs de tout milieu social et culturel, ainsi qu'à tous les scouts et guides du monde.
(14.00 euros, 124 p.)
ISBN : 978-2-343-10965-7, ISBN EBOOK : 978-2-14-002526-6

LA PENSÉE DE CHEIKH AHMADOU BAMBA FACE AUX DÉFIS AFRICAINS
Sow Cheikh Mar
Cheikh Ahmadou Bamba Mbacké a su déterminer une nouvelle vision aux yeux de ses contemporains en formulant d'une façon très claire des idées novatrices capables de faire bouger le peuple. Cette conception de la société dans sa globalité a permis «à chaque individu de devenir un centre d'initiative, de création et de responsabilité à tous les niveaux : celui de l'économie, de la politique, de la culture ; une conception qui ne soit ni individualiste, ni totalitaire mais fondée sur les communautés de base».
(Harmattan Sénégal, 24.00 euros, 238 p.)
ISBN : 978-2-343-10021-0, ISBN EBOOK : 978-2-14-002284-5

LE MODERNISME EN ISLAM
Introduction à la pensée de Sayyid Amir Ali
Diagne Mbengue Ramatoulaye
« Les thèmes abordés par le Professeur Ramatoulaye Diagne dans sa lecture de la pensée d'Amir Ali ont tous un lien indéfectible avec le pluralisme et la paix. (…) Dans la lecture de son ouvrage, on arrive à comprendre que le modernisme d'Amir Ali est une sorte de renouveau dans la pensée islamique. C'est un mouvement d'intellection qui intègre, dans une cohérence architecturale, l'usage de la raison, l'esprit du soufisme pratique ghazalien et la finalité de la prière qui concilie l'ascèse de l'âme à la transformation positive des sociétés. » Abdoul Aziz Kebe, Ancien Chef du Département d'Arabe UCAD-DAKAR.
(Harmattan Sénégal, 15.00 euros, 144 p.)
ISBN : 978-2-343-09977-4, ISBN EBOOK : 978-2-14-002211-1

MA RENCONTRE AVEC ALLAH
De l'obscurité à la lumière
Mbengue Adama Ousmane
Cet ouvrage traite surtout de la question essentielle du Mahdi qui vient pour apporter les solutions idoines en s'appuyant sur la Sharia mouhammadiya et la Tariqah ahmadiya afin d'offrir à tout individu le meilleur profil dans la société idéale qu'il compte établir.
(Harmattan Sénégal, 14.50 euros, 134 p.)
ISBN : 978-2-343-10299-3, ISBN EBOOK : 978-2-14-002277-7

Structures éditoriales du groupe L'Harmattan

L'Harmattan Italie
Via degli Artisti, 15
10124 Torino
harmattan.italia@gmail.com

L'Harmattan Hongrie
Kossuth l. u. 14-16.
1053 Budapest
harmattan@harmattan.hu

L'Harmattan Sénégal
10 VDN en face Mermoz
BP 45034 Dakar-Fann
senharmattan@gmail.com

L'Harmattan Cameroun
TSINGA/FECAFOOT
BP 11486 Yaoundé
inkoukam@gmail.com

L'Harmattan Burkina Faso
Achille Somé – tengnule@hotmail.fr

L'Harmattan Guinée
Almamya, rue KA 028 OKB Agency
BP 3470 Conakry
harmattanguinee@yahoo.fr

L'Harmattan RDC
185, avenue Nyangwe
Commune de Lingwala – Kinshasa
matangilamusadila@yahoo.fr

L'Harmattan Congo
67, boulevard Denis-Sassou-N'Guesso
BP 2874 Brazzaville
harmattan.congo@yahoo.fr

L'Harmattan Mali
Sirakoro-Meguetana V31
Bamako
syllaka@yahoo.fr

L'Harmattan Togo
Djidjole – Lomé
Maison Amela
face EPP BATOME
ddamela@aol.com

L'Harmattan Côte d'Ivoire
Résidence Karl – Cité des Arts
Abidjan-Cocody
03 BP 1588 Abidjan
espace_harmattan.ci@hotmail.fr

L'Harmattan Algérie
22, rue Moulay-Mohamed
31000 Oran
info2@harmattan-algerie.com

L'Harmattan Maroc
5, rue Ferrane-Kouicha, Talaâ-Elkbira
Chrableyine, Fès-Médine
30000 Fès
harmattan.maroc@gmail.com

Nos librairies en France

Librairie internationale
16, rue des Écoles – 75005 Paris
librairie.internationale@harmattan.fr
01 40 46 79 11
www.librairieharmattan.com

Librairie l'Espace Harmattan
21 bis, rue des Écoles – 75005 paris
librairie.espace@harmattan.fr
01 43 29 49 42

Lib. sciences humaines & histoire
21, rue des Écoles – 75005 paris
librairie.sh@harmattan.fr
01 46 34 13 71
www.librairieharmattansh.com

Lib. Méditerranée & Moyen-Orient
7, rue des Carmes – 75005 Paris
librairie.mediterranee@harmattan.fr
01 43 29 71 15

Librairie Le Lucernaire
53, rue Notre-Dame-des-Champs – 75006 Paris
librairie@lucernaire.fr
01 42 22 67 13

www.ingramcontent.com/pod-product-compliance
Lightning Source LLC
Chambersburg PA
CBHW071402230926
51846CB00008B/205
* 9 7 8 2 3 4 3 1 7 9 5 5 1 *